D1604080

The First Conglomerate

◇

145 Years of the Singer Sewing Machine Company

By

Don Bissell

Audenreed Press

The First Conglomerate

◇

145 Years of the Singer Sewing Machine Company

By

Don Bissell

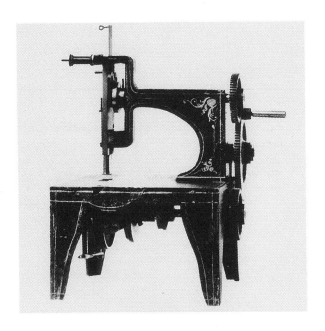

Audenreed Press

The First Conglomerate
145 Years of the Singer Sewing Machine Company

Copyright © – 1999 by Don Bissell

Publisher's Cataloging in Publication Data
Bissell, Don
The First Conglomerate: 145 Years of the Singer Sewing Machine Company – 1ˢᵗ ed.
      p. cm.
Photographs, selected bibliography, endnotes, author's working timeline and index.
LCCN, Library of Congress Catalog Card Number: 98-73207
ISBN: 1-879418-72-X.
        1. Business
        2. History
        3. Reference
        4. Singer Sewing Machine Company History
        5. Sewing Machine History
   BR145.2.S65 1996   270

Printed in the United States of America

Audenreed Press
P.O. Box 1305, #103
Brunswick, ME 04011
(207) 833-5016

For Kristen

Disclaimer

This book is designed to provide information in regard to the subject matter covered. It is not the purpose of this manual to reprint all the information that is otherwise available to the author and/or publisher, but to complement, amplify and supplement other works. You are urged to read all available material and learn as much as possible about the Singer Sewing Machine Company. For more information, see the many references in the Selected Bibliography.

Every effort has been made to make this work as complete and as accurate as possible. However, there may be mistakes both typographical and in content. Therefore, this work should be used as a general guide and not as the ultimate source of Singer Sewing Machine Company history. The purpose of this work is to entertain and to educate. The author and the publisher shall have neither liability nor responsibility to any person or entity with respect to loss or damage caused, or alleged to be caused, directly or indirectly by the information contained in this book. If you do not wish to be bound by the above, you may return this book to this publisher for a full refund less shipping costs.

Acknowledgments

This book is dedicated to my daughter Kristen who is the finest young lady any dad could hope for. My aunt and uncle, Genevieve and Leonard Morin, have been another calming force in my life. My thanks as always to fellow writers Ellen Geisel and Judy Finman for their editorial comments. And a very special appreciation to writer/poet/editor Cynthia Graves who reviewed key portions of the manuscript. Thanks to my brother Dave Bissell and to my close friends Don and Trudy Berichia, Howard Cohen, Dave Jensen, Mark Garrepy, Dave Orosco, Roger LeClerc and Terry Yuill.

I am also indebted to my many editors who helped me develop as a writer. I have always appreciated the assistance of the University of Southern Maine's Portland Campus Research Librarians and especially those extra efforts of reference librarian Ed Zimmerman who has for the last 15 years somehow resolved my most difficult inquiries. Thanks to Jerry Hostetter of the Singer Company and to Customer Service Manager, Vickey Merritt, for the informative Singer Company reports. A special thank you to Carl Machover for his longstanding support. Thanks to Robert Scott of Robert Scott Associates, Inc. for his valuable review of the manuscript. Finally, this work would not have been possible without Sam Harvey's wonderful memories and insight into the Singer Sewing Machine Company.

Author's Overview

Why write about one company's 145 years of successes and failures? What relevance does a study of business history have at all? Isn't there a historical business cycle to explain it all?

During the long years of modernism's onset, no facet of the Industrial Revolution has altered the present day more profoundly than the emergence of the modern workplace. All our divergent social and economic cultural patterns – our entire way of daily living – have emerged from a our inescapable linkage to our changing workplace. The changing workplace has demanded a more sophisticated workforce. In turn, sophisticated workers have demanded more leisure time, more recognition, and a greater share in what life offers. As the workplace changes, so do its workers. We are our workplace. Ask anyone to identify his or her self and he or she will respond by casting out a label identifying a work affiliation.

For the last century and a half, the evolving workplace has been the handmaiden to our dynamic lifestyle. And since the workplace itself progresses by producing the changing goods and services its workers demand, the relationship is symbiotic. History notes that the workplace has evolved mainly by producing and placing small appliances into the world's households. Of all the goods produced during the entire Industrial Revolution, none have been more influential than the first mass-marketed home appliance, the sewing machine.

Our way of life owes much to the sewing industry's evolution and comparatively little to the recent advent of the computer. When contemporary writers point to the computer as the defining tool of modernism, they ignore history. The computer's popularity, when viewed statistically, only now begins to rival that of the sewing machine. In the United States, a wealthy industrialized country, personal computers have crossed the threshold of only 15 percent of American homes. The sewing machine can still be found in twice that many U. S. homes.

A generation ago, nearly every American family owned a sewing machine. From a historical perspective, the computer is but a johnny-come-lately whose influence on 200 progressive years of the Industrial Revolution and the workplace has been minimal. During most of these years in which mankind stepped out of the high middle ages, the computer existed only in theory. Further, today's self-styled Information Age is no more than the predicted outgrowth of automation. (Singer company executives foretold of this future outpouring of data processing technology during the early 1950s.)

How do modern editorialists leap over this inescapable historical perspective? Mostly, they assert that present-day changes in social and business models represent an incipient and unique era in world history. Such assertions, which often take the form of "a new world order is upon us," rely on a supposed reformation ongoing in world commerce and in the global workplace.

However, these models of business behavior are not new. The Singer company history discloses that today's changing business methods merely embellish its own historical models. The present-day manifestations of the still-developing Industrial Revolution appear trifling when compared to the global upheaval leveled on world society during the nineteenth century. If today's Information Age theorists understood the historical relationship between economy and technology, they would not repeatedly point to a self-perpetuating *new world order*.

The Age of Information has not supplanted the Age of Automation. Progress in the workplace is not identified with the generation or management of information or data. The data always existed: its proliferation caused the computer to come about. The computer's ability to handle more information has refined the means of data entry, retrieval and storage – but this refinement has not created a new business or workplace model. The computer is no more than the latest tool or logical enhancement in the saga of industrial history.

The study of economic history reveals that a country's fortune and way of life will lead or lag according to its willingness to control emerging technologies. Presently, America's economic fortune seems spiraling downward into a well-worn path in economic history. Why has America failed the historical lessons of the Industrial Revolution? The economic revolution began in France's textile industry and then prospered under Napoleon's protectionist trade policies and his well-documented support of scientific research and development. Unfortunately, France, which brought forward the textile industry's automatic machines, lost itself in internal politics, betrayed Napoleon's legacy, and did not benefit from its countrymen's scientific genius.

Instead, England took hold of and reinvigorated automation's tools. In England, new technologies, like spinning jennies and power looms, flooded its fabric industries. When the technological mantel next crossed the Atlantic, Yankee ingenuity gained control over the economic revolution. Then, after years of affluence, America – like her many historical counterparts – decided to send her leading edge technologies onto foreign shores. The American news press has little criticized this latest transfer of technology into the international public domain. But, even before passing automation's mantel to a new generation of upstart foreigners, even before giving computer technology away, America paved the road by giving sewing machine technology away.

Must these historical cycles continually repeat themselves? Historian Will Durant ended a lifetime of historical research by asking: "Is it possible that. . . history. . . teaches us nothing, and that the immense past was only the weary rehearsal of the mistakes that the future is destined to make on a larger stage and scale?"[1] Sadly, the history of the Singer Sewing Machine Company becomes the saga of maturing industrialists struggling against the inevitability of historical destiny.

1. Durant, Will and Ariel, *The Lessons of History*, Simon and Schuster, New York, 1968, p. II.

Contents

While imprisoned by India's British colonial government during the early 1930s, Mahatma Ghandi learned to sew on a Singer sewing machine. Afterwards, he often referred to Singer's sewing machine as "one of the few useful things ever invented."

Chapter One

Introduction and Overview
145 Years of the Singer Sewing Machine Company

The Singer Sewing Machine Company, SSMC, was the first successful American multinational company and the first large-scale home appliance manufacturer. Its growth was spectacular. Within a few years after its 1851 beginning in a small Massachusetts workshop, it quickly grew into a flourishing international company. In relatively little more time, it became the world's first monopolistic conglomerate. For over a century, the company's prosperity relied on its single product line of Singer sewing machines.

During these first 100 years of growth and expansion, The Singer Company never failed to deliver fabulous dividends to its privileged shareholders. Even while garnering astronomical profits from its global customer base, this first appliance company somehow managed to engender an unheard of degree of client loyalty. Singer's customers, who set their precious acquisition in a safe location within the home, never questioned the company's wide profit margin. Generally, when someone bought Isaac Merritt Singer's little invention, he or she held on to it for life and passed this product loyalty on to succeeding family members. Such product loyalty on such a grand scale became a phenomenon in the industrializing society.

At the root of the company's unmatched success was Singer's practical sewing machine itself. Before Singer, no other sewing machine maker had delivered a manageable product: Singer's sewing machine stirred a revolution in the textile industry just like Henry Ford's Model T would later arouse the automobile industry. Singer's sewing machine was the world's first small appliance that relied on complex mechanical workings to operate flawlessly. It was the first home appliance to operate without tiresome adjustments and frequent repairs.

The technological breakthrough of a working home appliance, of a flawlessly operating mechanical device, has meant a great deal for the world's working classes. No other invention has so made over the workplace or done more to enhance the quality of life around the globe. No other home appliance or modern electronic computer has found its way into so many homes or has achieved as much global recognition as I. M. Singer's Sewing Machine. No other discovery has affected our modern way of life as has the sewing machine.

From an historical perspective, the sewing machine may well represent the most important invention of the nineteenth century. Its popularity was unprecedented. The sewing machine was the first factory-made home appliance to be mass-marketed: it introduced such sales techniques to the world. And more than any other company, The Singer Company defined original mass-marketing knowhow. The company's initiation and development of novel marketing strategies probably evolved from Isaac Singer's self-propelled sales efforts. To sell his machines at a time when only strong men operated large commercial sewing machines with difficulty, I. M. Singer personally recruited and paid high wages to attractive seamstresses to demonstrate his machines. Singer himself often hammered his onlookers with his message: "Even tiny, frail women can operate a Singer!"

To get his message out, Singer staged sewing demonstrations in a storefront on Broadway that just happened to be a few doors down from another popular attraction, Phineas T. Barnum's museum. One newspaper reported that Singer's attractive storefront demonstrators drew a bigger crowd than did Barnum's museum. During its first 50 years, the company's unique, high-powered sales methods outlasted fierce competition from an estimated 150 sewing machine makers. Even today's corporations still rely on the same novel marketing methods brought into use by this pioneering and venerable company.

Besides creating a new marketing strategy, the sewing industry also became home to a new, technically grounded workforce. It introduced manufacturing methods and policies that helped modernize the factory system. The Singer Company especially became known for its dedicated and well-trained factory specialists. Generations of well-directed and well-trained Singer employees, who often included all working age members of an entire family, energetically pursued the sales, manufacture and development of sewing machines. Their efforts, which were always grounded in a simplistic Victorian Age honesty and morality, resulted in an always reliable, easy to use product.

Another key element in the company's success was its ability to trust its customers. Where other machine makers demanded full payment up front, the Singer Company accommodated low-income Americans and even poorer third world inhabitants by introducing installment buying. It offered this low down payment purchase plan to whoever could be enticed to buy their little machine, no matter if the buyer lived under a straw roof in the farthest back country or jungle. No company before the Singer Company ever offered easy financing to so much of the world's poor. And this trust, which showed itself early in the company's history, not only sent sales skyrocketing, it delivered up greater profits by tacking interest loan rates onto a large profit margin. For example, before the Civil War Americans earned around $500 a year. Singer's sewing machine, which cost about $23 to make, sold for more than $100.

The company always stayed one step ahead of its competitors. When other sewing machine makers brought out competitive products, Singer's machines quickly offered more features that incidentally delivered more productivity. From the very beginning, the company's marketing skill first stifled its domestic and then all of its global competitors. According to Frederick Bourne, who headed the Singer Company from 1883 to 1905, "The Singer Manufacturing Company, from 1853 to October 1, 1895, [manufactured] 13,250,000 [sewing machines] and of this number 5,877,000 have been made in factories located in foreign countries."[1] The Singer Company created markets in foreign lands where none existed. The company's unmatched growth rose from the innovative marketing techniques it created for third world markets. It uncapped the less industrialized world's marketplace by making it possible for those with a mud-thatched roof over their heads to pedal away on a Singer. By offering credit to unlettered peoples, the company built up a large, grateful, global customer base. When Singer's sewing machine found its way into the hands of the poor, it eased their daily labors and improved their station in life. More important, it also raised their income making it possible to repay the Singer loan. By the turn of the century, newspaper writers customarily referred to Singer's sewing machine as *America's Chief Contribution to Civilization*[2], *The Herald of Civilization*, and *The Great Civilizer*.

The First Mass-Marketed Home Appliance

During its years of producing a single product, the Singer Sewing Machine Company's employment reached 86,000 men and women worldwide. This great workforce, unmatched during its time, operated out of a support network of 5,000 branch offices and sewing centers that eventually reached into 190 of the world's political entities. Each autonomously governed branch office adapted Singer company policies and procedures to local business practices and to local culture. Because of this operational methodology, most Singer customers believed their local Singer company stores and facilities were locally owned. Only local higher management understood that profits funneled back to corporate headquarters. The Singer Company hired, trained and staffed all of its operating facilities from highest management on down by recruiting from the local population.

The company never behaved like some centralized colonial power. In keeping with the high moral beliefs of its controlling founder, Edward S. Clark, it treated all its employees fairly without regard to race or creed. To satisfy its foreign-speaking global customer base, the company translated its sewing machine instruction and repair manuals into at least 54 languages. Even today, in many world languages, the word *singer* supplants both the verb and noun for *sewing* in the defining compound expression *sewing machine*. In such locales the only expression for sewing machine is a *singer machine*. The global spread of Singer sewing machines and its company factories and repair and instruction centers began evolving before the Civil War.

As mentioned, Singer families, like generational military families, have existed for over a century. For example, when World War II broke out in Europe, many of Singer's locally managed facilities employed three and four generations of workers from the same family. In Germany, as in all of its global operations, blue collar workers and all of upper management had been recruited locally. Because the company's entire local structure had been drawn from the local population, it appeared to be a local manufacturer. The Singer Company had become so ingrained in German culture that World War II German aviators avoided bombing European Singer manufacturing facilities believing them German-owned. When hostilities ended, relatively intact German Singer manufacturing facilities began producing sewing machines within a few days. When payday rolled around, Singer's returning German employees gladly accepted handfuls of sewing needles in payment for their labor instead of money. In postwar Germany, German people bartered with Singer Company sewing needles instead of the near valueless German mark.

The company enjoyed a high profile in eastern Europe as well. The late Russian leader Nikita Kruschev once remarked to Donald Kircher, then Singer's company president, that his mother used a Singer sewing machine to make all his clothes. And before Kruschev, Joseph Stalin's widowed mother earned extra rubles on her Singer by taking in sewing from townspeople. Before Stalin, Russian Czar Alexander III purchased Singer sewing machines to fabricate 250,000 Russian army tents. Besides its Russian and European operations, the Singer Company's presence in Brazil also spanned generations of satisfied customers. When countrywide rioting erupted in that country during 1964, looting destroyed most business store fronts and wreaked heavy damage to much of the country's manufacturing facilities. Throughout the turmoil, only The Singer Company's glass-fronted sewing centers and centrally located production facilities went untouched. The Singer Sewing Machine's popularity reached into every corner of the globe. The historical contribution of Singer's sewing machine has been underreported and undervalued. For example, in 1930, Admiral Richard Byrd, who personally allotted space for "only that being absolutely necessary," carried six Singer sewing machines on his Antarctic expedition. Even the Wright brothers used their mother's Singer to sew fabric on their airplane's wings.[3]

No invention, not even the modern personal computer, has come into more general or more global use than has the sewing machine. Personal computer sales have only recently approached those of sewing machines. An August 14, 1948, *Business Week* article reported that 25 million Americans owned sewing machines. More than a hundred years ago beginning in the 1870s, the Singer Company, which competed among six dozen other makers, reported average annual sales greater than a quarter million machines a year.[4] The company prospered by supplying its buyers with a trouble-free, reliable and user-friendly sewing machine. Unlike the uneven operations characteristic of its early competitors, Singer sewing machines, from the very first model, worked consistently and just as advertised.

Creating Happy Customers

Unlike its short-sighted competitors, the Singer Company invested the time and expense to furnish each of its clients with an initial turnkey setup. After stamping the sales order, a Singer man delivered each newly purchased sewing machine to its final destination. On arrival, he set it up and put it into good working order. Besides this easy startup, the company established nearby centers to furnish added companion sales, ongoing preventive maintenance and repair, replacement parts, and instruction. Eventually, the Singer Company trained upwards of a million users in the proper use of their machines. These aftermarket efforts fostered the growth of a satisfied and loyal clientele. From its first days, the company's astute marketing practices, its product support network and its quality production facilities worked in unison to carry the company into prominence. Once arrived, the company established a de facto monopoly over both domestic and foreign sewing machine marketplaces. The company did not relinquish its hold on the sewing industry until the early 1950s.

Besides its sales and support network, the Singer Company owes much of its successes to its manufacturing production processes that have consistently produced a quality, state-of-the-art product. To maintain production quality, and unlike other factories of its time, which simply hired bullies to manage helpless employees, Singer factories introduced scientific management techniques. The company developed career-designated and well-trained production supervisors. In an age of triumphant capitalism, this far-thinking, enlightened management looked to workers' concerns while simultaneously realizing matchless productivity levels. The company's dedicated, capable, well-treated workforce became an anomaly among its neighboring Philistine-run factories that characterized the early years of the Industrial Revolution.

Refining the Factory System

Within the sewing industry and especially within Singer's factories, the world's best machinists honed their precise technology to perfection. Even as early as 1860, the *New York Times* reported that, "It is estimated that more than $1,000,000 is paid annually by the sewing-machine companies to their mechanics alone."[5] According to historian Frank P. Godfrey, "The mid-nineteenth century U.S.A. used the term 'machinist' to describe men who are nowadays referred to as mechanics or engineers."[6]

In those days, machinery trades represented the same state-of-the-art technology as do the engineering and computer sciences of today. And like today's techno-wizards, Singer factory workers threw themselves wholeheartedly into their labors. Perhaps, no other company continually refined the factory system by incorporating the latest innovations in automation as did the Singer Company.

Besides treating its employees fairly and enhancing its production facilities, the company did not wait idly for new ideas and processes to arrive. It supported research and design efforts on a grand scale: throughout its first half-century of operations, the company's financial support for such efforts eclipsed those of all its competitors combined. By the turn of the century, its modern production facilities housed the most extensive research and design (R&D) effort of its time. This large-scale interest and investment in R&D kept it in the scientific forefront of its own as well as its support technologies.

Into the Modern Era and Decline

Throughout its 100 years of garnering legendary and monopolistic profits, the company maintained an aggressive, no-holds-barred policy in dealing decisively with its competitors. When viable competition arose, Singer usually countered with high-powered marketing while quickly producing a more enhanced and equally sophisticated product. Whenever possible, it purchased its competitors outright. It purchased every emerging discovery or invention related to the sewing industry. The company was never a follower; it never sat around waiting for its competitors next move. Its tradition of working pro-actively, of consistently developing innovative manufacturing processes, marketing innovations and state-of-the-art products evolved as the company's historic modus operandi. Its characteristic pursuit of science and progressive thinking became the life force and backroom foundation for its ongoing successes. (This company's lifeblood, that historically identified with original thinking coming out of the president's office, would be stifled by a modern boardroom philosophy some contemporary writers call "corporatism," a future-denying, no-holds-barred immediate profit taking).

The company also owed its century and a half of success to an ability to produce novel products that worked as promised and that arrived out of a structure admired for its fair dealing and high business ethics became synonymous with all persons and things linked to the Singer Company. Had Singer's latter day corporate elite continued to drive this established company policy, the company would have doubtless survived into modernity as the largest, most progressive conglomerate on earth – but this was not to be.

In the 1950s, the company's monopolistic grip over the sewing industry began weakening. It blamed uncontrollable market circumstances and the U.S. Government's relaxed trade policies for the declining profitability of its single product line. During the postwar boom years, foreign sewing machine competitors, like many foreign manufacturers of various other home appliances and commodities, established important inroads into all segments of the American marketplace.

Especially injurious to The Singer Company was the advent of the capable zigzag machines and an entire spectrum of low-cost Japanese and European sewing machine models. In the face of new foreign competition, most American corporations of the time sought salvation in diversification. Now, the Singer Company would also follow a similar path out of necessity. Singer had perfected the sewing machine's marketing, its R&D department had kept its product technologically competitive, and its service and retail centers enjoyed a well-trained, well-qualified, long-tenured workforce; but no single home appliance could now, during the post-WWII boom years, monopolize a marketplace filled with low-cost, often politically buttressed competition. Because of the new competition, the company's single product line no longer generated the revenue needed to feed its mammoth size and large workforce. As its revenues declined during these postwar years, the Singer Company began making low-key but usually successful investments into various supporting industries. As its diversification progressed, the Singer Company's expansion into data processing and related office equipment fields eventually produced a commanding foothold in Information Age technologies ranking alongside of giants like IBM and ITT.

By the 1960s, the Singer Company emerged as a major office equipment manufacturer. Since office equipment makers were also producers of business machines, the company expanded into the emerging fields of electronics and associated electro-mechanical devices. After acquiring several more large industries during the 1960s, the company evolved as a leader in defense electronics. The Singer Company had become a new conglomerate versed in aerospace and high tech technology. But when a worldwide recession struck in the early 1970s, the company's highly leveraged acquisitions slowed the revenue stream. The costs of obtaining certain key manufacturing industries and controlling interests in other select technologies now greatly diminished the company's usually profitable quarterly earnings. Disappointed shareholders railed for a return to former profitability. One way out would be to downsize; to rid itself of slow profits returning from its recent and costly acquisitions. To counteract what they viewed as complacency in a never-ending business slump, shareholders insisted in bringing in responsive corporate management to turn a profit quickly by selling off these diverse, low-profit and non sewing machine related holdings. Unfortunately, had this shortsightedness been curtailed, if the company's well-designed interests in key Information Age industries had not been squandered, the Singer Company would have shuddered with another explosive expansion unrivaled in the tiny universe of conglomerates. Singer company old-timers associated with the 1960s President's office believed their company had settled into a course guaranteeing an arrival as the data processing behemoth of all times. By the early 1970s, The Singer Company owned a lion's share of the base controlling industries needed to feed the coming flash fire of Information Age technologies. According to its disappointed old-timers, if the company had maintained its 100-year-old policies, had stayed the course, it could today be the greatest conglomerate on earth.

A Quiet, Well-Mannered Company

The Singer Manufacturing Company always maintained a conservative public demeanor. In a 1948 article, *Business Week* described the company as 'venerable, publicity-shy.'[7] In fact, it conducted all its business dealings in quiet, closed-door meetings. It customarily shunned the light of public notice. A completely honest, beyond-reproach code of ethics marked its business transactions. Industry leaders envied Singer executives' quiet, impassive and humane approach to the business world. This secretive, cash-rich conglomerate was known and respected all over the globe. For example, the same 1948 *Business Week* article went on to say, "You can't find out much more about the current business of this venerable and world-famous company, which dominates its field as few manufacturers have ever done."[8] Every one of its agents, whether stationed in South American jungles or small Mexican hamlets, always dressed in a proper business suit – white shirt and tie always *de rigueur*. For many years it was the most blue of blue chip stocks. During the 1929 Depression, its predominantly foreign sales base held Singer stock to $631.00 per share. Because of its high price, Singer stock generally traded in blocks of ten instead of the customary 100. Again according to *Business Week*, the company consistently paid dividends averaging fifty dollars per share beginning from its 1863 incorporation and continuing through the 1930's Depression years. Until recent years, no Singer Company annual profit and loss statement ever recorded a loss.[9]

Throughout more than a hundred years of predictable profitability, The Singer Company remained a tight-lipped and closed organization. Even as recently as the 1960s, when the company went public by joining the New York Stock Exchange, stockbrokers could not produce Singer company sales or production figures – the company had never released these confidential statistics.[10] Morever, actual financial statements were not printed or given out to its own stockholders during the entire early 1900s.[11] For such information, shareholders appeared at corporate headquarters and made their requests in person. For over a century, The Singer Company conducted its business in a professional, gentleman-like manner that garnered envy throughout the global business community. Perhaps its only moment in the limelight came in 1906 when newspapers carried front-page photographs of the recently completed 47-story, engineering marvel, the Singer Building in New York City.

How did this great monopoly and business empire come about? Unbelievably, the roots of this first conglomerate sprang from the unhappy melding of two unlikely business partners:

inventor Isaac Merritt Singer, and businessman Edward S. Clark. Edward Clark is one of history's forgotten great business innovators. Who was this giant who created and oversaw the world's first conglomerate enterprise? Edward Clark was a deeply religious man, a one-time Sunday-school teacher and senior partner in one of New York City's most influential law firms. This deeply conservative gentleman was also a risk-taking, innovative business maverick who fueled the company's dramatic rise by single-handedly directing the Singer Company's global mass marketing and product distribution network. Edward Clark's accomplishments appear more remarkable when understood as coming out of an era preceding reliable communications and fast-moving freight trains or sailing ships. Edward Clark was a great renaissance industrialist who defined the fundamental workings of the modern corporation.

Cast opposite this quintessential corporate leader was his full partner and Singer Company founder, Isaac Merritt Singer. I. M. Singer's life, which is usually glossed over as an oft-told Horatio Alger tale of street urchin becomes actor, becomes inventor, becomes wealthy capitalist. This legend sees a young Isaac Singer aimlessly roaming the countryside until suddenly inspired to invent a sewing machine that then evolves into the most significant business empire on earth – the world's first great conglomerate. But Isaac Singer's rush to prosperity relied on enormously complex circumstances managed by an even more enigmatic personality. During his lifetime, Singer's ingenuity kept his company in the forefront of new product development and a step ahead of his competitors. Singer's inventive mind has known few emulators. However, commingled with his unstoppable techno-genius, there was within I. M. Singer certain unmanageable devils.

During his financially prosperous years, Isaac Merritt Singer made his home in the heart of puritanical aristocracy, in the center of America's conservative, wealthy elite on New York City's Fifth Avenue. And in this center of morality, in full view of the high faithful, he lived with a woman he called his wife. Besides this open cohabitation and without regard to Victorian morals, Singer dated promising actresses, frequented prostitutes[12] and maintained simultaneous and lightly cloaked polygamous arrangements with at least three other young women and perhaps two more. According to historian Stephen Birmingham in his *Life at the Dakota*, "At one point, he [Singer] was married to five women . . . and was supporting as many as six mistresses on the side."[13] This polygamist, this former thespian and inordinately handsome man standing more than six feet in height, fathered twenty-eight children among five attractive women. All five women professed to be his lawful wife; but, surviving records show he married legally but twice. It is noteworthy that his last lawful wife modeled for the Statue of Liberty.

Besides his public philandering, Isaac Singer's personal behavior left much to be desired. For example, author Peter Lyon in his 1954 *American Heritage* article, "Great Stories of American Businessmen,"[14] said, "he [Singer] was hot-tempered, arrogant, and habitually profane." So despicable was this great inventor that according to historian Birmingham, Edward Clark's wife refused to allow her husband's full business partner into her home.[15] Because of this strained, contentious affiliation between the two business partners, discord fired the company. Clark and Singer disliked each other intensely. Only Singer's boundless creative gifts kept the difficult partnership alive.[16] The great innovator's ongoing enhancements to his little device always kept consumer demand high. On the other hand, Clark's social circles suffered mightily as the scandalous rumors of Singer's lifestyle spread. No other business marriage of convenience has been so Manichean, so dubious, or so disputable. No business venture promised so little chance of success. Yet, no other business partnership has succeeded so magnificently: never has so little elegance graced such great prosperity. Not before, nor since.

Isaac Merritt Singer. Actor, mechanic, inventor and industrialist.

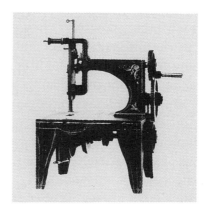

Isaac M. Singer's first sewing machine. Patent No. 8294, Machine for Sewing Seams in Cloth and Other Substances. Patented on August 12, 1851.

"The great inventor is one who has walked forth upon the industrial world, not from universities, but from hovels; not as clad in silks and decked with honors, but as clad in fustian and grimed with soot and oil." – *Isaac Taylor*

Chapter Two

Isaac Merritt Singer (1811-1875)
A Man of Successful Extremes

Isaac Merritt Singer was a complex man obsessively driven to extremes. Writers and historians usually dwell briefly on Singer's most notorious qualities, on his public philandering and on his polygamist lifestyle. As a group, they have not studied this great inventor's achievements. As noted historian Peter Lyon wrote ". . . chroniclers have likewise looked down their noses at Singer."[17] Writers have sneered at Singer's maladjusted home life, as if the hapless youth had himself chosen a life's path that lead to emotional self-destruction. Writers also overlook Singer's unequaled technical skill and interpersonal marketing artistry that both served early industry and its society so wondrously. Unfortunately, this great innovator's true genius has evoked little interest. Singer's reputation as a great inventor has not carried into our times. But this intelligent, boisterous, self-assured man could create, design, improvise and innovate in a careless, offhand and maddening manner. For more than two decades, Singer's ongoing innovations to his little machine guided his company along the leading edge of the changing technological frontier.

Besides his mechanical genius, Singer's marketing innovations led — in his own time — to the founding of a powerful financial empire. Perhaps, Isaac Singer never expected to become a powerful industrialist and moneyed capitalist. Singer's early obsession was with the fair sex and not with the pursuit of wealth; at least, not at the outset. The youthful Singer, who was always self-driven to excel, careened headlong over divergent but equally burdensome life paths.

The origins of Singer's complex personality and idiosyncratic behavior lie in the unevenness of his formative years. Although his ancestry traces to Hungarian Jewish origins, his family never accorded him this ethnocentric or any other close-knit kinship. Isaac M. Singer was the last of eight children to grow up within a troubled, dysfunctional, working class family. Isaac Merritt Singer was born on October 27, 1811 in Pittstown, New York, to Adam and Ruth Singer. Soon afterwards, the family relocated to Oswego, New York. Singer's elderly father, who found occasional work as a carpenter and farm hand, neglected Isaac, his youngest boy. At a time when most families honored religion, Singer's family, while outwardly Lutheran, was godless. Isaac Merritt Singer's upbringing differed little from that of a modern latchkey child left to his or her unguided meandering.

The most significant passage in Singer's life arrived during his tenth year. In that year, in 1821, his birth mother, Ruth Singer, divorced his aging father and left town, never to see her youngest son again. We can only guess at the long term effects of this tragic loss on Isaac Singer's life.

Although Adam Singer remarried, Isaac did not grow close to his new stepmother.[18] Outside his drab home life, the restless adolescent found little to excite his imagination in Oswego, New York. Oswego was then a developing frontier town founded only 25 years before. In later years, Oswego townspeople recalled Isaac Singer as a restless sort with a reputation as a quick study while apprenticing in a local machine shop. But the hard working life handed to him did not satisfy the Singer boy. Isaac Singer's journey into opportunity begins in 1823 when he was only 12 years old. Historians have generally written that teenage Isaac linked up with a company of actors passing through his hometown. The probable truth is that Isaac went to live with an older brother in Rochester, N.Y. Surviving reports show that I. M. Singer worked in the machinery trade during those years and in that city. His choice of studying the machinist trade was, perhaps, not arbitrary. The machinery trade held the same attraction to young people as does the computer industry for many of today's youths. The Industrial Revolution's flowering was accompanied by a fascination with the great changes in automation that enabled this great social and economic upheaval.

In 1830, while living in Rochester, NY, 19-year-old Singer auditioned for a traveling actor's troupe and landed a leading role as Shakespeare's Richard III. At his original audition, Singer reportedly recited portions of several Shakespearean plays entirely from memory. In December of the same year, Isaac Singer, the tall, handsome, articulate actor, brought an adoring female fan, Catharine Maria Haley, before a justice of the peace. Ms. Haley, who was only fifteen-years-old, had ostensibly been captivated during one of Singer's stirring performances in Palmyra, a New York town near Rochester. As a newlywed, married, the youthful Singer reluctantly left the low-paying acting profession to work first as a wood turner, then a store clerk, and later as a machinist's apprentice. After four months of service in another machinery apprenticeship, Singer undertook his own entrepreneurial enterprise after landing a contract to construct a lathe-like, factory production machine. One can only imagine how truly gifted this youth must have been to have entered into his own business venture with so little prior work experience.

For the next 20 years, Singer moved frequently while supporting himself as an actor and as a job-shopping machinist. His first child, a son, arrived in 1834. A year later, Singer moved his family to New York City reportedly to profit from that metropolis' many acting opportunities. However, in no more than twelve months' time, the ever-impulsive Singer again went on the road with still another acting troupe. According to Charles M. Eastley, author of *The Singer Saga*, "He worked for them (acting troupes) as a stage-hand, carpenter, ticket seller, advance agent, and occasionally (at first) acted small parts until his employers went bankrupt."[19] With his family in New York City and while performing on stage in Baltimore, Maryland, the charming, tall, red-haired, handsome Singer discovered 18-year-old Mary Ann Sponsler, a poor oyster fisherman's daughter. So as not to undermine a possible relationship with this obviously star-struck, uncompromisingly attractive small town girl, Singer neglected to reveal he was a married man. During a brief home visit a few months later, Singer again impregnated his legal wife and then promptly deserted her.

Singer chose to remain in New York City. After renting suitable quarters in a boarding house, Isaac offered a promise of marriage to convince Mary Ann Sponsler to join him. After relocating, Mary Ann belatedly learned of her lover's marital status and reluctantly agreed to pose with Isaac as Mr. and Mrs. Merritt.[20] In those Victorian days, men and women did not simply live together – not even in literature. The social pressure to disguise their immorality must have been enormous. Possibly, Mary Ann became Mrs. Merritt, the actor's wife, because of her fear of disclosing Isaac's betrayal to her very religious family. She may have simply been in love. Some writers have said Singer promised to end this temporary arrangement when he could afford to divorce his troublesome first wife. This nebulous union with Mary Ann would remain unlawful for twenty-five years and produce ten children. The first of their many children, William, arrived in 1837.

Before long, I. M. Singer resumed his vagabond acting career. Eventually, this second family soon joined him on the acting circuit. According to the historian Eastley, "They traveled about the country acting upon the stage. In fact, during their first fifteen years . . . they were nearly destitute having no local habitation nor any substantial means of support. They wandered about the country in a one-horse wagon."[21] One suspects that such a close-quartered gypsy's life must have produced a endearing relationship between Mr. and Mrs. Merritt. Singer himself once said, "By the gods! She is a good woman and a faithful wife, and I don't know what I would have done without

Ann."[22] And much later on, at the height of his capitalist career, it would be the faithful Mary Ann whom Singer's acquaintances and business colleagues would recognize as "the" Mrs. Singer.

Whether he was first an actor and later a mechanic only by necessity, as many writers have said, one cannot dispute the reality of I. M. Singer's inventive genius. Singer's mechanical aptitude first made itself known during 1839. While working alongside his older brother on a canal project in Chicago, Singer devised his first important invention, a rock drilling machine. Perhaps Singer had read of recent French enhancements to an ancient Chinese method of rope-drilling artesian wells. Using a similar scheme, Singer tethered horses to a large diameter, horizontally positioned wheel. The slow pacing horses simultaneously rotated and slammed a large metal drill into the rock. Historians have called this invention the forerunner of the rotary drill press. Singer succeeded in selling his 1839 patent for the then huge sum of two thousand dollars.

With this grubstake, Singer formed his own acting troupe, the Merritt Players of Chicago. The Merritt Players quickly booked Singer's live-in wife and her brother into leading roles. The troupe produced Shakespearean stage plays almost exclusively for nearly five years. During these traveling years, Mary Ann delivered three more Singer children. In time, the Merritt Players popularity ebbed until, with seeming suddenness, the entire troupe found themselves penniless in Fredericksburg, Ohio.

Singer wasted no time finding work in a Fredericksburg print shop where his fertile imagination once again leaped into life. While employed at hand carving wooden blocks into typefaces, Singer set about devising a machine to replicate his hand motions. Within a short time, Singer's inventive genius produced a labor-saving mechanical device to carve wood and metal typefaces. A local newspaper reported that the sophisticated, intricately operating contrivance, which Singer quickly patented, worked extremely well.[23] Armed with this new financial opportunity, Singer carried his "Machine for Carving Wood and Metal," back to New York City. On arrival, he solicited and secured financial backing from the A. B. Taylor manufacturing concern on whose premises he erected his newfangled machine. Unfortunately, this business venture returned nothing in the way of financial profit. Disappointed but still believing in the commercial viability of his machine, Singer nevertheless moved Mary Ann and their children to Pittsburgh, Pennsylvania. Singer's motive for this major relocation may have been a belief of a need for a wood type and sign-making shop in that major city. During these years of operating a small business, the Singer family enjoyed three years of middle-class prosperity until, with new patents in hand, Singer returned to New York City and its greater potential for his now enhanced invention.[24] It became apparent that a modest lifestyle, such as that of small businessman, would never satisfy a driven man like I. M. Singer.

On his 1849 return to the New York's lower east side, Singer never bothered looking up his legitimate wife and children who lived near his newly rented quarters. A 38-year-old Isaac Singer again called Mary Ann and their children to his side. Shortly after moving into a rented house, the longtime Merritt family ended their charade by changing their name to Singer. Their children's last names also changed without the benefit of a courtroom. On a visit to A. B. Taylor's, he saw his original carving machine neatly scraping bits of wood away as well as the day he left it. Singer felt pleased no doubt: at Taylor's he was now recognized as a real inventor.

Reports of invention and progress continued to suffuse newspapers. Stories of wild, overnight financial success flowed across every kitchen table. Horatio Alger helped spread these fact-based tall tales in his trademark rags-to-riches stories. And in Alger's day, exemplary men of ideas such as those introducing labor-saving machines, did emerge as powerful industrial giants in a fortnight. The stereotypical American image of Yankee ingenuity was in these days born. And no one promised to epitomize this characteristic portrait more than Isaac Merritt Singer.

George Zeiber: A Savior

Singer again began marketing his enhanced wood and metal type-carving machine. Unfortunately for Singer, a boiler explosion destroyed his only production model. The explosion also ended the lives of 63 hapless A. B. Taylor company employees. After the tragedy, a despondent Taylor decided not to rebuild Singer's intricate machine. Singer's dream seemed dashed. But the always ingenious and persistent Singer soon located another investor, George B. Zeiber. Zeiber, a successful bookseller, believed there was a niche for Singer's machine within the publishing industry. For a full share of Singer's enterprise, Zeiber advanced his life savings of $1,700 to rebuild the type-carving machine. For Zeiber, this risky investment began a business relationship that would consume the rest of his life. Perhaps, this relationship destroyed his life.

In June of 1850, Zeiber and Singer transported the reconstructed type-carving machine to Boston, where a large, well-developed publishing industry awaited. With high expectations, the two men put the machine on public display in a room leased within Orson C. Phelps's workshop at 19 Harvard Place in Cambridge, Massachusetts. Unfortunately, the sedate Boston publishing industry took little notice of the intricate contraption; and none were sold. While in Phelps's factory, I. M. Singer became interested in the Lerow and Blodgett sewing machines that Phelps manufactured and repaired. These machines, like all sewing machines of that time, closely emulated the mechanical stitching operations patented a few years before by Elias Howe. Such machine designs, though workable, were remarkable for – and thoroughly resented for – their high frequency of required maintenance and repair. Even when the Lerow and Blodgett machines ran peacefully, they demanded the vigilant hand of the most capable operator.

It was Phelps who originally suggested that Singer apply his wizardry to designing a general purpose sewing machine. At Phelps's urging, Singer studied the faulty and contentious Blodgett mechanism that produced a lockstitch by drawing threads from two separate spools. In a day's time, Singer approached Phelps with a rough sketch for a mechanism that would greatly simplify the sewing machine's operation. Phelps, an expert machinist himself, quickly recognized the feasibility of Singer's design and gave the project his approval. Just as quickly, the three men formed a partnership to support the new venture. Phelps furnished the work space, machinist tools and even the help of his workers. For his part, George Zeiber promptly contributed another forty dollars for Singer's living and miscellaneous expenses. Singer, like any modern consultant, brought his experience and design skills to the table. Zeiber reported that the three equal partners suddenly felt overwhelmed by the excitement and romance of invention.

Many years later, John Scott quoted Singer in his *Genius Rewarded: or The Story of the Sewing Machine:*

Phelps and Zeiber were satisfied that it would work. I had no money. Zeiber offered forty dollars to build a model machine. Phelps offered his best endeavors to carry out my plan and make the model in his shop; if successful, we were to share equally. I worked at it day and night, sleeping but three or four hours a day out of the 24, and eating generally but once-a-day, as I knew I must make it for forty dollars or not get it at all.

The machine was completed in 11 days. About nine o'clock in the evening we got the parts together and tried it; it did not sew; the workmen exhausted with almost unremitting work, pronounced it a failure and left me one by one.

Zeiber held the lamp, and I continued to try the machine, but anxiety and incessant work had made me nervous and I could not get tight stitches. Sick at heart, about midnight, we started for our hotel. On the way, we sat down on a pile of boards and Zeiber mentioned that the loose loops of thread were on the upper side of the cloth. It flashed upon me that we had forgot to adjust the tension on the needle thread. We went back, adjusted the tension, tried the machine, sewed five stitches perfectly and the thread snapped, but that was enough. At three o'clock the next day the machine was finished. I took it to New York and employed Mr. Charles M. Keller to patent it. It was used as a model in the application for the patent.[25]

As they watched this first practical sewing machine stitch along, the three partners felt a wonderful exuberance no less than the Wright brothers would experience after their first successful flight. In their elation, George Zeiber thought to name Singer's invention the *Jenny Lind*, after the famous Swedish singing soprano and coloratura. Ms. Lind's successful American tour had been P. T. Barnum's marketing brainchild. During 1850, Barnum's publicity machine made sure that a newspaper was fed a report of the *Swedish Nightingale*'s barnstorming activities along with a revue of her extraordinary performances. Zeiber soon reconsidered his idea and talked Isaac into calling his invention by the inventor's own name, Singer.[26] Perhaps the allusion to the little machine's *singing* appeared too great a marketing ploy to miss.

The great invention, Singer's original sewing machine itself, resembled a small desktop router table having an L-shaped arm that supported the vertical sewing needle and thread assembly. A side-mounted hand wheel moved a main gear that meshed with two smaller gears driving the above-table and the under-table mechanisms in a forced synchronism. Like many well-publicized contemporary startups, the Singer Manufacturing Company fabricated its first production models in a garage-size workshop. A 1911 Singer Company publication says: ". . . the place where the first machine was made for sale – was in Harvard Place, Boston, where several other sewing machine inventors, notable in their generation, had their home and worked out their ideas into more or less practical form."[27]

The initial response to Singer's creation proved far less than its three promoters expected. The years of touting impractical sewing machines had built up a wall of public distrust for such gadgets. Disappointed customers had engendered a widespread disapproval of sewing machines. But after two years of relentless marketing and public demonstrations, the practicality of Singer's machine overcame this prejudice. On June 25, 1853, an *Illustrated News* article reported that, "The sewing machine has within the last two years acquired a wide celebrity, and established its character as one of the most efficient labor-saving instruments ever introduced to public notice. [Previously] they were so imperfect, both in principle of construction and mechanical finish, that they were soon laid aside, leaving the deceived purchasers smarting under the imposition."[28] The article went on to describe this new technology's proper employment [sic], "We must not forget to call attention to the fact that this instrument is peculiarly calculated for female operatives. They should never allow its use to be monopolized by men."

Within two years of its introduction, the practicality of Singer's sewing machine furnished the entire industry the credibility it lacked. An article in the respected *Godey's Lady's Book* elicited a widespread demand for the Singer machine and probably opened the door for its following success.[29] Writing in 1880, historian John Scott said, "Many other machines, of more or less merit, were constructed before Mr. Singer made his machine, but all fell short of being practical or useful."[30]

In 11 days' time, Singer completely redesigned the uncomplicated Lerow-Blodgett mechanism. The Lerow and Blodgett machine operation ran the shuttle around in a circle while its horizontally held and curved needle stabbed into the vertically positioned cloth. Singer's innovation introduced a less complex straight-line path for the shuttle to follow and a straight up-and-down motion for a vertically mounted needle-bar that systematically skewered the flat placed fabric. Singer's close-tolerance machining of the toothed gears, which never jammed due to the forced synchronization, and his use of iron throughout the entire construction guaranteed the reliability of his machine.

Besides a novel presser-foot that held the fabric in place and freed both operator's hands, Singer introduced another clever and unheralded innovation, the yielding spring. The yielding spring permitted automatic adjustment to modulating fabric thicknesses and allowed the sewing mechanism to jump over seams without pausing or stopping. Additionally, it allowed continuous feed of the fabric and the ability to sew both curved and linear continuous stitches. Isaac Singer's machine was the first sewing machine to suspend a needle from an overhanging arm set above a horizontal table. On 12 August 1851, Singer received patent number 8294 for his improved sewing machine.

Isaac Singer followed up on his original design with continuing improvements he patented both here and abroad. For example, in May 1854 he patented a chain stitch sewing machine. Between 1854 and 1862, he received eleven more patents for improvements to his original lockstitch reciprocating shuttle machine. By 1867, he received three more patents for improvements to other lock-stitch vibrating shuttle machines.[31] In time he would accrue twenty patents related to various improvements to sewing machines. Taken altogether, Singer's innovations included: continuous feed-wheel, thread-controller, shuttle-thread controller and tension device, heel-and-toe action treadle with an attached flywheel or balance wheel for smooth operations (an idea probably carried over from the spinning wheel), latch under-needle, a binder, a ruffler and tucker, the yielding presser-foot, an embroidering attachment carrying a third thread, a wooden packing case that doubled as the machine's support, and a machine that produced a single-thread chain-stitch. Singer also developed an iron stand with a rocking treadle wide enough to hold both feet. Not realizing the value of this last idea, he failed to patent this invention.[32] Two years after its introduction and Singer company use, his competitors discovered this fact and freely incorporated the wide treadle on their machines. It was then too late to apply for a patent.

Singer's original invention could zip along at 900 stitches per minute; by contrast, an experienced and fast seamstress might get forty stitches in place in the same amount of time. Because of its iron construction, the Singer machine did not struggle with the maintenance and repair problems characteristic of less-rigid, less-precise wooden machines.

While Singer's machine proved entirely useful, it was not an overnight success. Singer single-handedly fought a well-developed dislike and distrust of sewing machines in general. Many different sewing machine manufacturers made unique models of sewing machines; none of these inventions operated very well. Isaac Singer's voice appeared to be one more barker in the sewing machine circus. Even one of his competitors, Blodgett, of Lerow and Blodgett fame and a successful and respected tailor of the time advised the struggling Singer that "sewing machines will never come into (general) use."[33] This widespread negativism seemed to little affect the persistent inventor. Singer seized on every opportunity to advertise his invention. Calling on his stage skills, he traveled to and demonstrated his sewing machine at fairs and circuses. In those early days of the Industrial Revolution, no one marketed as lavishly or as aggressively as did Isaac Singer. He was the first sewing machine maker to open an elegant sewing machine showroom appointed with all the trappings of the gilded age. A surviving pencil sketch shows a basketball-court-sized hall lined with dozens of sewing machines surrounded by appreciative onlookers. In this oversized showroom, I. M. Singer first trained and then retained young women as sales consultants to demonstrate his various sewing machine models. The message was clear: if a diminutive young woman could operate a Singer, anyone could. According to historian Kaemppfert, "Singer was the pioneer in the use of lavishly decorated showrooms."[34]

Singer's unusual marketing techniques eventually succeeded. Although Singer's sales efforts held no equal, the venture's success owes more to the efforts and direction of his working business partner, Edward S. Clark. Indeed, without Edward Clark's guidance and support, the I. M. Singer Sewing Machine Company would have died out as quickly as it fired up.

Prosperity Brings A New Lifestyle

Isaac Singer's prosperity did not arrive as easily as appears, but it arrived quickly after Edward Clark's veered the company into the right course. In 1853, after Clark came on board, the two men relocated their manufacturing facility from Boston to New York City.[35] In the Mott Street factory, I. M.

Singer devoted all his time in product development. Clark acted as company president with Singer as his second and as an individual research and development department. By 1854, the renamed I. M. Singer & Company produced the best sewing machine technically possible, thanks to Singer's efforts; the company emerged as the world's largest maker of sewing machines thanks to Clark's efforts. Within a few short years, the two partners became wealthy industrialists. Clark invested his profits carefully and wisely; Singer placed much of his newfound wealth in the service of his notorious lifestyle.

Although he was still legally married to Catharine Maria Haley, the public believed that Mary Ann Sponsler, who lived under the same palatial roof with Singer and their children, was the great capitalist's wife. One may wonder why the real Mrs. Singer never came forward to end the public charade of her now-wealthy and bigamist husband? Perhaps Singer's ongoing financial support kept her silenced. To onlookers, the counterfeit Singer family appeared little different from other wealthy families ensconced in an ostentatious home on New York's Fifth Avenue. Here in the heart of the great society, Isaac and Mary Ann and their children lived luxuriously with the help of many servants and a coachman to care for their six carriages and horses. Like his well-healed contemporaries, Singer enjoyed promenading in his ornate horse-drawn carriages that distinguished New York City's well-to-do. To mark his arrival within the city's elite, Singer personally designed a ostentatious 3,800-pound horse-drawn carriage. This street-liner held as many as thirty-one adults, with added rear seating for children and servants. Smaller sections held a nursery and a smoking room. Even New Yorkers accustomed to affluent displays must have gazed in awe at the brilliant yellow with glossy-black trim, nine horse-powered galleon as it lurched down crowded city streets on a lazy Sunday afternoon. The magnificent wagon made clear to all – Isaac Merritt Singer had arrived.

Besides these ostentatious displays, Isaac provided all his children, even those not living with him, with a high-priced education and excellent music tutoring. His live-in family enjoyed health care through full-time employment of a physician dedicated to their personal needs. However, though they had arrived financially, the Singers were unable to purchase acceptance within New York's higher social milieu. As historians say, this rejection had little or nothing to do with Singer's godless or immoral lifestyle. The old-moneyed high society that surrounded the Singer residence, which consisted of the 400 families that mattered, cared little for nouveau-riche upstarts like the Singers. This close-knit society remained shut to all but the most blue-blooded families. Singer's inability to penetrate high society arose from his lack of pedigree and not from his lack of social skill. But Singer's uneven, brusk character traits alienated those in social circles he should have been part of. For example, the Singer's did not socialize with their business partner, Edward Clark, whose religion-ingrained society disapproved of Isaac's infidelities and open-marriage. Nor did Singer's immediate neighbors wish to socialize with the wealthy industrialist they regarded as a garrulous and callous brute. In sum, the fabulously wealthy Singers never achieved the social approbation they most desired.

In 1860, Singer finally divorced Catherine, his legal wife of thirty years. After a great deal of backroom machinations[36] and on advice of her attorney, Catherine accepted Singer's miserly $10,000 buyout. She also admitted before a judge in open court that she was an adulterer; adultery then being the only accepted ground for divorce in New York State. Attorney Clark, no doubt solely concerned with appearances, had proffered the original proposal to Catherine. Doubtless the puritanical Clark wanted to raise his business partner's moral standing in the community. It is likely that Clark hoped to end the ongoing disdain for his commercial partner's lifestyle. Certainly the proper attorney did not enjoy justifying his personal business dealings to his conservative acquaintances and their Victorian Age credo.

With his long-awaited divorce finalized, both Edward Clark and Mary Ann Sponsler stood shocked beyond belief when Isaac reported he had no intention of remarrying. He would not marry his lifelong and faithful mate and put himself, as he told Mary Ann, 'under her power.' Isaac enjoyed Mary Ann's faithful company; but marriage must have appeared unattractive to the great polygamist who simultaneously maintained other longstanding liaisons. One of these liaisons, with Mary McGonical, was equally deserving of the stamp of respectability as was the cohabitation with Mary Ann. Ms. McGonical, whom Singer discovered on a trip to San Francisco, had borne five Singer children: one in each year of 1852, 1854, 1856, 1858 and 1859. Mary Ann Sponsler's children had arrived in 1852, 1856 and 1857. The now nine-year-long liaison with Ms. McGonical, who posed with the itinerant Singer as Mr. and Mrs. Matthews, was hardly a quiet one. After all, Singer had fathered five children with her and maintained a separate New York City home for his Matthews family. He provided for all of this family's financial needs as well. When in company of Ms. McGonical, Singer answered to her neighbors and friends as Mr. Matthews. But Singer's brazen hedonism, this delicately positioned house of cards, was about to tumble down.

On August 7, 1860, on a beautiful, sun-filled, summer day, while Mr. and Mrs. Matthews breezed along in a luxurious open air carriage, an event happened that set adrift the entire web of Singer's deceit. As the Matthew carriage coasted peacefully down Fifth Avenue, it passed close to a Singer carriage transporting Mary Ann Sponsler in the opposite direction. At the sight of this open infidelity, Mary Ann Sponsler forgot herself. Without thought for the consequences of her actions, the intolerant lady blasted off a socially unacceptable, stream of vitriolic anger at her unfaithful husband. Mary Ann's rage erupted like a cannon shot in the surrounding respectability of Fifth Avenue society. Onlookers gleefully reported the details of this public vilification of this important public man, of this great capitalist. To all, this one reckless public act confirmed the truthfulness of the interminable sordid backdoor murmurings. During an age when appearances meant all, this public display became too much for even the dissolute Isaac to bear.

Within the hour, a livid Isaac Merritt Singer returned to his 14 Fifth Avenue palace where he confronted an equally unrecalcitrant Mary Ann. The confrontation heated quickly, then turned violent. As tempers flared, Singer resorted to choking his wife-of-convenience into unconsciousness. When Mary Ann's daughter entered the fray with a voice of reason, he choked that young woman into unconsciousness as well. Now, the gentlemanly long-hidden truths about the great innovator were exposed to polite society. Mary Ann told authorities that Isaac often beat her physically and usually tamed her with verbal abuse. The resulting social and very public chastisement devastated the usually callous Singer. Perhaps, he feared the legal ramifications of his thoughtless actions even more. As a result, on September 19, 1860, 49-year-old Isaac Singer booked passage on a London-bound ocean liner. For his sole traveling companion, the socially outcast industrialist chose Ms. McGonical's 19-year-old sister, Kate.

European Departure

Notwithstanding the welcome company of his youthful, understanding traveling companion, this departure must have been more than doubly painful for Isaac. Not only would he no longer enjoy the company of both his *wives* the public had knowledge of, now he would no longer enjoy the company of a third but little-known common-law wife, Mary Eastwood Walters *Merritt*. Fortunately for Singer, the press had not discovered this third Singer family. With this Mary, Singer fathered a girl in 1851. While together, I. M. Singer and Ms. Walters opted for the then vacant alias of Mr. and Mrs. Merritt.[37] In all, at the time of his 1860 escape or self-banishment to Europe, I. M. Singer had fathered eighteen children among these exceptionally attractive younger women. Sixteen of these offspring were then alive. The detail-oriented Singer knew all of his wives by the name of Mary. Including Catharine *Maria* Haley. He apparently never chanced to call his wife of the moment by another woman's name.

On arriving in England, Singer first settled near his Cheapside factory. But finding little to occupy his interest, he soon rented temporary quarters in Paris. In this lively metropolis, he linked up with another young woman in her early twenties, Isabella Eugenie Summerville. The ravishing, Paris-born Isabella was divorced from an American named Summerville. One gossipy story of the time relates that the great capitalist had first dated Isabella's mother, Pamela Boyer, until his greater interest in

Isabella surfaced. During a return business trip to New York City, which was taken to formerly dissolve his partnership with Edward Clark, Isaac married the pregnant, Catholic-raised Isabella on a Saturday, the 13th of June 1863 in an Episcopal church. Later, Singer even allowed an Episcopal minister to baptize him. Contrary to some historians' reports, Singer did not marry to appease Edward Clark's sense of morality. The Singer and Clark partnership had dissolved a full week before on June 6. Doubtless his new paramour's Catholic religiousness was the death knell to Isaac's bachelorhood. On June 25, Mrs. Isabella Singer bore the first of six Singer children. One of their offspring, Paris Singer, became a prominent architect and earned notice by contributing to the establishment of the Everglades Club in Palm Beach, Florida. The newlyweds again setup residence in New York City, but not on Fifth Avenue. Isaac and Isabella soon learned that the moral majority's outrage had diminished little during Isaac's three year exile. They quickly realized they would not penetrate the city's fashionable social circles. Again, the absence of societal acceptance sent the Singers reeling back to Europe. The less affected Europeans enjoyed rubbing shoulders with the interesting misalliance of brute and loveliness. Isabella said she missed French society and culture. From their elegant home in a fashionable Paris neighborhood, the Singers catered to a limited social network of European nobility. In a less puritanical Europe, the unlikely couple managed to avoid complete social ostracism. With their home established, Isabella bore Singer's fourth child. Isaac had now fathered 22 offspring.

When the Franco-Prussian War of 1870 approached Paris city limits, the Singers moved out of harm's way to the small town of Paington in Devon. Now resettled in Britain, Singer began designing an expansive Greco-Roman mansion that he named The Wigwam. Singer wanted, like his aristocratic neighbors, to build a princely castle. He hankered also to stamp his new villa with a distinctly American individualism and image. However, before completion of his estate, on July 23, 1875, Isaac Singer died of a heart attack at the age of 64. He was laid to rest in Torquay, England, in a mausoleum he had constructed less

than a mile from his Paington home. Two thousand mourners
from around the world trailed along in 75 horse-drawn carriages
to form a mile-long funeral procession. The town of Paington
lowered its municipal flags to half-staff to honor its most famous
resident. After the great innovator's passing, construction on The
Wigwam ended. During World War I, the edifice saw service as
an American Women's War Hospital.[38] At war's end, the great
building began a slow deterioration. In 1945, Paris Singer
donated The Wigwam to the town of Paington, which put it to
use as its municipal center.

Isaac Singer bequeathed his huge $13 million estate into
60 equal shares to all his offspring and to all his former legal and
common law wives save one.[39] Isaac Singer had fathered children
with at least six women: Catherine Maria Haley, Isabella Eugenie
Boyer, Mary Eastwood Walters, Mary McGonical, Ellen Brazee,
Ellen Livingstone and Mary Ann Sponsler. The troublesome
Mary Ann Sponsler, who received little from her many lawsuits
against Isaac (thanks to the poor or corrupt legal counsel which
colluded with Singer[40]) received nothing at all in Singer's will. A
newspaper reported: "He (Singer) never covered his acts with a
cloak of hypocrisy, but recognized in his will all just claims upon
him."[41]

Isabella Singer, whom Edward Clark had personally
assisted in her claim to Singer's estate,[42] became a wealthy,
uncommonly attractive widow. Suitors of all descriptions flocked
to her door. High society welcomed her. The public sought her
out as they did famous actresses. She attracted Frederick
Auguste Bartholdi's interest and graciously modeled for his
Statue of Liberty. New York society, which had never accepted
her, would now look out at her every day of the year. Eventually,
she married an impoverished Italian Count who helped direct her
share of the Singer fortune into a socially active lifestyle.[43]

Possible Early Influences on Isaac Singer

In Isaac Singer's time, the public's imagination filled with
the latest advances in the Industrial Revolution. In 1850, the U.S.
Congress voted to add two more wings to the Patent Office that
was then bursting to overflowing with the warehousing of 17,000

models of gadgetry and carefully designed instruments.⁴⁴ This was the dawning Age of Automation. It was a time of revolution in mechanical craftsmanship whose entire engineering science then consisted of advances in the machinery trade. During the eighteenth century, the scientific literature feeding popular imagination was extensive. Practical developments, which usually arrived with the evolution of automata and ongoing enhancements of the automatic machine tools of the Industrial Revolution, filled every newspaper and elicited words of wonder over every dinner table.

Singer, like so many young men of his day, doubtless marveled at the new scientific discoveries. Besides the textile industry's spinning jennies, flax spinning machines, and automatic Jacquard looms, many important discoveries attracted the public's fancy. Some of these included the British Army's use of rockets as weapons; the discovery of infrared light; the electric battery; Eli Whitney's cotton gin; the hydraulic press; lithography; William Burt and his printing typewriter; Edwin Budding and his first lawnmower; John Howe's automatic machine that mass produced straight pins; railroad and ship steam engines; the revelation of atomic theory; the development of morphine; the process of canning food; the launching of *Nautilus*, the first submarine; and the almost weekly discoveries in pure physics, mathematics, chemistry and medicine. All combined to propel this incipient scientific culture into the limelight of public awareness and into the imagination of inventive men like Isaac Singer.

I. M. Singer claimed to have voraciously absorbed all of the available engineering and scientific literature of his time.⁴⁵ We must believe him. Singer, who was always driven to extremes, showed a consuming passion toward excellence in honing his machinist's skills into a refined expertise. Anyone studying the engineering drawings that Singer submitted to the Patent Office will be immediately struck by their precision and general professional appearance. If Isaac Singer inked these drawings himself, then we must see him as a skilled engineering technician of the highest order. Notwithstanding his great mechanical ability, which his many patents alone stand in testimony of, some historians have characterized Singer as a poor, untrained reader.

Peter Lyon's *American Heritage* article stated, "he [Singer] was practically illiterate."[46] While this may true, Singer may have been a slow reader; his demonstrated trade skills suggest that he slowly read and absorbed everything noteworthy in his field.

Singer's Farewell

I. M. Singer is often quoted saying; "I don't care a damn for the invention. The dimes are what I'm after." This statement alone does not explain Singer's hard-pressed, headlong pursuit of his interests. I. M. Singer struggled mightily to develop his upstart company. Singer himself often recited that during many downward plunges of his company's roller coasting years, he would have gladly divested his share for a small sum. But Isaac Singer stayed the difficult course into prosperity. He also maintained a burdensome course into an unsatisfying personal life. His fundamental essence may have simply been to seek out love, acceptance, and approval. Perhaps, his many youthful wives became surrogates for the youthful mother who deserted him: none succeeded in replacing a mother's love. Isaac Merritt Singer was a man of extremes: an extreme seeker of business and of financial success, of public and of private approbation, and of love and passion. He differed only in the extreme measures used to reach for the basic acceptance we all need. His invention and business legacy have changed our world and our everyday relationships for all time.

"The history of the world is but the biography of great men." — Thomas Carlyle.

Chapter Three

The Sewing Machine's Historical Significance
Briefly Revisiting Its Origins

The sewing machine's significance for the modern corporation's workplace and its overall evolution has not only been forgotten, it has never been recognized. Somehow, historians have overlooked the sewing machine's influence on modern industrial history. How did this happen? Why hasn't the sewing machine received its due alongside the other notable tools of the Industrial Revolution, such as the steam engine and the reaper?

As a group, historians agree that the Industrial Revolution, which they also refer to as the Age of Automation, or the Age of Machinery, opened the door to modernism. They believe the textile industry and its manufacture of cloth fabrics spearheaded this economic revolution both here in the colonies and in Europe. Their studies show how textile factory centers flourished as one scientific discovery after the other pushed this country's economic miracle forward.

Mainstream historical works aver that the Industrial Revolution came about because of the key innovations of spinning jennies, giant weaving looms, steam engines and the breakthrough discoveries of iron and steel. But why do these same history books rarely mention the 12 million sewing machines that came into use during these very same years? Such an oversight seems the more remarkable since the generations who lived during this era held the sewing machine in high regard. For example, mid-nineteenth century newspapers recognized the sewing machine's contribution to modernity and gave it its due. A *New York Times* 1860 feature article began: "To America belongs the honor of giving to the world many new inventions of great practical importance to mankind. Prominent among these are the Electric Telegraph, the Reaper and Mower, and the Sewing Machine. What the telegraph is to the commercial world, the reaper to the agricultural, the sewing machine is to the domestic."[47]

In the eyes of mid-century Americans, the sewing machine affected all facets of the developing Industrial Revolution and by extension, all facets of their lives and culture. If historians identify the Industrial Revolution with fabric production, why do their studies overlook the little machines that stitched all that enormous textile output together? Besides automating the making of canvas, sheets, drapes, curtains, rugs, blankets and towels, the sewing machine mechanized both the shoe and ready-to- wear clothing industry for all time. In the rush to simplify the compilation of progress, historians have dismissed *The Great Civilizer,* as Singer's machine came to be known, and failed to recognize the sewing machine's significance in ushering in the Age of Automation.[48]

While Isaac Merritt Singer may be the most colorful character with the most recognized name in sewing machine history, he alone did not create this important industry. Even in 1850, a full year before Isaac Singer invented his sewing machine, the marketplace offered a large variety of patented sewing machines. Until Isaac Singer came on the scene, all sewing machines were produced in small machine shops; sewing machine factories still did not exist.[49] Without doubt, I. M. Singer &

Company, which introduced sewing machine mass production and mass marketing techniques, spearheaded the sewing industry's evolution. The Singer Company's eventual leadership, monopoly and de facto control over its industry, attests to its central role in the furthering of the first home appliance industry.

Thanks to Singer, the sewing machine became the first small home appliance to infiltrate households both in this country's rural and urban locales and in all of the world's major cities and nameless hamlets. Long-lasting, uncomplicated, hand- or foot-powered sewing machines still sing away in every corner of the globe. The sewing machine's evolution created and guided the evolution of the home appliance industry. Advances in this home appliance's manufacture, which demanded the most advanced and precise production equipment, directed the factory system's progress. Modern-day corporate processes evolved from the factory system that was born within the Industrial Revolution. This entire evolution is intricately tied to technical advances in the sewing industry.

An Overview of America's Ascent into Modernism: Agriculture First

Unlike their British counterparts, American workers' acceptance of factory automation was immediate and widespread. In the United States, anti-technology, neo-Luddite mobs did not roam nascent urban centers: in America, progress was welcomed everywhere. The first sector of American society to feel the effects of technological advance were the farming communities. Within a relatively short time, America's agrarian society gave way almost wholly to mechanization. In the agricultural community, Automation's onslaught began when new mechanical monsters began plowing, threshing and reaping company-owned fields. In 1810, before mechanization, 2.3 million working Americans labored on small independent, family owned farms. But this traditional face of agriculture and its small garden parcels soon was transformed into large enclosed fields where production intensified under dedicated managers and scientific growing processes.

Small farmers toiling on homesteads located in harsh unremitting lands could not match the lower-cost harvest of their mechanized and corporatized competitors. As farming became less and less profitable, farmers migrated in an unstoppable stream to fast-growing urban industrial areas. The migration from the farmlands provided the Industrial Revolution and its factory system with its workers. But more than this simple observation, the modernization of agriculture established the fundamental business precedents on which the coming conglomerates and the Singer Company in particular would later capitalize on.

Many of these forward-looking techniques came out of Cyrus McCormick's originality in the manufacturing and marketing of his reaper. Using McCormick's 1833 reaper, one man following behind two horses accomplished as much as 20 field laborers. One can surmise that such a labor-saving device required little marketing and even less cost-justification. However, this is not so. Reapers were expensive and illegal patent infringers abounded. However, by 1860, a full 17 years after developing his invention, McCormick had built and sold only 3,000 reapers. Ten years later, McCormick's manufacturing production levels of 20,000 per year failed to meet demand.

McCormick succeeded, not by crying out for justice, but by beating down his many competitors through lowered costs. McCormick lowered operating costs by introducing mass production techniques; by careful marketing and well-devised on-site demonstrations; by locating his manufacturing facilities close to his client-base to save shipping charges; and by introducing an industry first, the buy-now pay-later installment payment plan. McCormick pioneered this risky sales agreement by allowing buyers to remit the balance of the purchase price of his expensive reaper in December, well after the profits from the harvest season were in.

The Singer Sewing Machine Company would later build factory centers near its globally dispersed consumers and it would also institute installment buying. In an era before sophisticated transportation and shipping, it simply made economic sense to fabricate in the same geographical location where most sales took place. Besides McCormick's precedent-setting establishing of a large scale, uniquely American manufacturing enterprise, he provided a uniquely American means of manufacturing that awaited the arrival of the textile industry to flourish.

American Manufacturing Revives the Industrial Revolution

Automation of the textile industry began with mechanical combing machines to straighten the animal fibers progressed to spinning jennies to string the fibers into yarn arrived at automatic looms to weave the fabric, and finally culminated in sewing machines that stitched the pieces of fabric together. These four major labor-saving innovations changed the basis of industry forever. Besides these inventions, other ancillary machinery played important supporting roles in bringing Automation forward. Some of these included machines for cutting fabric and leather, buttonhole makers and buttonhole installers, and large hot presses to smooth the fabric out. These new production machines, the factory system, sophisticated management, new marketing and distribution techniques finally coalesced to move working America out of its rural-based, cottage-industry era.

Why did this transition take place? During the early 1800s, America's frontierlike towns had no large-scale manufacturing or industry. But America's early settlers had a near unquenchable demand for British-made textile fabrics such as, blankets, sheets, linens, drapes, curtains, rugs, furniture padding and covers, for homemade and ready-to-wear apparel, and for tent and wagon canvas. During the early 1800s, England was the only source for these necessities. When hostilities broke out between the US and England in 1812, industryless America found no alternative but to recreate England's textile industry here.

But how would Americans develop this technology? British protectionist laws stood as strict sentinels over the transfer of its lifeblood technology and its associated trade secrets. These laws forbade the exporting of textile machinery or their associated proprietary machine-assembly drawings. England also barred skilled machine operators and tradesmen from leaving the country.[50] English law prevented workers from providing even an offhand description of their manufacturing techniques.

After declaring war on Britain, Americans suddenly found themselves without a supplier for their textile needs. With no recourse, a previously nonexistent American textile industry quietly began secretive startups. Capable British technologists like Samuel Slater, "the father of the American cotton industry,"[51] recreated a British spinning mill based on Arkwright's spinning machinery in Pawtucket, Rhode Island.

Arriving colonists included many skilled textile workers. In 1811, 100 Irish weavers landed in the port of New York on the same day.[52] As skilled immigrants moved the new technology forward, small tailoring shops began prospering especially in the Massachusetts towns of Waltham, Fall River and Lowell. These small manufacturing concerns quickly expanded into large-scale textile factories. Mill towns emerged where giant weaving looms, and even sophisticated Jacquard looms producing low-cost, intricate weaves, began reverberating with the incessant side-to-side slapping noise of flying shuttles. And in very little time, American textile centers began spewing fabrics of a quality comparable to British textiles. And why would this not have happened? Americans had simply transferred and stolen the technological mantle from Britain.

This transfer of Automation's technology introduced the Industrial Revolution in the United States. Before the arrival of textile manufacturing centers, America's commercial textile and garment industry workers numbered less than 10,000. Most of these worked out of their homes using rudimentary tools to spin, weave and hand sew their clothing and other fabric needs. Now, because England prevented her skilled mechanics from leaving its shores, hard-working Americans taught themselves textile factory production skills and, more importantly, they also taught themselves the machinery trade.[53] As a result, America's feudal-like home fabric industry declined as great textile manufacturing centers rose up.[54]These new automated manufacturing centers, which soon turned to steam power, quickly hastened the economic obsolescence of America's home-based fabric-makers and their spinning wheels.

Unlike their British counterparts, America's textile workers, who were also unfettered by bureaucratic complacency and politics, welcomed progress and innovation. Free from bureaucratic chains, American workers met the challenge of industrialization through logical innovation and by devising their own solutions to toward increased productivity. Yankee ingenuity now took on a special meaning and large, thoroughly American manufacturing centers quickly surpassed their British forbears in cost, quality and productivity.

As American textile productivity increased, America's retail stores began filling with inexpensive textiles and other low-cost manufactured goods. Immigrant factory workers sent letters to their ancestral rural homesteads boasting that for the first time in their lives every family member owned a pair of shoes. New urban families no longer bartered, borrowed, and exchanged labor with other semiskilled home workers. Textile manufacturing and its low-cost, widely available fabrics displaced a nonmechanized, relatively costly cottage industry. A millennia-old way of livelihood had unraveled in a historical instant.

As early as 1840, one half million Americans earned steady wages in commercial manufacturing facilities. Soon urban houses surrounded Automation's industrial centers. Yankee ingenuity gained respectability as it introduced greater efficiency to production machinery. Increased manufacturing efficiency produced lower-cost textiles. Lower costs brought on a skyrocketing demand for these necessary products. The job market responded to these economic forces and began changing. Factory centers called for specialized workers answering to technically skilled, new-styled production managers. Besides sophisticated management, America's new factory system introduced modular, interchangeable machinery parts (first pioneered by Eli Whitney),[55] mechanical power generation, and more humane working conditions. Modern, scientific managers overseeing fast-producing, machinery-driven factories now asked for professional administrative support and business management emerged as a career field.

The advance of automatic machinery, the spread of inexpensive transportation, the onset of retail credit, the formation of commercial shipping and distribution networks, and the growth of manufacturing facilities brought orders for increased production in related supplier industries like coal, iron, steel, and for all building supply vendors. But perhaps no facet of the Industrial Revolution changed the workplace more than when technically skilled laborers struck and lobbied for wages commensurate with their expertise. In 1852, when Singer began producing his sewing machines on a large scale, the first national labor unions also arrived in a major way. Rapidly growing factory centers, especially sewing machine manufacturers, quickly learned to appreciate its technically capable workers. A skilled, well-paid workforce became a middle class with its own lifestyle and a new purchasing power.

This then was the commercial state of the marketplace when the sewing machine arrived. The conclusion that sewing machine manufacturing played a central role in bringing about our modern way of life appears inescapable. Sewing machine manufacturing is the only significant industry that distinguishes British from American industry during mid-eighteenth century economic development. By mid-century the sewing machine becomes the only differentiating element in the American industrial experience. If America had not developed the sewing industry, its Industrial Revolution would have stagnated as Europe's did.

European writers understood why their once-dominant economy had faltered: the Industrial Revolution lost momentum in England when technological advances in the textile industry slowed. These writers believed that British technological progress faltered under the weight of the "American system of manufacture."[56] But more than effective production techniques, the present study believes that sewing machine technology bootstrapped American manufacturing and the Industrial Revolution forward in the colonies. The same 1860 *New York Times* feature article reported: "The sewing machines led to the invention of other machinery for their manufacture . . . the sewing trade [has attracted] some of the best mechanical and commercial talent in the country."[57]

Americans reinvigorated the stagnant Industrial Revolution and its factory system by advancing developments in precision machining, complex tooling and scientific manufacturing techniques. Yankee ingenuity, which especially honed its leading edge technological skills within the sewing industry, redefined the entire workplace. A changing workplace brought along an entirely new lifestyle. All modern peoples are offsprings of this workplace transformation and its prototypical business methodologies. Since the sewing machine claimed a central role in this transition, America's modern lifestyle owes much to the sewing machine's development.

Setting the Stage for the New Conglomerates
How did this transformation in our way of life come about? The business world of the Industrial Revolution fed off laissez-faire government policies. Governments around the globe responded slowly to the arriving industrial giants and the changing workplace. During this hands-off era, Americans viewed capitalism as a fundamental right. In these years of Manifest Destiny Americans believed in the righteousness of westward expansion and in breaking open world markets. In 1853, for example, Commodore Perry sailed into lower Tokyo Bay and forcibly opened isolationist Japan to American trade and influence.

Besides opening up foreign trade, America's Industrial Revolution succeeded because of its new breed of business men. These first corporate managers succeeded by controlling the means of production; by developing a skilled labor force; by investing in emerging technologies when they surfaced; by initiating innovative marketing strategies; or, failing all, they created monopolies through outright buyouts of their competition. Historians call these years the rise of the modern era in the United States.

As seen, the model for laissez-faire capitalism that now suffuses modern times arrived at the dawn of the economic revolution in America. And even at this early stage of capitalism, fast-thinking corporate raiders and robber barons backed by wealthy, profit-sharing bankers plied their trade.

The Sewing Industry Appears

The textile industry had kindled the Industrial Revolution's fires. But fabric manufacturing became an exact, leveled-off industry. So many pounds of wool became so many lengths of yarn. The advances in spinning technology had come to a halt: the 1828 invention of the ring-spinning frame was the last notable innovation in the textile industry.[58] As England's bureaucratically run industries faltered, American's precision manufacturing, such as its introduction of interchangeable machine parts, produced an economic resurgence. This new facet of Automation with its great variety of applications called for different, wide-ranging working skill sets. Skilled machinists were highly sought. For example, the Singer Company manufactured more than 3,000 separate commercial models of its sewing machines during most of its years of operation. Each machine presented its own set of construction plans, parts replacement, maintenance and repair difficulties. It is noteworthy that the Singer Company never monopolized the *commercial* sewing machine market – there were simply too many commercial providers of sewing machines.

For its first 75 years, most Singer sewing machine sales went to jobbers working out of their homes. The sewing machine revitalized the cottage industry by mechanizing it. Hand-sewers became machine operators. During this period of incipient national commerce, a tiny, almost negligibly small market existed for ready-made clothing. The demand for this rough-fitting, harsh-feeling, ready-to-wear clothing had historically come only from sailors and from settlers in western states. Because it was a shipping crossroad for Southern cotton manufacturers, New York City became the location of the first clothing factory in 1831. However, the ready-to-wear market, even with occasional offerings of quality clothing, remained small. So-called *slop shops*, which then existed in major shipping centers and seaport cities, hand-sewed most of its ready-to-wear clothing.

The Civil War created a demand for uniforms. By this time, sewing machines, and especially the Singer sewing machine, had become reliable, practical and affordable. The war's demand for uniforms alongside the sewing machine's newfound acceptance introduced standardized clothing and assembly line techniques in the garment industry. A burgeoning ready-to-wear industry set standard clothing sizes after measuring the anatomy of a thousand or so Union Army soldiers. The sewing machine's portability and ease of operation created the ready-wear clothing industry.

The sewing machine was more than a machine that decorated fabric or performed simple stitching: it was an actual tool of the Industrial Revolution that created its own worker skill sets. Its simple operation lent itself to widespread employment of relatively unskilled labor who developed into specialists. In early clothing manufacturing facilities, the sewing of a ready-to-wear coat would typically be broken into a hundred or more operations. By the turn of the century, sewing in garment-making factories, often described as sweatshops, became the usual occupation for arriving immigrants in New York City.

The sewing machine changed manual sewing, the biggest cottage industry of the early 1800s, into a machine-based industry. Now, America's home-based workers subcontracted their production not to their neighbors, but to large companies in their towns and cities. A distinctly different cottage industry of job-shoppers now rose up. As before, they furnished their own heat, lighting and comfortable working conditions. Like some modern, home-based computer users producing desktop publishing wares, the products of these new jobbers came out of the tabletop machinery of newfangled sewing machines. These subcontractors either bought or purchased sewing machines on installment buying plans. Modest tailor and dressmaking shops purchased several machines and soon blossomed by setting up small-scale mass production techniques. Experienced sewing machine operators owned sought-after skills. Because of its portability, user-friendly operation, and relatively low purchase price, the sewing machine enabled individual business startups as no home appliance had before. Even as early as 1862, 75,000 sewing machines had found their way into American households.[59]

The sewing machine not only brought old products to market faster, it introduced new products to the market. The sewing machine reduced selling prices below those of all manually sewn fabrics. The newfound functionality of sewing machines affected all fabric-based products such as hats, umbrellas, blankets, sheets, tents – anything requiring a stitch. B

Before sewing machines, only the affluent imported machine-woven fabrics for their carefully tailored garments. The typical American clothed himself with mother's careful crocheting and needlework. The sewing machine made small, user-specific, specially tailored clothing runs cost-effective. Sewing machines reduced the textile industry's labor costs and lowered retail prices while increasing sales and profit margins. For example, a hat bindery's new sewing machine stitched 374 stitches in a minute's time while its longtime hand sewers pricked along at an average seven stitches per minute. A commercial sewing machine stitched a man's shirt in one hour and 16 minutes; a seamstress needed 14 hours and 26 minutes to accomplish the same operation. An 1860 Connecticut shirtmaker's 400 sewing machine operators accomplished as much as 2,000 hand sewers.[60] A cost analysis showed that a complete payback, or return on investment, for the 400 sewing machine capital outlay, came within the first 98 days of their use. Sewing machines reduced 80 percent of the cost of sewing together almost any garment: sewing machines had arrived in a big way.

In typical bureaucratic fashion, only the Army Department resisted the new technology by steadfastly insisting on making its uniforms by hand. During the Civil War, however, the Army did begin contracting with machine-sewing concerns in order to clothe its hurriedly conscripted soldiers. These Army contracts went to large, established garment factories whose floors held row after row of industrial sewing machines. A sewing machine invented in 1858, which stitched the parts of a shoe or a boot together, also became important to the Civil War Army's war effort and to the stagnant shoe industry. Before the sewing machine, and according to historian Kaemppfert, "Shoemakers tools taken form the ruins of Roman villages and even from more ancient tombs differ little from those in use when the United States army shoe of 1860 was made."[61] An 1861 U.S. Census study reported that a single sewing machine enabled a cobbler to sew together 900 pairs of shoes in a 10-hour day. This was eleven times more productive than the usual man rate for attaching soles onto upper leather pieces. It is noteworthy that even Singer's original 1851 sewing machine had also been sturdy enough to sew leather pieces together. Following the Civil War and by the turn of the century, the sewing industry emerged as a billion dollar a year industry.

As the sewing industry grew, supplier companies like needle manufacturers, repair parts suppliers, cabinet makers and those making sewing machine attachments boomed with large unexpected production runs. These suppliers increased their production at an unprecedented rate. For example, since mechanical sewing devours three times more thread than hand sewing, thread manufacturers tripled their production. This growing industry produced new blue-collar specializations and a new breed of technically trained mechanics who flocked to good-paying jobs making intricate sewing machine attachments. Automation's progress rested on the leading edge technology of the machinist trade and the sewing industry which increased this demand to an unprecedented level.

When I. M. Singer introduced his refined machine to the domestic market, he eventually released a pent-up demand for a practical and reliable sewing machine. Shortly after his initial successes, Singer's company quickly gained a near monopoly over the domestic sewing machine market and then just as quickly escalated its overall dominance into a global one.

Within a 23-year time span, from 1853 to 1876, the sewing machine industry grew from annual sales of 2,266 to 262,316 sewing machines[62] and from a handful of major manufacturers in 1853, to at least three dozen by 1876. In twenty-five more years, 150 sewing machine manufacturers competed within U.S. borders alone. Between 1860 and 1900, foreign sales of sewing machines surpassed $90,000,000. The Singer Company, the first great conglomerate, the first great multinational company, led all competitors in units sold, foreign or domestic. How did the Singer Sewing Machine come to monopolize this highly competitive industry? The answer lies in the sewing machine's combative history.

A Brief History of Sewing Machines: Fifty years of product development

To understand the sewing machine's development requires an understanding of its classifications. Sewing machines are of three classifications related to the stitch they produce: a simple chain-stitch relies on a single thread stitch; a double chain stitch uses an upper-needle thread linked to a lower thread; and a lockstitch uses a double-thread configuration to interlock upper and lower threads. Since a chain-stitch requires more thread and unravels easily, a lock-stitch is the preferred method of seaming cloth.[63] *Isaac Singer's machine was the first practical machine to produce a lock-stitch.* Before the 1850s, sewing machines were generally unreliable, expensive and close to unproductive. Isaac Singer's sewing machine introduced modern sewing as we now understand it.

By the turn of the century, the U.S. Patent Office had issued more than 700 patents governing advances in sewing machine technology. This fact provides another measure of the sewing machine's stature in the workplace. Like all major technologies, the sewing machine evolved out of years of ongoing modification and enhancement.

The sewing machine originated in Europe but it matured as a thoroughly American invention. Both France and England awarded sewing machine patents years before American sewing machine inventors happened along. But Europeans did not assimilate this new tool of the machinery age.

In America, however, Isaac Singer's all-important patent ignited the fledgling sewing industry. In the wake of Singer's patent, no fewer than 100 American innovators quickly contributed enhancements that eventually culminated in the modern sewing machine. Nevertheless, only a relative few of these inventions deserve mention as useful contributors to and prime-movers of the sewing machine industry.

Early European Efforts: Thomas Saint[64]

On July 17, 1790, London-based cabinet maker Thomas Saint obtained British patent 1764 for a machine that, while designed to assemble "shoes, boots, spatterdashes, clogs and other articles,"[65] nevertheless introduced the concepts of modern sewing. The machine, whose operation emulated crocheting hand movements, employed a vertically mounted awl suspended over a flat table. A hand crank turned cam-linked shafts that forced the awl to pierce a hole in the leather. An eyeless needle with a notched end then pulled the spooled thread into the hole.

Thomas Saint also claimed his machine fed fabric automatically. But if it did, it did so intermittently and not continuously. Perhaps, if Saint's machine had used an eye-pointed needle the resulting tighter stitch may have brought about his success and upstaged Singer's invention by two generations. No one knows if Saint's machine remained a working prototype or if it was actually used in a productive setting.[66] According to historian George Iles *Leading American Inventors*: "[Saint's] machine was virtually forgotten for nearly sixty years. One inventor after another followed Saint. . . . only to miss points of excellence which Saint had included in his model." Iles concluded that Saint's stitching machine never gained popularity, "Simply because its inventor offered people a good thing before they were ready for it."[67]

Thomas Stone[68]

On February 14, 1805, a Parisian by name of Thomas Stone, obtained a patent, a *brevet d'invention*, for: "a machine for joining the sides of segments of all flexible matters." Mr. Stone claimed his machine, "will be particularly serviceable in preparing clothing for the army and navy."[69] A published report of the time declared that a single user of Stone's invention produces as much as "one hundred persons and a needle." No other record of Mr. Stone's possible prosperity survives. After Thomas Stone, many rudimentary stitching machines found limited application in commercial settings. Unfortunately, these poorly functioning apparatuses attracted little public interest and for the next 25 years automatic sewing devices never caught on.

Barthelemy Thimmonier (1793-1857)[70]

The first workable sewing machine did not arrive until 1830. Barthelemy Thimmonier, of St. Etienne, France, aspired to an academic career in higher education. Unfortunately, this intellectually gifted youth lacked the money to continue his education and instead found his livelihood in the trades. In those days, the most skilled, most demanding and most rewarding occupation was tailoring. In 1825, Thimmonier opened his own tailor shop and, because he rarely stepped into the light of day, was considered odd by his neighbors. The French tailor, like a solitary writer, apparently enjoyed his isolated lifestyle and the challenge of technological innovation, or tinkering.

Thimmonier secretly busied himself with inventing a mechanized sewing contraption. Without the slightest background or training in mechanics, the quiet tailor spent four years puzzling over the enigma before him. Then, in 1829, he felt confident enough to seek a financial backer, M. Ferrand, a tutor at the local L'Ecole des Mines, to help his project along. In his thirty-seventh year, Thimmonier publicly revealed the product of his secret tinkering, a sewing machine constructed entirely of wood. On July 30, 1830, he received a patent for his creation.

Thimmonier's machine, which produced a chain stitch with a crochet-like hooked needle, was the first useful sewing machine. Its main drawback was the lack of an automatic feed. The cloth had to be carefully advanced by hand. History relates that Thimmonier conceived of a mechanical sewing machine from listening to the incessant side-to-side slapping sound of shuttles flying through his neighbors' looms in his boyhood town of Amplepuis. As in all late medieval towns of the time, weaving was the primary cottage industry, and nearly every living room in every home had a loom in operation.

By 1841, Thimmonier, now with additional backing of a government engineer by the name of M. Beaunier, placed 80 of his mechanical marvels in a Paris factory that soon began stitching ready-to-wear clothing for the French Army. Nevertheless, not everyone welcomed this new technology. Thirty years before, weavers had lost their jobs to automatic Jacquard Looms and Hargreave's Spinning Jennys. These jobless weavers banded together to attack the textile manufacturing centers, where they destroyed the new automatic machinery. Again, Thimmonier's machines rekindled the fears of worker displacement and an antitechnology mob came in the night to destroy Thimmonier's fast-flying sewing machines.[71] These neo-Luddites were probably French tailors reacting to the increased specialization filtering into the changing workplace. Their fears were well-placed. Tailors and their wide-ranging, diverse skills would not be needed and, moreover, would not keep pace with the new mechanical marvels of the machinery age. The workplace was becoming too complex and too specialized for such all-purpose generalists. One historical account relates that the factory holding Thimmonier's machines was twice burned to the ground.[72] As with Jacquard, history relates that Luddites barely spared Thimmonier's life on at least one of these occasions.

As a result, Thimmonier emigrated to England.[73] Undaunted by the possibility of new attacks because of the strong Luddite fervor also prevalent in Britain, the French inventor secured additional British and American patents for later enhancements to his original machine in 1845. In a 1848 partnership with yet another financial backer, Jean Marie Magnin, Thimmonier opened the doors of the first sewing machine manufacturing company. The company produced the newly patented Thimmonier machine, which reportedly used metal parts while railing along at 200 stitches per minute, or fourteen times faster than manual sewing.[74] Thimmonier had succeeded in producing a chain-stitch where the loops reside on the cloth's top side.

However, the unfortunate timing of the 1848 revolt in Paris ended this well-conceived enterprise of the first commercial sewing machine manufacturer. Perhaps the associated negativism and added promise of violence from the Luddite-led movement helped end this advance into Automation. Thimmonier's invention, which he patented in the United States in 1850,[75] never became popular and was largely sidestepped by attendees at the British Great Exhibition of 1851. Frederick Bourne, who would head the Singer Company beginning in 1883, remarked, "his

[Thimmonier's] machine had no important features that were of value as compared with the sewing-machines of that date."[76] Though he owned many French and British sewing machine patents, the inventor with a scholarly bent, Barthelemy Thimmonier, died poor and unremarked on July 5, 1857.

Early American Efforts: Walter Hunt (1796-1860)

The first American attempt at creating an automatic sewing machine originated with John Knowles of Monkton, Vermont, in 1818 or 1819.[77] The surviving record says only that Knowles' machine ostensibly emulated hand sewing movements. Despite this first failed attempt, the American inventors who followed Knowles emerge as the giants of the modern sewing machine industry. The first of these was Walter Hunt. During 1832 to 1834, Walter Hunt, of New York City, supplied an important innovation to sewing machine's ongoing invention by moving the thread hole from the center to the end of the needle. With this enhancement of an eye-pointed needle, Hunt's machine became the first to create a lock-stitch.[78] However, of greater significance for Automation was the fact that Walter Hunt's sewing machine was the first to *not* emulate hand stitching or hand motions.[79] Hunt's inventiveness amounted to a maverick departure from the normal means of invention at this time in the history of technology.

Hunt's machine created a straight lock-stitch by vibrating an arm whose first motion forced a curved, eye-pointed needle to pierce the fabric. As the needle receded from the hole, it left a loop of thread. Next, an underneath shuttle fed thread from a lower spool through the loop left by the upper thread. Hunt, who apparently did not understand the value of his accomplishment -- he was then trying to market several of his more promising devices – sold his *patentless* invention for a nominal sum to a blacksmith, George A. Arrowsmith, of Woodbridge, New Jersey. Arrowsmith tried to market the device and engaged Hunt's brother, Adoniram F. Hunt, to construct the novel machines for him.[80] The Hunt-Arrowsmith sewing machines, which the duo built and marketed in New York City, achieved limited sales and a near-negligible financial return. Like Hunt, Arrowsmith did not try to secure a patent. The blacksmith later offered three reasons for not patenting Hunt's machine: he considered the patent filing fee too extravagant, he mentioned the undeniable difficulty of selling sewing machines and he finally alluded to his inability to raise the two to three thousand dollars such a business startup would cost.[81] Walter Hunt had not sought a patent because he reportedly felt his machine would prove unpopular by sending too many hand sewers into unemployment.[82] Hunt later claimed he also neglected to patent another of his inventions, the eye-pointed needle. This patent had gone to Englishmen William Newton and Thomas Archibold, in 1841. But Hunt's failure to patent his sewing machine is akin to IBM's failure to hold on to the rights to either its personal computer or its software operating system.

Walter Hunt was a Quaker known for his altruism toward his neighbors. His obituary, which appeared in *Scientific American* on July 9, 1860, reported his sole occupation to have been that of an inventor. His patented inventions include a coach alarm, the fountain pen, a bottle stopper, a knife sharpener, a heating stove, an ice boat, a nail-making machine, a breech-loading rifle, a hand gun, a rotary street-sweeping machine, a paper collar mill, and a reversible metal heel. An interesting testament and footnote to Hunt's genius came out of a request from his patent illustrator, Mr. Richardson. Richardson agreed to forgive Hunt's longstanding debt with him if Hunt would give the patent rights to any invention he could make out of an old piece of wire. In three hours time, Walter Hunt devised the safety pin.[83] If, in 1844, he had spent $60 to patent his sewing machine, Walter Hunt would have changed the course of history, would have quite possibly prevented the "Sewing Machine Wars" and would have become a wealthy man. Instead, Elias Howe, Jr., became that prime mover.

Elias Howe, Jr. (1819-1867): Isaac M. Singer's Main Antagonist[84]

Many innovators and sewing machine makers emerged during the late 1840s and early 1850s. Still, none offered a productive, problem-free, easy-to-use and automatic sewing machine. Historians generally agree that Isaac Singer was the first

to accomplish this.[85] Unfortunately for Singer, a less-reliable but
more important sewing machine invented by Elias Howe, Jr.,
preceded his. In the resulting legal contest, Howe and Singer
became longstanding antagonists. Frederick Bourne, who would
later head the Singer Company for 16 years, said of Howe's
accomplishment: "Prior to Howe, all the sewing machines
patented made the chain or tambour stitch, or attempted to
imitate sewing by hand, making what might be called a
backstitch."[86] Howe first patented the lock-stitch-stitch sewing
machine. The lock-stitch was a tight stitch that held up well.
Unfortunately, Howe's invention, his wood-framed sewing
machine, did not operate well. As historian Scott concurs,
"Howe's machine was not, even in 1851 (when Singer's machine
came along), of practical utility."[87]

Elias Howe grew up among eight brothers and sisters on
a farm in Spencer, Massachusetts. Howe's introduction to
invention and the world of ideas came very early. One of his
uncles, William Howe, had invented a structural truss used in
house and bridge construction as well as a machine that sliced
palm leaves into strips for hats. Tyler Howe, another uncle, had
many inventions including the spring-supported bed.

As a youngster, Elias Howe was described as "long-
haired, high-cheek-boned, and puny,"[88] and full of playful humor.
Howe learned the machinist trade while engaged in his family's
home-based business, which may have been a grain-grinding
operation or gristmill.[89] The Howe family also job-shopped for
nearby textile factories. Beginning at the age of six, young Elias
sat with his siblings and pushed wire teeth into cards used in
cotton-spinning machinery. Howe said later that his family
engaged in other 'machinist-like' home industry. In 1835, at 16
years of age and attracted by the new manufacturing centers,
Elias Howe migrated to the textile industry in Lowell,
Massachusetts. Here, he worked on hemp-carding machinery.
The operation of these machines ostensibly gave him the later
idea of drawing threads through fabric.

In 1837, a job loss brought on by a nationwide financial
panic emboldened a 18-year-old Howe to move to Cambridge,
Massachusetts.[90] In Cambridge, he worked for the well-respected

machinist, Ari Davis. Davis was the widely known inventor of a dovetailing machine and proprietor of a small machine shop that repaired precision chronometers and surveying instruments. Davis's shop also manufactured intricate scientific and marine instruments. James Parton in his *Famous Men: Triumph of Enterprise, Ingenuity, and Public Spirit*, said of Ari Davis: "It pleased him to say extravagant and nonsensical things, and to go about singing, and to attract attention by unusual garments."[91] Parton also added that Ari Davis once chided a group of machinists and an unnamed financial backer engaged in developing a knitting machine in a heated conversation during which Davis said, "Why are you wasting your time over a knitting machine? Take my advice, try something that will pay. Make a sewing machine." To which the finance man replied, "If you [make a sewing machine]. . . I can make an independent fortune for you."[92]

When one of Davis' workers, a 20-year-old Elias Howe, overheard his employer's comments, it set the young man on the path of his life's work.[93] Beginning in 1843, a poverty-stricken Howe devoted his spare time devising such a machine that promised to earn a fortune for its creator. Howe's undertaking, which was guided solely by close observation and work experience, must be seen as enormously ambitious. Historian George Iles says that Elias Howe ". . . never studied the abstract principles which underlie mechanical construction."[94]

A close friend and former schoolmate, George Fisher, financed the venture. Fisher, a coal and wood merchant, moved Howe's family into his own home while additionally supplying the project with $500.00 of capitalization. Historian Iles reports that Fisher used funds from a recent inheritance. For his munificence, Fisher retained one-half interest in Howe's sewing machine. Later, during litigation with the Singer Sewing Machine Company (SSMC) and while testifying on Howe's behalf, Fisher said: "I was the only one of his neighbors and friends in Cambridge that had any confidence in the success of the invention. He was generally looked upon as very visionary in undertaking anything of the kind, and I was thought very foolish in assisting him."[95] We can only marvel at George Fisher's two-year-long support of his friend Elias Howe.

Howe, who apparently suffered from a hereditary physical disability, often felt too tired to work for more than a few days a week. The contemplative life of inventor may have appealed to him more greatly than the drudgery of daily work. As James Parton related: "Steady labor was always irksome to him; and frequently, owing to the constitutional weakness to which we have alluded, it was painful."[96] Elias may have suffered from migraine headaches.[97] In fact, Howe claimed work exhausted him and on retiring for the evening often wished he could lie in bed for "ever and ever."[98]

Several historians relate that Howe's careful observance of his wife's sewing motions, which supplied the family's main source of income, encouraged him to keep on fiddling with his contraption. After five years of off-and-on tinkering and on September 10, 1846, Elias Howe obtained a patent for the first two-thread lock-stitch sewing machine. This machine duplicated his wife's hand motions. In summary, Howe's machine made more effective use of the eye-pointed needle and the under-thread shuttle invented by Hunt twelve years before. Unlike his predecessors, Howe introduced greater precision by constructing his machine almost entirely of metal. Howe's sewing machine consisted of an uncomplicated operating assembly propelled by a palm-sized handwheel. The machine oscillated an eye-pointed needle fed from a spooled thread supply. A second thread spooling from an underneath shuttle and bobbin assembly formed the lower lock-stitch loop. The only real drawbacks to Howe's machine were that it did not run continuously and it only stitched straight seams. While it did clip along at a reported 250 stitches per minute,[99] the machine needed resetting by manually advancing the fabric whenever the end of the baster plate arrived. The fabric was held by, or stretched between, holding pins. As a result, the length of the baster plate determined the length of the stitch.

Howe boasted that his automatic sewing machine accomplished eight times more than the most proficient seamstress. By comparison, a modern home maker's lock-stitch sewing machine, using a straight up and down needle action, will clip along in forward or reverse directions at 1,500 stitches per minute. Modern commercial sewing machines run up 5,000 stitches per minute. Elias Howe understood that the existing sewing contraptions framed in wood and strung with wire could never provide the precision or strength to pierce fabrics consistently. Perhaps, Howe's most important contribution was this realization that an automatic sewing machine needed the close-tolerance precision of metal construction. Unfortunately, Howe's machine operated poorly and intermittently yet his working prototype succeeded in attracting more venture capital.

He put his machine on display and paid a tailor three times his normal wage to demonstrate it. (The tailoring industry was strictly politicized against modernizing its industry). Howe himself once competed with his machine against five seamstresses in Boston's Quincy Hall and won.[100] And while the public appreciated this new technology and marveled at how it so easily turned out wool suits, it did not purchase a single machine. Perhaps, the $300 selling price, which was more than an average family's six months of income, was simply too high a deterrent.[101] Large sewing manufacturing concerns within the textile industry, which the ongoing anti-Automation chorus from the hand sewing and tailoring industry may have warded off, also evinced little interest. The added high cost of initial capitalization remained a huge encumbrance: an industry analyst of the time projected that a shirtmaker would require 30 of Howe's machines to produce a profit. Additionally, Howe's machine was limited in functionality: it could not stitch along curves or follow at an angle. According to Frederick Bourne, who published a wide-ranging study of his industry in 1895: "It is not claimed that any machines made after the model of the original Howe machine were ever put into practical use."[102]

As with Isaac Singer, success did not come easily or quickly to Elias Howe. Many have argued the validity of Howe's claims; but none have questioned his obstinate nature and exceptional staying power. Although he tried, Howe never manufactured or marketed his sewing machine profitably. He had truly expected to earn a fortune for his great idea; his disappointment was all-consuming. Without understanding the reason for his sewing machine's commercial failure, Howe raised money by selling half his patent rights to his father for $1,000. He used this grubstake to carry his sewing machine to England. The British, he believed, had a well-developed textile industry that might prove receptive to his labor-saving device. In England, however, he was unable to reconfigure his machine to fit British manufacturing needs. In frustration, Howe sold his invention to an London manufacturer of umbrellas, corsets and leather goods, William F. Thomas of Cheapside, for 250 pounds. Thomas, who later became a millionaire industrialist, employed Howe to refine his sewing machine for use in his British factory to sew heavy leather. He paid Howe an ignoble weekly wage of three pounds per week. In 1846, Thomas obtained British patent 11,464 for a sewing machine that was simply a copy of Howe's patent. Because of the likelihood of Thomas lawsuits, the Thomas patent would greatly limit the manufacture of sewing machines in England.[103] The effect on the decline of British industry is incalculable.

In England, and just as he had in America, Howe promoted his machine by claiming that it replaced five of the swiftest hand sewers. His claims fell faint amid still-lingering Luddite fears. In 1849, an impoverished Howe found himself in a British debtor's prison. Eventually, he returned home to his ailing wife, Elizabeth, in Massachusetts. On arriving, he discovered his wife of eight years, who had suffered from consumption for two years,[104] lying on her deathbed. Some say she passed away moments after his arrival. Following her funeral, Howe placed his children with friends and returned to work as a machinist.

Elias Howe Goes to Court

While still recovering from this great personal tragedy Howe learned that during his absence, sewing machines had grown in popularity in the United States. In fact, nearly two dozen American manufacturers now made sewing machines that, in his view, merely emulated his basic design. Everywhere Howe went, he saw sewing machines infringing on his basic patent rights – rights that he had thoughtlessly pawned at the end of his stay in England. Now, real anger drove the characteristically kind and sociable Howe. Elias Howe somehow raised the one hundred dollars needed to repurchase his patent-letters as well as his prototype machine that he had pawned in England.[105] After regaining his American legal rights, he sent out businesslike letters to all his transgressors asking for tribute or royalty payments. Initially, sewing machine makers looked favorably on Howe's formal financial request; But they soon formed a united front disavowing Howe's claim.[106] This forced Howe to initiate numerous legal proceedings.

Because Singer's company emerged as the most successful sewing machine manufacturer, Isaac Singer became Howe's most targeted defendant. When Singer revealed the existence of the Walter Hunt machine, all sewing machine makers aligned with Singer's defense that Howe's machine added nothing to the old out-of-patent Hunt sewing machine. The great disdain of Howe's claims remained strong for years to come as seen in Singer Company historian John Scott's 1880 essay: "The honors and emoluments of the great sewing machine invention passed to a man who neither had invented a single principle of action, nor applied a practical improvement to principles already recognized; and Elias Howe, Jr., acquired the power, by simply patenting another man's invention."[107]

Earlier in 1854, the Commissioner of Patents, Judge Charles Mason, who decided in Howe's favor over Hunt's claim seemed to concur: "The papers in this case show that Howe obtained a patent for substantially this same invention (Hunt's) in 1846."[108]

One must laud Howe's tenacity. In those days, there was little precedence or assistance in collecting the royalties due a person. For example, Howe probably knew of Oliver Evans' "automatic flour mill," a 1790 invention that turned grain into flour. Unfortunately, this useful machine had returned Evans no more than a whisper by way of royalty payments. Evans had held his basic patent for this new method of agricultural mass production for 14 years. During this time, and to Oliver Evans' great consternation, automatic flour-grinding mills came into general use throughout the US. Lacking Howe's determination or financial backing, Oliver Evans was unable to corral his copycats.

After years of support, George Fisher, who had always been Howe's main financial backer, finally collapsed under the perceived hopelessness of an expensive sewing machine litigant's war. Undaunted, Howe now interested a wealthy man, George W. Bliss, to buy out Fisher's interest. According to historian George Iles, Bliss acted as a willing hatchet man, thoroughly enjoying the courtroom wars, while Howe turned his attention to manufacturing and improving his sewing machine.[109] The litigation against Howe's infringers progressed slowly as legal battles often do. When Howe took on Isaac M. Singer, all the litigants rallied behind this new source of legal strength.[110]

I. M. Singer, who was not an easy man to get along with, intended on blocking Howe at all costs. Singer's legal representative and partner, Edward S. Clark, a well-qualified attorney was also a formidable opponent. The Howe vs. Singer & Company litigation continued at a slow, expensive rate. In an effort to overturn Howe's patent, Singer ferreted out the ancient, never-patented Hunt machine. One of Hunt's machines was found in disrepair in a forgotten corner of George Arrowsmith's blacksmith shop. Singer hired the aging Walter Hunt to rebuild his machine.

Singer's ploy, which raised industry hopes that Howe's patent would soon be invalidated, overlooked the fact that Walter Hunt's original machine never operated very well.[111] In fact, very little was known about Walter Hunt or his sewing machine. If Singer had not dug up the old Hunt machine, it is likely that history would never have learned of Hunt's sewing machine. In its 1854 finding for Howe against Hunt (and Singer) the patent commission decided: "The plaintiff's patent is valid. Other machines are infringement . . . . There is no evidence in this case that leaves a shadow of a doubt that, for all the benefit conferred upon the public by the introduction of sewing machines, the public is indebted to Mr. Howe."[112] Years later, a 1890 Singer factory fire consumed Walter Hunt's sewing machine.

Howe had won his patent infringement suit against I. M. Singer & Company. The inescapable truth was the Singer machine employed the eye-pointed needle to produce a lock-stitch − a lock-stitch indistinguishable from that created by the Howe machine. With the court's favorable decision in hand, Howe now asserted that all sewing machines after his merely added efficiency or another (albeit useful) attachment to his basic, patent-protected sewing machine. Soon, all sewing machine makers began coughing up royalty payments that eventually raised Elias Howe, Jr.'s, income to $4,000 per week. During a failed attempt at renewing his patent license in 1867, Howe reported his accrued fees and royalties earnings had reached $1,185,000.

What became of Elias Howe? Always an idealist, a 42-year-old Elias Howe enlisted as a private in the 17th Regiment of Connecticut Volunteers when the Civil War broke out. Historian Iles reports that Howe turned down an initial offer to wear a colonel's uniform.[113] Instead, Howe put his good horseback-riding ability to use and rode contentedly as his company's postmaster. It would be instructive to have heard his criticism of the Singer Company's war slogan: "We Clothe the Union Armies − While Grant is Dressing the Rebels."

Occasionally, when the government could not meet his regiment's payroll, Howe lent the required funds. Just before he died in 1867, Howe created the Howe Machine Company in Bridgeport, Connecticut. (Singer's Bridgeport factory, which covered 13 acres and boasted 517,000 square feet of manufacturing spaces, easily outsized Howe's). Every sewing machine produced by Howe carried his likeness etched in a brass medallion inlayed in the bed plate. Throughout his working life, Howe continued to design and market his improved sewing machines. One of Howe's enhanced machines earned a gold medal at the 1867 Paris Exhibition.

In 1867, the same year during which his patent expired, Elias Howe, Jr., passed away on October third. He had contracted Bright's disease, a chronic kidney inflamation, while visiting his daughter in Brooklyn.[114] He was 48 years old. Howe, legend has it, walked around carrying a shuttle in his hand always hoping to fall upon yet another patentable idea for his sewing machine.[115]

The Other Howe Sewing Machine

History often confuses the handful of Elias Howe sewing machines manufactured much later in Bridgeport with those of his commercially successful brother. During these early years of the sewing machine's introduction, this other Howe sewing machine began enjoying regular sales. But this was not Elias Howe, Jr.'s sewing machine. Elias' older brother, Amasa B. Howe, made this completely separate machine. Amasa Howe had opened the Howe Sewing Machine Company in 1853. Unlike his brother's poorly functioning prototypes, Amasa's machines garnered the first prize in a sewing machine competition at the 1862 London International Exhibition.

The "Howe sewing machine," while not Elias Howe Jr.'s original machine, had also evolved out of Elias' patent; But it also owed its derivation from patent infringements from prior Bachelder, Wilson, and Singer patents. Throughout the years of litigation between Howe and Singer, the public erroneously believed the "Howe Sewing Machine" built by Amasa had been put up against the Singer Sewing Machine. According to records filed with the Patent Office, Elias Howe made only three sewing machine prototypes. These were similar to those produced by Amasa, his older brother. To Amasa, Elias' prototypes seemed too similar and he also initiated litigation against his brother. Amasa also succeeded in preventing Elias from using Amasa's trademark name the "Howe Sewing Machine." As a final blow to Elias, the courts decided that Amasa B. Howe was the original inventor and developer of the Howe trade name and its associated sewing machine.[116] In retrospect, it is entirely possible that Elias Howe, who many believed had stolen Walter Hunt's idea, had never heard of or even seen the Hunt machine. According to historian Godfrey, Howe was amazed to learn of the Hunt machine during the unfolding courtroom proceedings against Singer.[117]

Allan B. Wilson.[118]

In 1849, a 25-year-old American cabinetmaker, Allan B. Wilson, invented and patented a sewing machine whose main innovations included a four-step mechanical procedure for advancing the cloth after every stitch, and a stationary, long-lasting, bobbin-held thread feeding through a rotary hook. Wilson's rotary hook replaced the reciprocating shuttle. The four-motion feed eventually found its way into all sewing machines. Reportedly, Wilson accomplished these innovations without once poring over a single photograph of a sewing machine. Respected historian Grace Cooper claims that Allan Wilson was the most original and creative sewing machine inventor.[119] Even Frederick Bourne admitted, "To Allan B. Wilson must be awarded the highest praise as an inventor, and for the ingenuity displayed in constructing and improving the sewing machine."[120] Wilson's enhancements eventually became universally employed by all sewing machines. However, even by 1870, Wilson had realized only a fraction of the estimated $2 million reaped by the de facto owners and infringers of his patents.

Other manufacturers criticized Wilson's first sewing machines for their lightweight and consequent unsuitability for commercial applications. By comparison, Wilson's machine weighed less than seven pounds while Singer's pushed the scale up more than 50 pounds. Later, Wilson became a partner of Nathaniel Wheeler, and the Wheeler and Wilson Company went on to become I. M. Singer's main competitor. Wheeler and Wilson eventually employed around 1,500 employees in their Bridgeport, Connecticut, manufacturing plant.

Grover and Gibbs[121]

A final sewing machine innovator deserves mention in this brief historical overview. In 1851, Boston tailor William O. Grover patented a machine that sewed a double chain-stitch. Five years later, Virginia farmer James A. E. Gibbs patented the automatic chain-stitch machine. Gibbs came by his invention after spending days puzzling over a sewing machine illustration in a 1855 issue of *Scientific American*. After teaming up, Grover and Gibbs developed a noteworthy and successful sewing machine enterprise. The enhancements produced by Grover and Gibbs represent the last important additions to the sewing machine's basic design.

The Modern Sewing Machine Arrives: A Summation.

Now, thanks to Walter Hunt, Elias Howe, Jr., Allan Wilson, Isaac Singer, William Grover and James Gibbs, the fundamental concepts and methods for all later models of sewing machines had arrived. These main sewing machine innovators would soon become main players in the great Sewing Machine War. This economic conflict, which arrived at the dawn of America's Industrial Revolution, would establish important lessons and business precedents for all later corporations.

To purists, automatic sewing machine theory as first propounded in Elias Howe's dominating patent has not changed after all these years. In this view, Elias Howe, Jr., fully deserves recognition as the *Father of the Sewing Machine*. According to these pedants, not even the latter day addition of electric motors and foot controls have added in any substantial way to Howe's fundamental operating principles. Others step back by honoring Walter Hunt as the real innovator who introduced automatic sewing machine theory into the light of day. As mentioned, Allan Wilson is also held in high regard as a sewing machine innovator. One wonders why Isaac Merritt Singer's name never receives mention in these discussions? Isaac M. Singer's little machine, the first practical sewing machine, essentially gave the sewing industry its credibility. Additionally, Singer's ongoing innovations enabled his company to keep pace with all his competitors. Historians have instead surmised from Singer's ramshackle emotional life that the failed thespian's only gift was not his inventive genius but his marketing skill.

The entire sewing machine industry lacked credibility until Singer's serviceable machine came along. Howe's bulky machine and its limited operation had not been commercially-viable. The useable Singer machine differed little from the Howe machine. The Singer machine relied on a long shuttle like Elias Howe's machine but used a heart-shaped cam. Howe's wheel-driven machine used a curved needle that approximated regular movement. Singer's 1851 patent for a heart-shaped cam allowed a straight needle to oscillate in a precise up and down motion. This major innovation resulted in glitch-free, continuous operation. With Singer's machine, users no longer interrupted their sewing every few minutes to accomplish minor adjustments or to advance the fabric. Fifty years after its introduction, Isaac M. Singer had finally turned the sewing machine into a useful appliance.

One wonders how Isaac Singer reacted to Elias Howe's initial demand for a $25,000 tribute? In comparison to his well-honed, precision-fitted machine, Elias Howe's sewing machine functioned poorly and, moreover, Howe's machine was nowhere in use – it was merely a prototype! Did Singer believe that Howe's contraption compared in any meaningful manner with the unerring reliability of his *great civilizer*? Even if he accepted at the outset the validity of Howe's claim, Singer had not yet realized real profits from his obvious accomplishment and had no means of meeting Howe's demand. He had little choice but to litigate. When Howe followed up Singer's refusal to cooperate with a lawsuit, Singer approached Jordan, Clark & Company, New York's most prestigious law firm.

With legal representation, this penniless backroom inventor became a main litigant in the ongoing sewing machine war. When Isaac Singer engaged lawyer Edward S. Clark, the entire legal deliberation was wrested from his hands. Besides handing over his legal problems, Singer also handed Clark operational control of his successful startup company. When Isaac Singer reached out for legal help, he stepped into the most uneven business partnership that history has ever recorded. Out of this always tension-laden business partnership of Singer and Clark would come the world's first great conglomerate.

"The society of money and exploitation has never been charged, so far as I know, with assuring the triumph of freedom and justice." – Albert Camus

Chapter Four

The Edward Clark Era (1851-1882)
A Policy Base for the Future

Besides presiding over New York City's most prestigious law firm of Jordan, Clark & Company, Ambrose L. Jordan also served as the state's Attorney General. The elder Jordan kept close tabs on his law firm through his son-in-law and partner, Edward S. Clark. Ambrose Jordan no doubt enjoyed a close relationship with his youthful partner. On graduating from Williams College in 1830, Clark had studied in Jordan's law office, then located in Hudson, N.Y., before moving on to law school. After being admitted to the bar in 1833, Clark set up his own law practice in Poughkeepsie. Four years later, the two men again reunited to form a law firm partnership in New York City.[122] Besides their successful practice, Jordan pursued his political ambitions while the younger Clark dabbled in real estate.

One wonders why a penniless Isaac Singer, then being sued by Elias Howe, the most successful litigant in the ongoing sewing machine war, felt comfortable enough to approach this high-priced, well-respected law firm. Historian Peter Lyon relates that Ambrose Jordan had originally helped Singer obtain his original sewing machine patent but found the man too personally distasteful to represent again. As a result, when Singer approached him, Ambrose Jordan referred him to his son-in-law.[123] Another historian, the always accurate Professor Davies, claims that the two men, Clark and Singer, had a prior business involvement that had led to Clark's financial interest in one of Singer's inventions, the type-carving machine.[124] Perhaps one of these prior associations gave Singer the impetus to approach this high-powered lawyer without the hint of a retainer in his pocket.

Isaac M. Singer and Edward S. Clark: A Dubious Partnership

On that day in 1851 when 40-year-old I. M. Singer set foot in 40-year-old attorney E. S. Clark's waiting room, neither man expected this first meeting to take control of both of their lives. After listening to his near-bankrupt client, Clark proffered his services in return for a set of circumstances that essentially gave the attorney complete operational control over Singer's enterprise. Without funds for his legal defense, Singer had little choice but to play into Clark's hand.

Singer must have felt relieved that the attorney even took him on. Would any lawyer in his right mind take on a financially destitute player in the 'sewing machine war'? What could be Clark's motive? After all, Elias Howe's patent appeared to be holding up. Moreover, the courts had steadfastly sided with Howe. Did Clark think he could surmount the ever-thickening quagmire of litigation? Clark probably hoped he would eventually litigate away Singer's legal problems: perhaps he saw greater profit in the free publicity his firm would receive by simply joining in the well-publicized legal fracas known as "the great sewing machine war." Perhaps, like Singer, he saw himself as an emerging captain of industry in the Horatio Alger mold. And why would he not have? He enjoyed investing and was an active property owner in the West Side Association. He was steadily multiplying his assets and these were the risk-taking, rags-to-riches days, the days of fabulous overnight successes. When Isaac Singer walked into Edward Clark's office, the attorney no doubt visualized Singer as a heaven-sent instrument of profit, a once-in-a-lifetime opportunity. Perhaps, his father, Nathan Clark, a successful factory owner, had enlightened his son on how fleet-footed real business opportunities are. No matter the reason, Edward Clark, at least in this instance, did not let opportunity turn its bald head to him.

      After listening to the great inventor's plight, Clark offered his legal services in return for a full third interest in Singer's fledgling and stone-broke company. Isaac Singer's business venture had within moments acquired another major partner. George Zeiber, who had been Isaac's earliest financial backer, still retained a full-third partnership in Singer's company. While this decision must have been trying, Singer no doubt understood that only Clark's legal maneuvering would prevent Elias Howe's forthcoming lawsuit from forcing him out of business. The inventor of the first practical home appliance had been left without other recourse.

      Sometime after Clark came on board, the Singer Sewing Machine Manufacturing Company changed its name to I. M. Singer & Company. This happened after Singer prevailed upon Clark to buy back the Singer Company's handful of small investors. Clark managed the payback by borrowing from friends and relatives and by borrowing against his own credit to its limit. Because he risked all his assets, we must believe that this money-loving conservative attorney understood the enormous potential of Singer's faultless little machine. In the partnership agreement with Singer, Edward Clark, the careful, capable lawyer, placed control of the company's marketing and financial departments into his own hands. Clark also received half ownership of all of Singer's future patents.[125]The company savior became the controlling partner. This partner would create a company business legacy whose grip would remain undiminished after his death 31 years later. Edward S. Clark, and not Isaac M. Singer, would now steer the little desktop wonder into prominence. Isaac Singer, according to Clark's imposed manifesto, would continue as a glorified product manager employed as his tiny machine's chief designer and architect.

On the legal front, Clark somehow managed to push Howe's complaining into the background while he placed a grandiose business plan into play. For example, in 1852, Clark used the company's limited funds to open branch offices in Boston, New York City and Philadelphia. Clark probably justified this expansion because of Isaac Singer's introduction of the No. 1 Standard. The No. 1 was a more robust model of Singer's original machine.[126] Clark's business acumen, which doubtless recognized the usefulness of Singer's latest creation, now began to unfold. Indeed, later company records support Clark's decision: the No. 1 Standard remained popular for nearly 20 years and boasted of sales surpassing several hundred thousand machines. As their recently opened branch offices began delivering up new sales orders with regularity, the two partners quietly perceived they were sitting on a business powder keg.

In their view, only one problem remained, George Zeiber. Both men wondered why they should share this coming gold rush with anyone else? Why share a full third of the hard-earned fruits of their labors with anyone who was not actually contributing to the risk and hard work? Zeiber's only contribution had been the loan of a limited amount of cash during Singer's early days. For this small contribution, Zeiber held legal paperwork giving him a full third share in Singer's enterprise. Do we believe Isaac Singer enjoyed sharing his company with a silent partner? Especially one whose only contribution would be to suck away a large share of the coming profits?

George Zeiber, the only major investor remaining after Clark's successive payoffs of Singer's debts, had carried Singer through his critical make-it-or-break days, steadfastly held onto his one-third interest in this new technology. In fact, Zeiber, himself a mildly successful, middle-class, small business man, doubtless understood the sewing machine's potential. After many entreaties, which had no doubt come from both Clark and Singer, Zeiber adamantly refused to sell out.

Unfortunately, during the late winter of 1852, George Zeiber fell gravely ill. During this smalltime publisher's weakened condition, he received an unexpected visit from the famed Merritt Players' star elocutionist. While lying weak, actually struck down with a raging fever, Singer suddenly materialized at Zeiber's bedside. Singer claimed to have rushed over after speaking with Zeiber's physician, Dr. Anderson. Zeiber knew his physician occasionally treated both Singer and himself and probably believed the great inventor had indeed just spoken with the good doctor. History has left us Singer's grave misrepresentation of the facts to his bedridden benefactor: "The doctor thinks you won't get over your sickness. Don't you want to give up your interest in the business altogether?"[127]

On learning that he lay in his deathbed, the suddenly despondent Zeiber quickly agreed to sell his share in Singer's company. Zeiber later related he wished only to buy off his debts and assure his heirs of some minimal legacy. In March of 1852, George Zeiber delivered up his full third share of the company to Singer and Clark for $6,000 in cash. Less than a year later, I. M. Singer & Company reported their capital assets exceeded one-half million 1853 dollars.

Zeiber had been stricken with undulant fever that he probably contracted from bacteria-laden meat or milk. This Malta fever, also called Mediterranean fever, was often fatal in the nineteenth century and Zeiber had good reason to fear Singer's contrived assertion. George Zeiber eventually recovered from his fever; but he never recovered from Singer's deceit. Instead of finding an attorney, the good-hearted Zeiber, like some movie actor's fan, took to following his one-time partner and friend. Surely, this great capitalist must some day share a small portion of his great wealth with the one benefactor who had made it all possible? Surely, the great I. M. Singer, who often brought needy strangers into his home, would ease his conscience by rewarding a friend who had so thoroughly believed in him that he unhesitatingly forked over his own financial grubstake? After a few years, Singer did ameliorate Zeiber's whining by retaining him in a low level position within his conglomerate. However, throughout his long employment with I. M. Singer, George Zeiber never gave up hope that the great industrialist and innovator would one day find compassion somewhere in his soul. Hopefully, his ongoing presence would give Isaac an opportunity to atone for his great deception and properly indemnify Zeiber's years of financial and emotional support. Nevertheless, the years slipped by and the great elocutionist never once nodded his head in his former business partner's direction. Looking his former partner in the eye probably held no interest for the great man. In yesterday's business empires, as in today's, a business ace silences most magnificently when falsely played.

Years later, Zeiber confided that he despised Singer and Clark equally. In Zeiber's final view, his former partners shared a mutual all-consuming greed. In fact, Zeiber called them "birds of a feather."[128] In retrospect, one must surely assume that Edward Clark must share in the backroom complicity in the Zeiber buyout. Apparently, Clark's morality disappeared when attractive business deals came along.

Prosperity Arrives

With Zeiber out of the way, the two partners concentrated on their expanding business empire. In 1853, they awarded themselves half ownership in their grand undertaking by supplying each other with 2,500 company shares that they valued at $100 each. Singer now contented himself with management of his manufacturing facility and with developing technical improvements to his little machine. In 1854, Isaac introduced the No. 2 Standard. This heavier machine came in response to customer demands to work with large pieces of fabric.

In 1856, Singer produced the No. 3 Standard.[129] This toughened, more robust machine stitched leather pieces together for carriage makers and harness makers. In this same year, I. M. Singer & Company introduced its first machine targeted solely to the homemaker, the relatively lightweight Turtle Back Sewing Machine. An improvement on these machines arrived in 1859 with the introduction of the Letter "A." With the introduction of this model, home-based sales of Singer sewing machines took off. Clark marketed the Letter A until 1865. From 1865 to 1883, the company sold four million of its "New Family Machine."[130] After 1883, so called round bobbing sewing machines flooded the home market.

As he brought forth these remarkable devices, we assume that Isaac Singer had found himself, had finally settled comfortably into his life's course, had found contentment in the pursuit of mechanical invention. After all, I. M. Singer had finally earned recognition as a great inventor. And perhaps Isaac was content to leisurely pursue research and development. He treated his fellow machinists in his R&D Department with equanimity. These men who worked shoulder to shoulder with Isaac regarded him as 'a good story teller' and they also jointly agreed that the great inventor most always went out of his way to be "companionable."[131]

With Zeiber gone and Singer in his place, Edward Clark now assumed his role as the company's director. By overseeing the financial and commercial side of the fledgling business, Clark enjoyed de facto control over day-to-day operations.[132] By setting corporate policy, he established the company's long term direction and vision. Clark's first goal was to expand the company's customer base. Because of the high selling price of these first sewing machines, only well-capitalized commercial concerns purchased them. The Singer machine's heavy industrial weight also deterred prospective home users. As a result, most of the company's revenue derived from commercial accounts. Now, Clark determined he would break open the stagnant retail appliance marketplace.

Original Sales Tactics

Edward Clark knew he had a fine, fault-free consumer product. He only needed to educate the consumer on how wise a purchase the Singer sewing machine really was. To get the word out, Clark hired sales agents whom he carefully screened. He selected only those individuals who showed a rare blend of verbal and of mechanical skills. In addition, successful candidates had to demonstrate personal honesty and paramount loyalty to the company. To inculcate this belief, Clark expounded on the idea that their product was actually raising their customer's way of life. This modern labor-saving device brought leisure time and a new means of income that quickly raised its users out of poverty. Clark advertised that a single homemaker could earn a thousand dollars in a year's time. No one lost in this win-win interaction. How could buyers demur if the product would quickly pay for itself and elevate their station in life? How could sales agents not be enthusiastic about each signed purchase order that in the end represented the highest form of social responsibility? In addition, Clark demanded that his agents hold sufficient mechanical knowledge to accomplish sewing machine repairs, and lastly, they needed the easy deftness of a carnival barker in demonstrating the sewing machines.[133] In choosing dedicated, capable sales agents, Clark showed his understanding of consumers and their needs. There was a great deal more depth to this great capitalist than we can imagine; he was not merely milking a get-rich-quick scheme.

Domestic sales soon flourished. Nevertheless, Edward Clark did not ease comfortably back in his office chair. Instead, like some great whirlwind he concerned himself with all of the details surrounding the Great Civilizer – no matter how niggling. For example, he convinced Singer to add ornamental gold striping to his basic black model. One of his first marketing ploys followed Singer's example by renting a store front where a diminutive young dressmaker quietly sewed on a Singer sewing machine. Every day, this young lady attracted crowds of interested onlookers. Moreover, onlookers enjoyed watching the little lady easily outproducing many experienced seamstresses engaged in manual sewing. Clark personally wrote advertising copy directed at ministers' wives offering to sell them a Singer at half price. If the preacher's wife introduced one of his machines into her sewing circle, Clark reasoned, then all the church's ladies would follow suit. This tactic was one of Clark's most successful sales ruses.[134]

When the Wilson and Gibbs sewing machine increased in popularity, Clark directed his agents to accept trade-ins of his customers' older models toward the purchase of a *greatly improved* new Singer machine. In this way, he attracted new customers while holding on to his own by allowing them to upgrade to a newer and comparable Singer machine at less cost. To prevent the build up of a second-hand Singer sewing machine market and an unwanted availability of used repair parts, Clark directed his agents to simply destroy the trade-ins. Clark's customers could not afford but to remain loyal. By making their sewing machine affordable and by providing nearby maintenance, the Singer Company developed a base of dedicated customers that would grow and sustain the company for more than a century.

Many Civil War veterans had witnessed the Singer machine's utility at first hand. Clark had donated a thousand Singer sewing machines to the Union Army's Civil War effort. Clark's munificence was more brought on by flat wartime sales in the states than by actual spirited involvement in the war effort. Because of competition from a previously unknown competitor, James E. A. Gibbs, the Singer Company produced the first lightweight sewing machine intended for home use in 1858. Company employees referred to their new, lightweight product as the Grasshopper. While the Grasshopper first sold for $100, the price dropped quickly to $50 to compete with the new, low-priced Wilson and Gibbs single-thread chain-stitch model.[135] Clark's innovative marketing created a sales bonanza that soon propelled the company into a leadership position over all sewing machine makers. Clark's pioneering sales ideas have withstood the test of time and call out to us every day. All of Edward Clark's marketing innovations have been carefully described in Ruth Brandon's fine Singer sewing machine company history, *A Capitalist's Romance*.

Branch Offices

To expand his sales arm, Edward Clark began opening branch offices throughout the United States. Each branch office employed a manager, a repair mechanic, a product demonstrator (who was usually an attractive and youthful seamstress) and a sales agent. No home appliance manufacturer had ever supported his product in so complete a fashion. The nearby presence of branch offices, which supplied maintenance, repair, supplies and even training, gave Singer's customers complete confidence in their purchase.

In pre-Civil War years of nascent consumer commerce, only I. M. Singer & Company, among all other sewing machine makers, had the financial means or desire to sustain full-time and remotely based agents. These dedicated employees furnished a full range of customer and after-market product support that advanced the finest word-of-mouth advertising of all.

Branch managers quickly learned to abide by Clark's code of conduct and military chain of command. As in the military, Clark delegated all local authority to the area agent in charge. For example, he allocated funds for his autonomous agents to design and purchase local advertising. He expected his agents to deal with local laws and local tax issues. These corporate policies eventually developed a cadre of agents having a fine blend of professionalism and autonomy that always supported a well-defined company goal. No employee succeeds as well as when complete responsibility for success rests with the individual.

Clark further supported his geographically remote employees by maintaining a distribution network that guaranteed fast delivery of repair parts. As the good Singer word spread and as sales climbed an ever-steepening incline, branch offices struggled to meet an ever-mounting demand. By 1859, the company boasted fourteen well-managed, highly successful branch offices.

For a time, branch managers felt secure because of their territorial sales rights guarantee — which Clark had sold to them. Businesses of the time often relied on employee vesting to guarantee the reliability of remote branch offices. Nevertheless, during 1856 Clark recognized how self-limiting territorial rights were in a fire sale. As a result, he discontinued the common practice of selling these rights to individuals.[136]

Installment Buying

Edward Clark was a forward-moving and original-thinking business man. When sales tumbled in response to the recession of 1856, Clark introduced installment buying.[137] With this sales incentive, Clark guaranteed I. M. Singer & Company's ability to attract all possible customers no matter how far-flung or how limited in income they might be. The Singer Company salesmen left listeners no excuse for not committing to a sales transaction. In 1857, the world's economic situation worsened due to continued irresponsible speculation in US railroad shares. As this great worldwide recession progressed, Clark sought to prop up declining sales by refining the hire-purchase and installment payment plan. For five dollars down and as little as three dollars per month, a customer could rent-lease a sewing machine until it was paid.

In 1871 France, installment loans sometimes relied on weekly payments as low as sixty cents. While Clark had no known industrial business or marketing experience, his novel introduction of the hire-purchase plan for a relatively low-priced home appliance drove the company's sewing machine sales upwards dramatically. Other appliance makers did not catch on to installment buying until well after the Civil War ended. This unchallenged sales technique allowed I. M. Singer & Company to penetrate more easily into the domestic market and to essentially conquer all of the foreign market. Other domestic sewing machine makers either chose not to trust low income foreigners or they simply lacked the financial means of supporting widespread consumer loans. Now, even those who had only wished for this great labor-saving device smiled in disbelief as the Singer man crossed the threshold of their home. (Note that the Cowperthaite and Sons furniture store had been the first to introduce installment selling in 1807). For unknown reasons, Clark's success with installment buying found no emulators. Among all its competitors, I. M. Singer & Company alone developed mass-credit and mass-marketing methods that allowed it to prosper during this great time of economic uncertainty.

Domestic Expansion

As Singer's domestic sales multiplied, Clark reinvested his incoming revenue into ongoing capitalization of his company. As a result, company assets grew to dizzying heights. Clark, who sometimes lost himself in operational minutiae, somehow never failed to grasp the larger picture. For example, as production increased, the logistics of supplying I. M. Singer & Company's Mott Street factory through crowded New York City streets simply became too time consuming and too expensive. When Inslee Hopper, one of his vice presidents, pointed these problems out in 1872, Clark gave the young man the go-ahead to open a large, state-of-the-art manufacturing facility in Elizabethport,

New Jersey. This facility, which was bounded by a railroad on one side and a waterway on the other, ended the delivery and distribution problems caused by the city's congested streets. This new facility spread out over 72 acres and employed some 3,000 machinists and factory workers within its 1,805,100 square feet of floor space. In 1873, I. M. Singer & Company relocated its corporate headquarters to New Jersey near its flagship manufacturing facility. At this time, the Elizabeth plant became the largest factory in the world producing a single product. Its $4,000,000 start up cost came entirely out of the company's cash reserves.

Overseas Growth: The Multi-National Corporation Emerges.
Edward Clark first made known his interest in foreign sales in early 1855. While many other American companies had fished foreign markets, I. M. Singer & Company became the first American company to report a profit from foreign marketplaces. Like other major businesses of the time, the company's desire for foreign investment grew out of a simple motivation and belief that viewed technologically undeveloped Europe easy prey to American ingenuity. This widely held belief often filled business editorials that understood one unassailable fact, the Age of Automation had crossed the Atlantic: Yankee ingenuity in perfecting the machinery trade had shown its superior hand. Some believed that America's success in developing sophisticated mass-manufacturing techniques arose because she had not been mired with bureaucratic trade apprenticeships, as mechanics in Britain were, and, besides, many felt that energetic Americans were always open to novel ideas and techniques.[138]
Clark knew his company's manufacturing know-how easily eclipsed that of his European competitors. His American manufacturing labor force owned an expertise that produced technically superior products at a lower production cost. All foreign manufacturers competed at disadvantage. In 1861, at the outbreak of the U.S. Civil War, American manufacturers tried to replace the loss of southern markets through sales to a product-hungry European marketplace. Historical records show that

around mid-century no fewer than 600 American-based businesses undertook various ventures in foreign locales.

While the business editorial press put forth great prognostications of these attempts at foreign export, no single company enjoyed wild, unimaginable profits from European sales. The promise of profits were many but the actual bankable returns remained small. The truth was that America's inventions were widely recognized and widely desired in Europe and in undeveloped countries as well, but no one had really figured out how to change this latent demand into actual sales. In this suspected coming global mercantilism, and in contrast to the printed hyperbole of uncontainable future successes, only the actuality of sobering failure reached non-editorial print. For example, Clark knew of the bankruptcy of Samuel Colt's pistol-making facility in England. Colt's pistol manufacturing represented the most advanced technology of its day. Many manufacturing processes devised in Colt's factories were taken up and refined by sewing machine makers; these included: interchangeable parts, semiautomatic machine tools, accurate measuring devices, and specialized jigs and tooling.[139]

In America, Colt's company was known as the most successful armament maker of its day. Even so, Colt failed at replicating his American sales in the then most industrialized economy in the world, England. In 1853, Colt finally ended this overseas venture that historians have remembered as the construction of the first American plant on foreign soil. Colt described his foreign experience as a "constant drain on resources and energies." Besides these unfathomable and undefinable pitfalls experienced by Colt, foreign investors like Clark struggled with a uniquely European political reality. For example, in 1857, another Ludditelike anti-Automation revolt broke out in England led by Northhampton shoe workers. This disturbance happened as sewing machines began infiltrating Northhampton's shoe manufacturing facilities. Powerful anti-automation sentiments ran high among European workers. Automatic machinery's encroachment into the textile industry had displaced many lower class Europeans. During these years, job losses brought on by Automation often deepened following reactionary labor strikes both in England and in France. For example, as late as 1859 a newly formed European labor union tried to stop sewing machines from being introduced in shoe manufacturing.[140]

As a result, Clark's first overseas venture had not been a pleasant one. Clark expected the introduction of the Great Civilizer to resonate among Frenchmen as it had with Americans. The company's first large scale foreign fishing expedition never got off the ground. Clark's choice for his first important foreign agent guaranteed the failure of this venture. At best, the company's association with Charles Callebout[141] survived as a drawn-out and expensive learning experience. In March 1855, Clark sold his first foreign manufacturing patent to Parisian Charles Callebout. In his enthusiasm, Clark even made known his wish to build a factory in Paris. Clark, who expected immediate and overnight results, catered to this first French franchisee by meeting Callebout's every need in hopes of easing the Frenchman's startup. Clark even provided machine shop tooling, along with an experienced machinist.

Despite the Singer Company's munificence, Callebout proved unmotivated, untrustworthy and unreliable. The careless Frenchman even held back revenues and failed to report sales figures. Callebout continued his defiance by abrogating his contractual agreement by promoting and selling competitive sewing machine brands. As a final blow, he even brought legal proceedings against his American employer. Eventually, I. M. Singer & Company signed an agreement with Callebout in 1858 by which they paid the Frenchman a small royalty while keeping his contract in force. The Singer Company put up with Callebout's tactics, and honored their contractual bargain until their franchisee's patent rights expired in 1870. During these years, Callebout continued to use his patent ownership to sell Singer machines. Eventually, the Singer Company withheld its newly enhanced products from Callebout and entered direct competition with their own French agent. As a final letdown to the entire French initiative, the French courts ended the ongoing litigation between Singer and Callebout by deciding that all of Singer's French patents belonged in the public domain.

It is noteworthy that Callebout managed to sell 335 machines to Russia's military establishment. These were possibly the first sewing machines seen by Russians.[142] Because of the Callebout experience, Clark changed company policy and forbade the selling of the Singer Company's foreign patents rights. None of these were ever sold again. Further, Clark decreed that all patent negotiations must be carried on in complete secrecy. Fortunately, Clark had learned not to sell territorial rights and they had not sold these in Europe.

Commission Houses

Besides warped sales representatives like Callebout, foreign marketplaces often meant business dealings with the "commission houses." Like other American companies, the Singer Company asked 'commission houses' to represent their products on foreign lands. Usually, because of the language barrier and the hindrances of peculiar local laws and customs, American businesses relied on these factory outlets and their indigenous sales agents to move their products. These trading centers, which charged large commission fees as their first and overriding general rule, represented any of the products its clients cared to ship to its warehouse. These local outlet centers simultaneously represented several different sewing machine makers and generally pushed those products that coughed up the best profit margin.

On a return from a European trip, Isaac Singer reported that one of the commission houses, which had agreed to market Singer machines only, continued to stock all of their competitors' machines as well. On hearing this news, Clark now gave up on these far-flung intermediaries and became the first American businessman to terminate this easily made but poorly rewarded affiliation with foreign commission houses. Clark, as he had done domestically, now selected and hired salaried agents to represent his products overseas. History had long ago taught this very same lesson: ancient Sumerians traders first propounded the need for foreign-based company men dedicated to managing and marketing their own proprietary wares. Soon, dedicated, company-trained and properly attired Singer Company representatives announced their presence from newly opened branch offices. Clark gave his foreign branch offices, which also served as company retail stores, the same laissez-faire authority enjoyed by his US sales network. He empowered his foreign agents-in-charge to their own judgment in adjusting for cultural differences. He encouraged them to act autonomously and gave them free reign in dealing with local corruption and law makers. He also supplied funds for local advertising. This policy soon returned the expected results. Foreign sales began to blossom.

A strong, well-oiled, globally dispersed retail organization solely reliant on Singer products emerged. In short time, dedicated Singer company salaried foreign agents found their way into Canada, Mexico, Russia, Scotland, England, Spain, France, Germany, Sweden, Puerto Rico, Cuba, Curacao, Venezuela, Uruguay and Peru.

Foreign Markets Become Self-Sufficient

Edward Clark became the first American capitalist to succeed in developing foreign markets on a large scale. Clark had created the first successful American multinational business.

But had Clark really taken a great risk? Clark's decision to invest in foreign facilities more heavily than ever attempted by an American company had come during the height of the Civil War. As the war escalated, Clark's domestic sales declined while his foreign sales increased to more than 40 percent of total sales.[143] Clark knew complexities of the foreign marketplace had proved too formidable for hundreds others like himself. Nevertheless, he persisted and relied on his basic instinct, on his quality product, on a steadfast confidence for his capable agents, and on the ultimate importance in raising the plight of the world's poorer class. During 1865 alone, American makers shipped $2 million in sewing machines overseas.[144] We are too far removed to know if Clark had followed an inner vision or if he had, like modern day computer makers, simply responded to the worldwide interest in his little tabletop wonder.

Toward the end of the Civil War, Singer's European sales increased beyond the production capacity of Clark's American facilities. In 1867, George Woodruff, the company's London agent, grew so exasperated at not having enough products to sell – he wanted at least 100 "A" machines per week – that he arrived unannounced at New York to personally make his needs known to both vice president Hopper and Clark. Impressed by Woodruff's visit, Clark instructed Scottish-born George Ross McKenzie, another important company man, to accompany Woodruff on the return trip.

McKenzie, who would later succeed Clark, was instructed only to establish a small experimental factory somewhere in Europe.[145] McKenzie's choice of building in Scotland raised many eyebrows. But McKenzie had not chosen his homeland as The Singer Company's first manufacturing site because of nationalistic feelings. Scotland boasted a freedom from the many limiting political and economic factors found in most European countries. Additionally, the Scots owned longstanding iron smelting facilities, textile plants and a reliable, world class shipping industry. McKenzie later said that inexpensive freight costs and the docile work force had been the deciding factors in his decision. American labor, whose wages remained low at the end of Civil War, had begun to exhibit signs of militancy. By contrast, Scotland's workers seemed happy for any work, no matter how low the wages. Glasgow, at the time, was one of Europe's major industrial cities. This large city was the home of experienced factory workers – not unskilled backwoods farmers.

The Singer Company's smallish Glasgow facility, which sold lock-stitch machines produced at one-half the cost of similar British models, soon expanded into larger quarters in nearby Kilbowie. At its completion in 1885, Kilbowie's 5,000 employees could turn out 10,000 machines in a week's time.[146] This was a modern facility whose design, as evidenced by its large research facility, welcomed changing technology. (Later, the town of Kilbowie became known as Singer). Profiting mostly from lower European wages, Kilbowie produced Singer machines at 30 percent less production cost than the company's Elizabethport facility. In time, the Kilbowie plant expanded into nearby Clydebank and became known by that name.

Five years later, Clark opened a foreign manufacturing facility in Montreal, Canada. During the 1860s, British sales of all makers' sewing machines had not surpassed 10,000 machines a year. By 1870, Clark's well-trained sales agents alone were now selling 26,000 sewing machines a year in Britain. This success encouraged Clark to build a manufacturing plant in Bridgeton, UK, in 1871. Eventually, this facility would turn out 3,000 machines a week.

Effects of Multinational Marketing

Foreign-based manufacturing offered lowered wages, greatly reduced transoceanic shipping charges and an overall reduction in production costs. It is also to Clark's everlasting credit that his foreign marketing successes arrived without his ever pleading to American politicians for assistance and without once begging American consuls to intervene in local political problems. In years to come, nearly all American companies would establish European facilities and markets using Edward Clark's precedent-setting business methods. Clark's foreign marketing methods had proven themselves and became a de facto business paradigm: sewing machine sales had created the first domestic mass market for this first home appliance and now this same appliance delivered the first international marketplace. According to Mira Wilkins in her *The Emergence of Multinational Enterprise*, "Singer was the first American international business, anticipating the Standard Oil companies, General Electric, National Cash Register, and International Harvester."[147] By definition, a multinational business is one that operates in more than two countries.

The Sewing Machine Combination:[148] The World's First Strategic Alliance of Large Manufacturing Concerns.

Edward Clark played a central role in creating the world's first combine. The combination, an association of industries with common interest, became an important dimension in the evolution of American corporations. This collaboration among the sewing machine's main players created a de facto monopoly in the service of its participants. Since combine members controlled all of the sewing machine's major patents, all other sewing machine makers paid a licensing fee for their use to the combine. The combination limited any one of its competitors to producing no more than 1,000 sewing machines in twelve months. It did so by granting a given competitor no more than 1,000 licenses per year. How did these longtime Sewing Machine War antagonists become successful business partners?

The sewing machine war began with Elias Howe's first legal actions. In a short time, these litigations involved every sewing machine maker. During these years of legal sparring, I. M. Singer & Company was fast becoming a retailing behemoth. Due to its legal wrangling, its road to prosperity was not a smooth one. As it advanced, its formidable antagonists threw up every legal roadblock human ingenuity could possibly conceive in hopes of ending the company's very existence or at least forcing it to give over a significant portion of its large profits. Many suggested that Singer's competitors ally in one big front against the one company that threatened to monopolize their entire industry.

Still, these verbal threats did no damage when compared with the endless string of lawsuits. During 1856 alone, I. M. Singer & Company found itself embroiled in nearly two dozen lawsuits with other sewing machine manufacturers. Because these legal proceedings convened in various legal venues scattered throughout the northeast, it became difficult to deal effectively with them. This famous "Sewing Machine War," which regularly carried the day's headlines also sold newspapers. In time, Edward Clark concluded that the public confrontation was simply too harmful to the sewing machine industry as a whole. To the public, the sewing machine war appeared to be a financial playground for a group of greedy industrialists. As a result, the open mudslinging and quibbling gave all sewing machine makers a poor image. Besides this public scorn, which Clark believed affected everyone's sales figures, he recognized there was not enough time or staff to properly litigate the merits of each case.

During their first three years of partnership with Clark, Singer had secured 25 patents for various improvements to the company's product line. However, as soon as the patent office awarded the patent, someone stepped forward to level a patent infringement suit. Because of this widespread litigation and the public quagmire involving sewing machine makers, many businesspeople and economic analysts of the time believed that no single sewing machine maker would ever survive commercially.

In hopes of resolving this impasse, Clark reached agreement with Elias Howe, Jr., in May of 1854. On July 1, Singer and Clark paid Howe $15,000 and further agreed to pay Howe a licensing fee for every sewing machine they made. With this bothersome legal suit behind, Clark began moving his company toward ever greater prosperity. But Clark's hard won freedom to act was short-lived.

During 1856, the company entered into another round of lawsuits. Clark recognized that four main concerns owned the industry's most important patents: the Grover and Baker Sewing Machine Company, the Wheeler and Wilson Manufacturing Company, the I. M. Singer and Company and Elias Howe, Jr. Now in 1856, all four main litigants, who each held an indeterminable legal position, found themselves at one another's throat once again. Because of the strong arguments each could make in their own defense, no one could really ascertain how the courts would decide. The Sewing Machine War had turned into an expensive gamble even these high rollers could hardly afford. Each judgment brought cause for further appeal and more litigation. The situation had become unmanageable.

Orlando B. Potter, a future New York senator, but now a lawyer representing Grover and Baker,[149]first proposed the idea of pooling together the major patent owners. Potter recognized that years of judicial proceedings had achieved nothing except to create fodder for more legal proceedings. To Potter, the only possible resolution was to bring the major litigants together in a mutually rewarding alliance.

As fate would have it, these four major players and their legal entourage met face to face in Albany, New York. On a hot, humid early spring evening the group checked into the same hotel, Congress Hall. None looked forward to the months of uncomfortable, summertime courtroom deliberation. Before retiring, these main litigants met in conference, loosened their collars, and talked into the late night hours.[150] It was then that

Potter played his ace. Each of these strong-willed industrialists had already spent small fortunes trying to control their individually conceived innovations. Perhaps, no one had spent more than the I. M. Singer & Company in retaining control over its precious little machine. Since each large manufacturer owned important patents, their legal positions persevered against paper theories of industrial theft. Each regarded the others as true usurpers.

Imagine Isaac Singer's scorn. Who more than he was most responsible for actually creating their industry? Can we imagine Singer willingly signing over his legal claims to his 25 patents, of sharing his hard work and ingenuity to three hard-boiled courtroom adversaries who had simply followed in his wake? Can we picture his working alongside those who sought to bankrupt him by continually assailing him through their high-priced attorneys, men skilled in applying every conceivable legal machination? We know of Singer's disdain of and prior battles with Elias Howe. Singer had signed over first a half that became a third, and then the entire control of his company because of Howe's lawsuit. We can only speculate on how the two other big manufacturers must have shared in Singer's reluctance to give Elias Howe his due. Howe's machine remained impractical: Howe had not sold more than a handful of his machines, if any at all. One historian claims that Howe had actually constructed only three prototypes. In his opponent's eyes, Howe had done no more than patent Walter Hunt's idea. And Howe had asked for a $25 levy on each sewing machine made in America!

And what of Elias Howe's position? Howe felt he stood to gain little from the proposed alliance. Wheeler and Wilson and Grover and Baker had begun paying his $25 licensing fee. After all, did he not already own the sewing machine's basic patent rights? Even the sewing machine itself? Wouldn't more legal proceedings before courts that had steadfastly sided with him continue to affirm his primacy? But how could Elias Howe's grip, his absolute control over the entire industry, continue over every enhancement that added to the machine's ongoing evolution? And the same manufacturers who had begun sending royalty checks were now suing Howe for various patent infringements.

The impasse seemed destined for the litigation hall of fame. Edward Clark now sided with Potter and argued that the continuing press coverage of their bickering did their industry more harm than good. Potential purchasers, like buyers of any home appliance, feared buying from a company whose continued existence was questioned daily by the print media. For everyone's mutual benefit and financial reward, the incendiaries fueling the sewing machine war had to be buried. Regardless of the shared resentment, Potter and Clark finally cajoled these four major players into repressing their hostilities.

The resulting "Sewing-Machine Combination" or "Albany Agreement of 24 October 1856" gave each of the four litigants licensing rights to mutually share all of their distinct patents and technologies in the manufacture of their machines. Eight main patents became the common property of all pool members. This was history's first patent pool. Each member paid the combine a set license-fee for every machine produced. Technology had found a way to benefit the powerful few through the controls of patent licensing. In his 1895 study, Frederick Bourne reported: "There was no pooling of any other interest in the combination excepting that of the patents; no restrictions were placed on the price at which the machines were to be sold, either at wholesale or retail, but the market was open to fair competition on the merits of the several machines, and the result was to be the "survival of the fittest."[151] However, evidence abounds that indicates these main players also cooperated in price fixing and in other mutually beneficial policies.

Elias Howe probably gained the least from the combination. Although shares in these companies profits, his levy on every sewing machine they produced now fell to $5.[152] In return, the combine acquiesced to Howe's demand that the coalition's membership must always consist of a minimum of 24 sewing machine manufacturers. With this provision, Howe expected to prevent any one manufacturer to gain a monopoly over the industry. Perhaps, he hoped to lessen Singer & Company's grip. In any event, Howe satisfied himself by collecting a third of the $15 fee combine members paid on each sewing machine sale. Between 1856 and 1867 the combine collected $2 million from this royalty arrangement. The combination paid Howe his third, banked a small percentage to fund future legal proceedings and then divided the balance. Each combination member retained its autonomy and competed – within limits – openly against his strategic partners.

With the time-wasting legal proceedings behind them, these major manufacturers now produced sewing machines at an unforseen rate. The agreement effectively brought stability to the sewing machine industry.[153] Within a few years, their joint annual production surpassed 100,000 machines. By 1860, sewing machine makers sent out no fewer than 3,000 sales agents to knock on the doors of American households. The Singer Company added more salesmen to bolster its foreign salesforce.[154] In 1870, the Singer Company reached a milestone by producing 127,823 machines in a single year's time. The company's closest competitors were the Wheeler & Wilson Mfg. Company, with a production run of 78,866 machines, and the Howe Sewing Machine Company (not Elias Howe, Jr.'s, company) with an estimated output of 45,000 machines.

The combine remained strong for 20 years. When Howe's patent expired in 1867, the combination quickly dropped him. The association itself did not die out until 1877, when the last major patent, a Bachelder patent, expired. J. Bachelder's important patents included a continuous feeding device, a horizontal table, and an overhanging arm. At this time, the joint output of all sewing machine makers approached 500,000 machines per year. The Singer Manufacturing Company accounted for more than half this number and enjoyed a monopoly over three-fourths of the entire world market. When the combine lost control of all patents, all makers quickly lowered their prices in an effort to discourage the many new sewing machine maker startups that then joined in the open competition.

In 1870, no less than 69 sewing machine makers sold their wares in the United states. Ten years later that number grew to 124. Nevertheless, even with new competition, the enhancements to the sewing machine continued to come from the long-established combine members who could afford the necessary

R&D efforts. The sewing machine had arrived in nearly every American home, it had become as omnipresent as today's television sets.

The Changing Factory System

Besides R&D advances and economic controls, combine members remained solvent by reducing production costs as a direct result of developing economical manufacturing techniques. The success of precision machining under the guidance of scientific management is the sewing industry's least publicized contribution to our civilization. The well-designed sewing machine became the first mass-produced and mass-marketed home appliance to come from the Industrial Revolution. In the process, the sewing machine's manufacturers revitalized and completely made over the stagnant production methods left over from the high middle ages. Feudal-like Theory-X management did not work with a newly skilled work force that gained more and more autonomy as its industry prospered and its skill grew in demand. The introduction of scientific management and the use of interchangeable, mass-produced machined parts transformed the entire face of the industrial revolution and its factory system.

Sewing machine makers, and especially the Singer Machine Company, brought about most of the improvements in manufacturing processes. The pressures of the open market forced these prosperous, successful and highly competitive manufacturers to innovatively reduce the bottom line. The resulting manufacturing innovations Americanized the workplace forever.

One of the first defining characteristics of the American factory system was precision machining. The germs of manufacturing exactness had been planted in the workshops of colonial arms suppliers. Armament manufacturers were the first to welcome close-tolerance machining techniques. For example, colonial muskets with varying bore sizes each required their own specially formed and specifically sized shot balls: each rifle boring called for its own individually crafted and measured shot. Precision machining resulted in standard-sized barrels that in turn enabled shot to be mass produced. Mass production introduced experienced, speciality-skilled workers to the factory system. This workplace specialization, which was characterized by workers dedicated and knowledgeable in a single work function, advanced the technological envelope. By limiting the big picture, workers focused, not on a myriad of duties, but on enhancing their own productivity. In the sewing machine manufacturing factories, dedicated machinists known for particular skills emerged.

In fact, the sewing machinist trade, as in the computer's early days, sent out urgent calls for qualified workers. Singer company president Bourne asserted: "In no branch of manufacture has the use of automatic machines and tools of fine precision become more essential than in this. The special tools required to make various parts of some of the many varieties of sewing-machines . . . require greater inventive talent and ingenuity."[155] Another respected historian, Victor S. Clark, arrived at the same conclusion concerning 1850s sewing machine manufacturing: "The expansion of this [sewing] industry depended upon using automatic tools in place of manual skill, and technical necessities forced it to follow the mechanical and administrative precedents already adopted by makers of firearms, clocks, and similar articles."[156]

Soon, a highly specialized blue collar work force populated the newly created sewing centers. A Singer company report explained: "The increased use of sewing machines in American factories . . . has taught manufacturers that by sub-dividing the work on machines they can use inexperienced help. A girl that can do nothing but run a sewing machine can be taught in a day or two to stitch one particular part, and in a few months she will become more expert at doing that part than would an all-around operator."[157] For example, early ready-to-wear clothing manufacturers devised more than 150 different skill positions in the making of one shirt. New machinery specialists replaced weavers. These widely talented, gifted weavers, whose skills always kept them in managerial positions, lost their ranking to lesser-skilled, but more focused production machine operators and setup men. Before scientific management and production machines, textile manufacturing centers, which comprised all of the Industrial Revolution's industry, had been no more than large sweatshops driven by philistine managers. Manufacturing centers like Singer's introduced career-designated managers on a large scale. Scientific management produced greater productivity levels while creating a stable, trained and willing workforce. The sewing machine industry greatly affected the course of the Industrial Revolution in America? Until the sewing industry refined the American factory system, there had there been no similar shift in the history of manufacturing management. Until the "American Manufacture System" arrived, Automation's factory system had continued relatively unchanged for nearly 200 years.

Incorporation: Clark and Singer dissolve their partnership.
Edward Clark and Isaac Singer ended their 12-year-old partnership during an informal meeting on June 6, 1863. Clark brought an end to the troubled partnership after details of Singer's polygamist lifestyle and many offspring from these illicit affairs became public knowledge. While Clark felt the company needed Singer's continued technical guidance, he nevertheless openly blamed the company's lagging sales not on the ongoing Civil War and the accompanying financial recession, but on the negative publicity generated by his partner's notoriety and his mindless womanizing.[158] (Records show that I. M. Singer & Company exported $2 million worth of product during the Civil War and was then producing 21,000 sewing machines a year. The sewing industry had become one of America's most important industries[159]).

A week after ending his affiliation with his business partner, Singer married for a second time. Isaac no doubt wanted to legitimize his relationship with Isabella Summerville. Nevertheless, it was too late to resolve his past into a present day legitimacy. Rather than deal with the strain of social unacceptability, the newlyweds again retreated to Europe. At the time of his departure, Singer retained 40 percent of his company's stock and converted 10 percent to cash. While he also held a seat on the Board of Trustees, his usual absence generally put him outside the company's day-to-day operations.

(1863-1876) Inslee Hopper, a Singer Presidency?

After removing his partner, Edward Clark incorporated the company. It is noteworthy that Singer would not allow Clark to take the title of Company President. The incorporation agreement provided that neither Clark or Singer could hold that office during the other's lifetime.[160] To fill the office of the president, a capable 26-year-old Newark agent by name of Inslee A. Hopper was chosen as the company's figurehead president.

Many writers have questioned the youthful Hopper's capabilities. With the strong-willed Edward S. Clark hovering in the background as the chairman of the board, assessing Mr. Hopper's effectiveness is difficult. As reported in Davies, *Peacefully Working to Conquer the World*, Hopper's selection arrived in this way. Singer first approached Hopper, who apparently also acted as corporate office manager and the Newark Branch Office manager,[161] asking: "Clark won't let me be president – and I swear I won't let him . . . I think if you were married we would make you president. Don't you know some nice young girl you would like to marry?[162] Inslee Hopper did know some young lady, and was quickly married within two weeks' time.

Hopper's promotion to the Singer Company's presidency brought an immediate $10 per week salary increase[163] and a bonus of 175 company shares.[164] We might conclude that Hopper's youth and lack of corporate level managerial experience presented no threat to either Clark or Singer. Surviving company records report that Hopper contributed little during the Singer Company's board meetings.[165] Apparently his actions spoke louder than his words. During his years at the conglomerate's helm, Hopper oversaw the tremendous expansion of the company's production facilities during U.S. Civil War years. In one of his few terse remarks to fellow board members, he pronounced the company's expansion of its production facilities as his most important imperative. Generally, Clark responded favorably to Hopper's actions as company president. It appears likely that Hopper was sophisticated enough to exercise his own autonomy while loyally following Clark's policies.

Inslee Hopper, son of a Baptist preacher, had first entered Singer employment as an office boy and messenger. He became known for his conservative beliefs and boundless enthusiasm. In time, he secured a position in the finance department. Besides this employment in the corporate offices, he apparently simultaneously managed the Newark branch office. His rapid climb into important positions not usually presented to a 26-year-old shows Hopper's abilities. At Clark's request, Inslee Hopper traveled to Europe in the spring of 1864 to inspect all Singer facilities.[166] During this trip, president Hopper came to terms with the difficult legal proceedings involved with the infringement on the company's foreign patents.

One setback had been the French court's recent ruling that placed all Singer patents in the public domain. In his meetings with his various foreign agents, Hopper listened to their difficulties and broadened their powers and responsibilities as needed. As a result of these conferences, he established the position of a general continental agent. He also named the new London agent, 31-year-old George Woodruff. During his first year, Woodruff, who became highly respected in the company, brought in 175 new, mostly British-based sales agents. Edward Clark is known to have highly approved of Hopper's selection of Woodruff.

When his American employees tested Hopper by striking for an eight-hour-long work day, he threatened them with a lockout.[167] Hopper safely boasted that Singer's many foreign manufacturing facilities could absorb all of Elizabeth's production requirements. Workers quietly acquiesced at the end of Hopper's one week deadline.

Hopper guided the enormous domestic expansion production facilities the company undertook during the years following the Civil War. It had been Hopper's idea to move out of New York City, out of the overloaded Mott Street plant, and into larger, more modern facilities in New Jersey. When the company incorporated in New Jersey at this time, its board members took on the title of directors. During his tenure, Hopper was most responsible for overseeing domestic production while

Edward Clark and his right hand man, George Ross McKenzie, concentrated on developing foreign markets and facilities.

Inslee Hopper became quite successful in his personal life and served as a board director for a bank and an insurance company. Mr. Hopper, who also served on the Singer Company's new board of directors, retained his position until Singer's death in 1875. In 1875, the corporate officers brought their salaries up to $25,000 per year. At the time of their incorporation thirteen years earlier, their wages had been set at $2,000 a year. For these staid, hard-working men to take such an action indicates of how successful the new conglomerate was becoming.

Edward Clark, who always retained de facto control of the company, finally relieved Hopper of his title and responsibilities in September 1876. According to historian Davies, Inslee Hopper had chosen early retirement. Shortly after his departure, Inslee sold all his Singer stock and refrained from further dealings with the company. Mr. Hopper suffered a stroke during 1879 and died two years later at 44 years of age.[168]

Edward. S. Clark: A Final Appreciation

For Edward S. Clark, the journey to prosperity had not been an easy one; at least from an emotional perspective. His wife, Caroline, continually admonished her husband to break off his relationship with the despicable Singer.[169] Besides his wife, Clark also felt the social sting of openly accepting his partner's well-known immorality. Edward Clark had graduated from Williams Law School, where most of his fellow students were men called to the cloth; that is, missionaries or preachers. Imagine how Clark maneuvered within his social circles in constant validation of his dealings with Singer. How can anyone explain to such an audience his business relations with the devil incarnate? Even if this devil held the tool of the century in his hand? Would contemporary society understand, would it glibly look the other way, if some flagrant polygamist and womanizer of underage girls held the rights to the personal computer?

Clark, history has taught us, loved the business world and its financial rewards above all else. After all, he lived in the Age of Capitalism. No doubt he recognized the opportunity of a lifetime when the dissolute Singer walked into his office. Clark must have seen in Singer the very creativeness and cunning found only in old Satan himself. And this observation continually proved out as Singer came forth with one new patent after the other. During 1857 alone, Singer patented twelve ideas. By the terms of their agreement, Singer had perforce signed over a full 50 percent share of his patents to his business partner. A man would have to be crazy to pull his cup away from such a fountainhead.

To Clark, the sewing machine's obvious utility guaranteed to save labor such as no machine before. Yet, despite their great commercial success, the two Singer & Company partners held each in equal disdain. As George Zeiber said, "The one as heartedly hated his partner as the other. . . . There was no personal friendship between them."[170] Singer was known to ridicule Clark's bookkeeperish appearance (and especially his ill-fitting wig), and Clark often lamented aloud about the immoral Singer family, "Curse them! I'm making them all rich!"[171] Yet, Clark had been unable to walk away from this first world-class business empire whose architecture he had personally designed. As a prime mover in his industry, what workplace changes he must have witnessed and must have felt directly responsible for? The 1860 census records indicate that a third of all New England area seamstresses had by then lost their jobs to the sewing machine. Clark must have glowed in the intense heat of his personal contribution to these heady times.

Company Policy Established: Clark's Legacy.
During his tenure as the company's de facto chief enforcement officer, president, marketing manager, financial controller and operations manager, Edward Clark set forth executive policies that firmly established the company's historic course. Clark's initiatives and innovations have survived as a precedent-setting business plan that secured more than a century's worth of monopolistic profits. Boldness characterized his business dealings. In 1877, Clark unexpectedly and dramatically cut the retail price of the "New Family" model in half to $30.[172] With this unprecedented move, Clark greatly

magnified his market share. Few understood Clark's machinations. But soon after his price reduction, all sewing machine patents expired. With patents in the public domain, anyone could clone well-designed Singer or any other manufacturers' machines. Edward Clark's foresightedness had gobbled up most of the pie before it had been put up for grabs.

Even at the end of his company tenure, when there seemed little more for his company to achieve, the 1882 introduction of the "High Arm" family machine led to an explosion in Singer sewing machine sales.[173] The popularity of this quietly operating machine secured the Singer Company's market dominance position for another following generation. The high arm machine came while the company already produced all but one-fourth of all the sewing machines made in the world. For example, in 1880 England the Singer Sewing Machine company completely dominated that country's entire home sewing machine market. In the early days, Edward Clark had to land many financial loans to keep the company above water. But once established, Clark built up a large cash reserve. It was Clark who established the company's financial policy of investing roller-coaster profits into low-yielding but safe securities. Clark then called on this cash cushion during economic downturns. The resulting solvency enabled the company to ride out Black Friday in 1873, the Panic of 1907, the Great Depression and two world wars. As a result, instead of raking off profits, Clark ensured his company prospered entirely independent of bankers.

When the company expanded or diversified, it used its own funds. For a century, the Singer Company owned all of its branch offices and factories outright – including the real estate they occupied. It was Clark who successfully countered shareholder's overtures to skim off great cash reserves as profit. In these great Robber Barron days, Edward Clark's monetary policy kept high-powered thieves and their bankers away from company doors. Edward S. Clark had created a stable conglomerate of plenty: a great business empire comfortably lodged behind secure gates of solvency that would keep profiteers at bay for another century.

The great conglomerate's staying power arose out of Edward S. Clark's personal legacy. This legacy lives on in every modern corporate boardroom. The business paradigm he established consists of sophisticated marketing techniques, installment buying, a product upgrade or trade-in policy, a responsive and resourceful corporate chain of command, fully equipped local dealerships ably guided by autonomous management, well-trained and dedicated company personnel who relied on nepotism to maintain a work family atmosphere, ongoing self-capitalization requiring no high-cost borrowing for modernizing plant equipments and purchasing support materiel, generous support for research and development, and a well-oiled, well-structured distribution network.

Clark also showed that these business models must always be changing, must always adapt to the changing business climate. He showed that advancing technologies must be intentionally developed to assure a continual flow of high-quality, low-cost, technically modern products to market. Clark asked all employees to contribute their ideas and proposals for technical changes or sales approaches. (Note that Clark's company team concept has recently resurfaced in the latest management quality improvement schemes). This first great capitalist leader expected every employee to contribute their utmost, to be entirely dedicated to the company that fed them.

Clark's corporate policies forced his boardroom to recognize and accept change and, most importantly, he forced his directorial team to accommodate this change. Clark kept the company apolitical: throughout its long history the Singer Company rarely looked to government for support. Instead, succeeding company corporate officers followed Clark's lead and delegated its agents to solve these matters locally and within local jurisdiction. Usually, this resident general agent in charge was himself native to the area. These agents breezed through doors that often remained closed to foreigners.

Edward Clark imbued his company with his own Yankee thrift and in the process freed it from stifling bank loans or other profiteering financial ruses.[174] Clark established the secrecy code of never releasing company information to non employees. No one, except an occasional visiting politician, was allowed inside company property. Clark's insistence on producing high-quality products by employing state-of-the-art workmanship was another important company legacy.

Clark's tradition carried on in the men who worked closely with him and who succeeded him. His employees believed they were delivering the self-help tool that opened Horatio Alger riches to every world citizen. What higher endeavor could one engage in? These Victorian age businesspeople held a childlike belief in their useful product, in their God-directed and socially responsible work. Their works within this great Singer Company ameliorated the plight of the world's poor by delivering the *Great Civilizer* to them: by delivering their great enrichment tool they would – in time – eliminate global poverty.

A Final Appreciation

Edward S. Clark was born in Athens, New York, December 19, 1811. He built many New York City apartment houses including the famous Dakota. Clark began construction of this magnificent apartment building in his seventieth year. Over time, it would become one of New York City's most elegant addresses. He gave his alma mater, Williams College, a museum known as Clark Hall and established the Edward Clark Benevolent Society to provide financial assistance to his employees.[175]

He died in Cooperstown, NY, where he had lived since 1854, from typhoid malaria in October 1882. His wife predeceased him by many years and he also buried two of his three sons. He left a large estate valued at $25,000,000. Over the years, Clark's offspring used his legacy to support worthwhile philanthropies, such as funding art museums and supplying ongoing support to various historical societies.

Frederick Bourne has left a telling portrait of this first great capitalist: "Mr. Clark was of a very modest and retiring disposition, and never permitted himself to be brought prominently before the public." Bourne continued, "If occasion called he had an easy flow of rhetoric, and with a pen his diction was pure, terse, and to the point. . . . he had an inherent love of equity."[176]

Edward Clark established company policies that carried and nurtured the company into the twentieth century. His simplistic company mission was to ensure the production of a high quality product and then to advertise the dickens out of it. After Singer passed away, Edward Clark's unfettered leadership turned the Singer Sewing Machine Company into an unstoppable, monopolizing amoeba whose stranglehold over its competition lasted for 100 years.

Clark's policies have survived as the fundamental guiding principles of the world's first conglomerate. All large corporations have sanctified these principles by later emulation. Under Clark's guidance the company's heyday arrived and would grow unchained and unabated. Edward S. Clark, the father of the modern business paradigm, provided I. M. Singer & Company its soul.

"I know of no more encouraging fact than the unquestionable ability of man to elevate his life by a conscious endeavor." – Henry David Thoreau

Chapter Five

The George Ross McKenzie Era: (1882-1889)
Company Dedication Rewards

After Edward Clark's death, The Singer Sewing Machine Company, which now dominated its industry, experienced nearly 90 years of multinational expansion and growth. This prosperity came about because Clark's spirit carried steadily forward on the successive shoulders of five capable company presidents. Under the guarded leadership of these Singer company presidents or CEOs, the company progressed precisely as if Edward S. Clark's equitable hand remained in the background. Clark's successors succeeded by remaining faithful to the company's tradition of producing bountiful quantities of quality products while laboring honestly within a perfectly moral atmosphere. This Victorian Age value system, accompanied by a forceful and anticipatory guiding hand sustained the Clark legacy for another century. These would not be easy years, each company president would come to grips with Herculean labors.

The first of Clark's capable successors was the hard-driving Scotsman, George Ross McKenzie. He was one of the company's original employees who had worked closely with Edward Clark. Alongside Mr. Clark, McKenzie had wrestled with the Gordian vagaries of foreign manufacturing and marketing. The entire management family relied on McKenzie's sophisticated grasp of the subtleties of foreign enterprise. Because of Clark and McKenzie's efforts, the Singer Company became the first American company to succeed in any meaningful way on the continent.

George McKenzie had always been a behind-the-scenes key man who always figured somehow in the company's prosperity. It was only when Clark dissolved his partnership with Singer and incorporated the company that the Scotsman stepped into the limelight. At that moment, Clark selected the 43-year-old McKenzie, then listed on the company rolls as a factory worker, to serve on the Board of Directors. Other board members at this important juncture in company history included newly installed president, Inslee Hopper; newly promoted vice president, William Proctor, who had joined the company as a mechanic in 1853 and later married one of Singer's daughters, Voulettie; and newly elevated secretary and non-practicing New York City physician, Dr. Alexander F. Sterling, who, like Clark, had married one of Ambrose L. Jordan's daughters.

Familialism became in these early days the Singer Company's modus operandi. The Singer Company's reliance on nepotism began at the highest level, in the corporate offices themselves, and then reached downward to all employee levels. For example, the company employed George McKenzie's son-in-law and three sons. One of Inslee Hopper's family members, a nephew, rose to general manager level after inventing a single-thread sewing machine and otherwise proving himself through hard work and dedication.[177]

McKenzie's Career

McKenzie's fellow board members must have regarded the hard-working Scotsman as the consummate company man. George Ross McKenzie had immigrated to the United States in 1846 at the age of 26. On arrival, he found employment either as a carpenter or cabinetmaker with some small manufacturer in

New York City. During 1851, and only months after its relocation from its Boston startup location, he joined Singer's fledgling manufacturing company as a cabinetmaker apprentice. McKenzie soon earned recognition for his commitment to his craft and for a noted ability to organize his work.

McKenzie must have enjoyed working for Singer and must have had great faith in the sewing machine he helped make. There can be no other explanation for the great risk he took in 1855. During a brief conversation with an obviously despondent Isaac Singer, McKenzie learned that the company was temporarily in need of $5,000 operating capital. Hearing this, the thrifty Scotsman, who then earned $11.50 a week, quickly ran from the premises, promising to return in short time. Within the hour, McKenzie handed a surprised Singer the needed loan of $5,000. Apparently, McKenzie's good name alone allowed him to borrow without collateral half the money from a bank to which he then added all of his own savings. To help his employer through this financial crisis, McKenzie also volunteered to work for half pay until the company's finances improved.[178]

McKenzie's investment endeared him to his employer. And in time, as the company prospered, so did the dedicated Scotsman. The two men, McKenzie and Singer, developed a close bond of trust. For example, in later years we find McKenzie handling Singer's personal and confidential matters such as locating a domicile for Mary Ann Sponsler after her divorce from Singer.[179]

During Inslee Hopper's presidency, McKenzie, no doubt enjoying Clark's assistance, moved up to Vice President and General Manager. While serving the company as a general agent, McKenzie once said: "[general agents] commenced working at the bench, and it has only been through steady hard work and trying to do it right at all, the we hold the positions we do today."[180] At a board meeting, McKenzie grabbed the floor to deny emphatically he was not the "dammed dishonest man," Isaac Singer (who was in attendance) had once accused him of being. Instead, McKenzie asserted, he was someone whose 'character is his capital, who would not have it injured by any man however rich he may be!"[181] And this was probably so. Before coming to Singer, McKenzie had unceremoniously left his previous employer after clearing his name of some false accusation. Over the years, McKenzie matured   from a capable journeyman cabinetmaker and went on to distinguish himself as a trusted and able manager. It was McKenzie whom Clark trusted with the company's first foreign fishing expeditions. As a high level manager, George Ross McKenzie made his mark early in 1867 when he accompanied British agent George Woodruff on the latter's return trip to Europe. Clark had tasked the Scot to locate the first Singer Sewing Machine Company foreign manufacturing test site.

McKenzie's selection of Clydebank in Scotland, a site near the Scot's ancestral home, must have raised boardroom concern. But McKenzie's decision was sound. At that time, Scotland was renowned for its shipbuilding yards and large merchant fleet that plied the world's trade routes. Besides the convenience of lowcost shipping, Scotland offered a well-developed iron smelting industry and a hard-working population of intelligent, semiskilled factory workers accustomed to low wages. McKenzie's selection of Scotland proved itself many years later when the overriding success of the enormous Clydebank manufacturing facility was copied by one of Singer's main competitors, the Howe Sewing Machine Company. In 1871, the Howe company opened, without fanfare or explanation, a large manufacturing facility in Glasgow. Doubtless, the company hoped to emulate its biggest competitor's successes in foreign lands.

In 1868, General Manager McKenzie recognized the need for bolstering the R&D department. He no doubt understood the important contribution I. M. Singer had made in keeping the company in the forefront of emerging technologies. To counter the loss of the great innovator, he hired Thomas J. Jones, a technical expert and experimental inventor, to keep abreast of and assimilate emerging technologies into the company's production facilities.[182] He paid the well-respected Jones the enormous salary of $100 a week; or about $25 a week more than he paid his factory superintendent. This salary arrangement signifies more that any theoretical pronouncement that invention had become a careful, orchestrated discipline. The days of trial-

and-error and happenstance inspiration had ended. Now, precise and goal-oriented engineering guided product development.

By 1869, Singer factories could not keep up with the worldwide demand for the company's faultlessly operating sewing machines. Because of lowered production and shipping costs and the greater profit margin, McKenzie decided to expand the company's foreign factories. For example, within two years time, the company's Bridgton facility became the largest manufacturing facility in the United Kingdom.[183] A year later, the company passed another landmark when its foreign sales surpassed its domestic sales.[184]

As global sales proliferated, it was McKenzie who insisted on continually upgrading all company facilities to keep them as modern and as efficient as possible. The Scotsman, unlike the heads of other American-based foreign companies, showed no reluctance in outfitting his foreign manufacturing facilities with the latest American manufacturing techniques.[185]

McKenzie also enlarged on Clark's initial efforts at standardizing the company's operations and facilities.[186] The Scotsman first pulled the reins on the mom-and-pop store mentality of bookkeeping by introducing modern accounting procedures. Trusting few, he first introduced company auditors to check randomly on the company's far-flung and autonomous operations. McKenzie instituted careful bookkeeping practices for branch offices to follow. He demanded a weekly reckoning of all out-of-pocket office expenses. In 1881, McKenzie insisted agents use sound judgment in conducting company business. For example, he advised against selling to those low-income customers who appeared unable to support time payments. As general manager overseeing the company's 40,000 employees,[187] McKenzie proved himself time and again and especially while guiding the company's great commercial triumph abroad.

McKenzie's Presidency

The selection of McKenzie to fill the company president's chair after Edward Clark's passing in 1882 appears unsurprising. Board members knew the deeply religious Scot to be enormously hard-working, well-organized, practical to a fault and unapproachable in his personal ethics. The new president's personal qualities soon surfaced in company policies designed to bring about a highly moral, cost-conscious and dedicated workforce. Like his predecessor, the new president expected his workers to cooperate as caring members of one large, cohesive family. A hard-working family working in an atmosphere of amity guaranteed the company's daily successes and eventual longevity.

On attaining the president's office, McKenzie refined the company mission and vision statement that eventually identified the Singer Company for generations to come. In McKenzie's vision, the company's most important commitment was to its employees. To this end, McKenzie introduced profit-sharing for all employees. The Scot also insisted that all employees receive just and equitable treatment. His policy statement promised that employees at all levels must be treated as carefully as the company's customers and the public at large. This stated purpose came at a time when the Industrial Revolution's factory system was being criticized for its demeaning handling of its workers, and of its minor children in particular.

In 1882, the company's corporate offices sent out a letter advising its canvassers to be fair and agreeable to customers and to maintain all machines on time payment in good working order.[188] In this way, the Singer man developed a reputation for fairness over the his entire sales route.

Besides basking in the limelight of unheard-of productivity and profits, McKenzie's presidency also faced serious global issues of widespread political and financial unrest. For example, in 1882, Italy, Austria-Hungary and Germany formed their Triple Alliance; England flexed its colonial power muscle and seized Cairo, Egypt; Ireland's struggle with radical politics emerged with the murders of Secretary Lord Frederick Cavendish and Under Secretary Thomas Burke; and around the world, but especially within the United Kingdom, labor unions continued to strengthen.

Of overriding importance to multinational investors like the Singer Company was the emerging face of European nationalism. During the early years of McKenzie's presidency, protectionist politics discovered its voice throughout Europe. European newspaper editorials frequently belabored the extent of American financial interests in the Old World and warned of the "the Americanization of Europe." This clamor was so forceful that many felt that all foreign holdings of all American enterprise appeared at great risk. McKenzie himself wondered aloud at his own company's future in the face of the expected changes in European economic policies. As nationalistic tendencies strengthened, many European countries enacted new laws and tariffs designed to limit foreign profiteering. During McKenzie's tenure, England passed laws enabling it to tax foreign corporation profits.[189]

A noteworthy unfolding in German nationalism especially threatened Singer Company profits. Besides the clouded events in Europe, McKenzie, even at this early stage, understood that his Russian assets were similarly at great risk. A surviving letter to McKenzie early in 1883 warned of a possible Soviet revolution coming from the spreading influence of the communist movement. In response to Europe's stifling economic policies, McKenzie remained competitive by increasing the Singer Company's local presence. He strengthened his foreign national companies thereby establishing their greater importance in local politics and economies. He also energized his stagnated sales force. For example, in 1882, McKenzie expanded on his European presence by breaking ground for the Kilbowie manufacturing facility; this was the company's first truly substantial overseas investment.[190] When Austria-Hungary raised its tariffs on sewing machine imports, McKenzie countered by increasing local production through expansion of local manufacturing facilities.

It is noteworthy that in meeting these challenges, McKenzie never resorted to political subterfuge. He did not rail publicly against the foreigner's one-sided trade policies nor did he challenge their unfairness in the courts. Instead, he pushed his workforce to greater dedication, greater effort, greater excellence. McKenzie's quiet strength set the precedents the company would always fall back on in adverse times and in difficult situations.

In 1883, McKenzie responded to a collapsing marketplace brought on by a global economic downturn by testing previously untouched Asian markets. By opening these new marketing channels, he hoped to find a "commercial safety valve" to combat slow sales and to unload his warehoused stockpiles. McKenzie intended to provide new markets to support the company's continuing growth and product surplus. The Singer Company was now a behemoth manufacturer; the Glasgow plant alone could now produce 10,000 machines a week. This enormous output required a large and stable customer demand. In the face of the new European nationalism and its unfair protective tariffs and the continuing decline in European revenues, McKenzie recognized he needed new, welcoming markets to sustain the Singer Company's massive size. As a result, McKenzie decided on an all-out commercial incursion into Asia.[191]

To the Scotsman, Asia seemed like a vast, neglected sewing machine goldmine. McKenzie also believed that his competitors, who were established in Asia, were weathering the current financial crisis through steady Asian sales. Unfortunately, after five years of bombarding Asian countries with every conceivable marketing ploy, McKenzie shook his head over the red-penciled bottom line and gave up. The company failed in China simply because the Chinese people did not like the machine-tight stitch and preferred their own loose stitching. During five years time, no more than a few thousand Singer sewing machines could be found across the entire breath of this densely populated country. With great regret, McKenzie gave up entirely on his China venture.

However, the company's experience in Japan provided a glimmer of hope. At this time, Japan had begun opening itself to the West. In a sudden turnaround, Japanese leaders beckoned the industrial world and began influencing its population to become more Westernized. Japanese women, servicemen and police now began wearing fashionable Western-style clothing. Still, while the Japan market appeared promising, McKenzie did not commit large resources to it. Perhaps, if the world economy had rebounded in time, McKenzie would have relied on the usual company procedures of establishing self-contained Singer

Company agents and branch offices. Instead, he allowed a wealthy sewing machine dealer in Tokyo to maintain a representative Asian presence. The Singer Company's incursion and conquest of the Asian market would have to wait for other more propitious days. Such days would arrive 15 years later.

McKenzie faced challenges at home as well. When the city council in Elizabeth, N.J., defaulted on interest payments on a bond held by the Singer Company, McKenzie retaliated by stopping tax payments to the city. When Elizabeth council members increased political pressures on the company, McKenzie ordered a lockout. Without paydays, 3,300 Singer employees and Elizabeth residents no longer paid local city taxes on income. Without tax revenue, McKenzie believed Elizabeth would be forced to reduce municipal services; perhaps even shut down. In a well-publicized statement, McKenzie, with his Board members backing him, claimed he would close Singer's Elizabethport operations "as silently in the night as the Arab folds his tent and steals away."[192]

The Scotsman's unyielding posture soon defused the standoff. However, the likelihood of more problems with the Elizabeth city council, encouraged McKenzie to expand the Glasgow factory. After all, foreign manufacturing was cheaper. Surviving statistics show that the expenses related to Kilbowie's production capability of 10,000 machines a week were a full 30 percent less than those of Elizabethport.

During the McKenzie years, the press suddenly began noticing the demeaning aspects associated with the factory system. Published accounts of widespread child labor and other abuses began delivering up an outcry from the highly moral Victorian population. Often mentioned was the mind and hand-numbing drudgery imposed on hard-working and low-paid sewing girls.[193] In England, "the English semptress (sic)(became) regarded as the type of all that was wretched and helpless. Bitter were the newspaper denunciations of the(ir) employers."[194] As a result, labor reform became a deepening domestic issue.

In 1886, four years after McKenzie came into power, the American Federation of Labor consolidated 25 different trade unions. In Chicago, workers striking against the other American conglomerate, the McCormick Harvesting Machine Company, set off a bomb after police succeeded in dispersing them. The public feared the emerging labor movement whom they believed militant radicals controlled. Through these unsettled times of labor unrest and economic uncertainty, president McKenzie somehow kept his multinational company profitable and at peace with itself.

A Final Farewell

George Ross McKenzie, the one-time immigrant carpenter, never forgot his roots. He often visited and donated charitably to his tiny native village in Scotland, Kingussie. Townspeople remembered that a 14-year-old McKenzie had become his mother's sole support after his father's death. The youthful McKenzie first found work herding cattle to distant and better-paying markets. Before his twenty-first birthday, he parlayed his saved commissions from these successful cattle drives into the purchase of two small general stores. The thrifty Scot seemed on a path to small business success. But McKenzie was a deeply religious man. So committed to the Calvinist creed that when townsfolk purchased an organ for the local Presbyterian church, McKenzie moved out of town in a huff. Shortly afterwards, he sailed to America.

Years later, McKenzie built a new church in Kingussie and made certain there was no space allotted for an organ. He also built two Presbyterian churches in Jersey City. George McKenzie lived on a 3,000-acre estate in Sullivan County, New York, which he called Glen Spey. McKenzie had worked alongside Edward Clark for two decades. The loyal Scot had sustained his benefactor's vision of creating a highly respected, fair-dealing, and long-lasting organization. For example, when the London agent presented him with a Meerschaum pipe, McKenzie caused his board of directors to set company policy outlawing gift-giving among employees.[195]

McKenzie, more than his predecessors, helped solidify the moral atmosphere that came to identify the company. McKenzie's policies forced the sales staff to engage clients fairly. Under McKenzie, The Singer Company's marketing methods matured and neared excellence. His investment in R&D and in a clean, technologically modern workplace became a model for the successful, trouble-free corporation. His R&D efforts produced noteworthy accomplishments. Chief design engineer Philip Diehl introduced the first electric Singer sewing machine at the 1884 International Electrical Exhibition.[196] Under McKenzie's guidance modern accounting practices arrived. In 1885, he introduced traveling examiners who reported only to corporate headquarters.[197] He introduced novel programs to guard against embezzlement. He demanded that general agents return a profit or find other work. He ended the practice of selling to anyone regardless of their ability to repay. Real-world assets replaced inflated paper profits. The Scot enhanced and made corporate practices responsive by setting up autonomous oversight committees to watch over the finance and production departments as well as the company's many agencies. With these new management tools, McKenzie brought centralized control to the Singer empire.

In 1889, McKenzie found himself worn out and quite ill. In truth, he had struggled with his failing health for more than two years. Now, he decided to retire from the Singer Company and its Board of Directors entirely. After retirement, he survived three more years before dying on January 6, 1892 at the age of 72. He left an estate valued at $3,500,000. At this time, company assets surpassed $40,000,000. (Edward Clark's heirs held shares that claimed half this fortune). George Ross McKenzie was a self-made, extraordinary man who used his term at the conglomerate to instill a culture of justice and fair play. He brought Edward Clark's legacy forward and supplied the company with its fair dealing image. In the process, his company's sales soon eclipsed those of its main competitor, Wheeler and Wilson.[198]

For more than three decades George McKenzie had been instrumental in opening branch offices in Australia, New Zealand, Africa, Austria-Hungary, Britain, China, Scotland, Brazil, India, Switzerland, Italy, Belgium, France, Spain, Canada, Carribean, the Philippines and an added presence in Japan. During the 1880s, McKenzie's foreign marketing techniques were copied by other American companies.[199] When the tireless, trustworthy Scotsman, George Ross McKenzie, retired, the Singer Sewing

Machine Company was the most prosperous sewing machine company in the world, a vast multinational enterprise. McKenzie's legacy included a cash reserve guaranteeing the company its vaunted "freedom of action."[200]

The Scot was the only company president to work his way up from the factory floor. He had fine-tuned corporate structure making it more responsive and proactive. As quoted by historian Davies, McKenzie boasted to his 1885 stockholders meeting: "[the company is] in every country of the world in the unquestioned leadership and control of the sewing machine business."[201]

"The measure of a man is what he does with power." — Pittacus

Chapter Six

The Frederick Gilbert Bourne Era (1889-1905)[202]
Prosperity Continues

As the new century approached, the Singer Sewing Machine Company continued to make and sell its one product in competition with an estimated 150 other sewing machine manufacturers. A partial listing of these competitors includes Wheeler & Wilson, Wilson & Gibbs, Fisher & Steiner, the Reece Company, Lawrence M. Stein Company, Arbetter Felling Machine Company, Pfaff, Gegauff, Bergmann & Huttemeir Brosser, Frister & Rossman, Grimme, Haid & Neu, Kohler, Kayser, Natalis and Stucchi. All of these mostly German-based manufacturers would be no match for the next Singer CEO, a true Renaissance man.

After George R. McKenzie's death, the Clark-McKenzie tradition passed into the capable hands of 36-year-old Frederick Gilbert Bourne. Once again, another pacesetting capitalist surfaced to challenge changing times and to guarantee the first conglomerate's continued growth.

Frederick G. Bourne was a minister's son who first worked as a clerk in New York City's Mercantile Library. The young Bourne also enjoyed singing in choir at Old Trinity Church and in a local glee club. During one of his performances, a well-known music patron, Alfred Corning Clark, took notice. Alfred, who was Edward Clark's heir, was himself a fine tenor and regularly invited talented singers for gatherings in his mansion. After several hours of music-making, the group dined together and then relaxed while discussing world events. It is into this high circle that Frederick Bourne found himself. And, while his singing voice had opened this important social group to him, it was his after-dinner grasp of world events that impressed Alfred Corning Clark.

In time, Alfred hired the engaging Bourne to manage his father's estates and to oversee the construction of the Dakota, his deceased father's elaborate apartment complex. When Edward Clark died in 1882, the Board of Directors honored the elder Clark's will by allowing Alfred to fill his seat. But Alfred Clark did not immerse himself in the company's policy making and instead sent Frederick Bourne to attend company board meetings as his proxy. Bourne soon entered the company's direct employ as a stenographer. With Alfred always in the background, Bourne began climbing to more responsible positions of secretary and then vice-president. When George McKenzie retired, Alfred Clark influenced the board to move the 32-year-old Bourne into the company's vacant presidency.

It must be noted that the Singer Company shares remained largely in the hands of the directors, their descendants and their family members. At the time of the Bourne election, Alfred Corning Clark remained the largest shareholder. As an unfortunate but a probable aside, historian Davies hints that the possibly terminally ill George McKenzie may have been unwilling to step down.[203]

As seen, the implication of favoritism surrounds Bourne's appointment. During the McKenzie years, Bourne served as company secretary and was possibly involved in various company business during this time. Bourne's qualifications to assume command of the great conglomerate must have appeared limited.

Doubtless, he demonstrated exceptional leadership abilities while managing the Clark family estates and other real estate developments and while completing occasional secretarial duties as Alfred Clark's proxy. Still, what experience did Bourne have with the day-to-day operations of a large multinational company? With precision machining? With supervision of management? With international manufacturing and marketing? With corporate policy? Or with dealing with internal politics of foreign powers?

However, despite his limited background and preparation, history has proven that Frederick Gilbert Bourne was the right man in the right place at the right time. The selection of a youthful outsider to head the US's first successful multinational company would prove a master stroke. This unlikely, little-experienced youth would guide the company out of horse-and-buggy days into modern times and unexpected prosperity.

Difficult Times Welcome the Young Lions

When coming to power in 1889, Frederick Bourne assumed control of a company that had manufactured a total of 13,250,000 machines since its 1863 incorporation. Of this number, near 50 percent had been produced in Singer's foreign manufacturing facilities. The Singer Sewing Machine Company enjoyed a reputation as a large, well-respected multinational company. The first American company to succeed so well in the foreign marketplace.

After his whirlwind inaugural tour of the company's global facilities, Bourne reached two conclusions. Despite McKenzie's ground-breaking efforts toward maintaining modern facilities, many Singer buildings and factories showed signs of age. But not only its facilities showed signs of wear; most of the company's high level management neared their retirement years. In Bourne's view, the great age of Singer pioneers must come to a close. New blood must invigorate this venerable company and its complacent workforce.

Besides these two problems, he would somehow have to deal with the continually compounding problem of ever-growing European nationalism. Europeans now spoke loudly of the

"American invasion." In their view, American manufacturers controlled their marketplaces with no fewer than 500 low cost factory-made products.[204] Historian Mira Wilkins notes, "In London, in 1901-1902, three publications appeared, entitled respectively *The American Invasion, The American Invaders*, and *The Americanization of the World.*[205]

For the Singer Company, foreign manufacturing and sales represented the bulk of the company's assets and revenues. Bourne recognized that newly drafted foreign tariff laws cast all of the company's foreign operations into uncertain seas. Adding to the mounting European political pressures was the deepening worldwide recession. This financial depression landed full force in 1893 when US gold reserves fell below $100 million, or just enough to cover 20 percent of the paper money then in circulation. The resulting fast-paced security sales by foreign investors proved to be one of the catalysts for the ensuing panic.

This financial crisis would not abate for another four years. During these economically troubled times, 600 banks and 15,000 small companies closed their doors. To further complicate matters for individual manufacturers, large-scale mergers became commonplace. As a result many large corporations came into being.[206] Darwin's theory seemed to have relevance in the economic sphere.

A time of change had arrived. In response, Bourne enlivened his stagnating empire with fresh new ideas. Like most arriving CEO's, he surrounded himself with a personally selected management team. In his selection process, the brash, youthful president bypassed long-tenured employees and instead elevated well-educated young people into responsible management positions. For example, Bourne promoted 35-year-old MIT graduate Franklin Park to manage the Clydebank facility. He selected 33-year-old Edwin H. Bennett, an engineer out of Cornell University, to manage the huge Elizabethport factory. (Bennett's father had held this same position until retirement).

Bourne also brought Douglas Alexander into his employ as his personal secretary. It is noteworthy that as Alfred Clark had first discovered Bourne singing in a glee club, Frederick Bourne noticed Mr. Alexander while the latter sang as a solo baritone during a church service.[207] In time, Douglas Alexander would succeed Frederick Bourne and oversee the company for 44 years. Besides Alexander, all of Bourne's young executives earned positions as directors within a few years. Under Bourne's firm grip, these young lions would move the company into a new era.

An Autonomous Sales Department Arrives

During 1890, the company reported sales of 800,000 machines. It held $12.8 million in cash reserve, another $14.5 million surplus and more than $20 million in accounts receivable.[208] Singer sewing machines, which somehow managed to survive the cost-cutting measures of its numerous but financially strapped competitors, now accounted for 80 percent of all sewing machines sold the world over. Nevertheless, Bourne reflected the company still operated haphazardly, much too loosely for the young president's bent toward precision and harmony such as one finds in the great musical masterpieces.

Very often, the company's fortunes in a geographic area rested completely on the whims of the local agent in charge. While McKenzie had brought structure to branch offices' cost accounting, a great deal of company operations remained unregulated. Local agents, for example, determined their own advertising schedule and marketing needs. Bourne determined to bring structure to this hit-or-miss methodology.

In 1891, Bourne created a standalone advertising department. Soon, the new department introduced relatively costly and novel advertising such as company calendars, handouts, posters, thimbles, and tape measures bearing the trademark red "S." "Nation Cards," which usually depicted a female Singer employee in her native dress, also arrived in 1891. Beyond the obvious artistic merit of these lithographs, Bourne's sales agents employed the carefully orchestrated picture cards to illustrate various product selling points.[209]

The Ultimate Importance of R&D[210]

Bourne believed his Research and Development Department offered little organizational structure and had stagnated. He decided the principal reason behind the failings of his many competitors was their negligence in maintaining a technological edge. Most companies accepted innovation in a traditional and unsophisticated manner. Often they relied on occasional flashes of insight and creativity. By contrast, Bourne expanded on McKenzie's idea of supporting a focused and large scale R&D department: "The experimental department is one of the most important and expensive. Here, the inventor's idea is carefully wrought into form and receives preliminary tests of its efficiency."[211] Bourne then elaborated on the extended development time that often follows a commitment to the original idea: "After all this expensive preparation and experiment, the invention may soon be replaced by something better and be abandoned."[212] This commitment to long term R&D and the added willingness to accept failure discloses an unexpected intellectual maturity for a young man. At Singer, Bourne brought more structure to invention.

Like today's home appliances, the sewing machine underwent constant change and enhancement. Since 1842, during the five decades following its introduction, the patent office had issued 7,439 patents relating to sewing machines. Bourne reflected that, with few exceptions, in the 20 years following the end of the sewing combination in 1867, only two of the original sewing machine makers had contributed significant improvements to their product: the Wheeler and Wilson Manufacturing Co. and, of course, I. M. Singer & Company. Bourne further noted, that only these same two companies produced sewing machines sophisticated and durable enough to run at the high rate of speed provided by the recently developed steam power engines.[213] Besides steam power, Bourne also recognized the importance of electricity and gave this new technology its own home by spinning off this department into its own separate company, the Diehl Manufacturing Facility.

Bourne's R&D department succeeded in keeping the company competitive. Its delivery of three new family sewing machine models known as the Class 15, 24, and 27 became the company's mainstay product line at the turn of the century. During 1889 alone, R&D managed to link the new electric motors to the foot treadle[214] and they also produced an automatic buttonhole machine.[215] In 1892, Singer developed a commercial grade zigzag machine. But for unknown reasons, the company failed to develop a domestic model. Such an all-purpose machine had to wait until 1948 when both Pfaff and Necchi found a profitable niche in selling zigzag machines to the American domestic market. The year 1900 witnessed the introduction of the "The Singer 66." This popular, smooth-operating model sped along at 2,200 stitches per minute.[216] In 1904, the company increased its competitive edge by introducing unique automatic features to enhance its Class 71 buttonhole machines.

Refining the Factory System

Besides bringing in efficient management and design engineering, Bourne enhanced and smoothed out his production departments. A few years after Bourne's retirement, a company flyer reported the results of its refinement of the *American system:* "One of the most important departments of the modern Singer factory is that for designing and constructing tools required accurately to make thousands of different kinds of sewing machine parts so that every one of a kind shall be exactly duplicate and interchangeable with its fellow."[217] The great benefit of machining interchangeable parts is to manufacture pieces at geographically separated locations and bringing them together at some central location for final assembly. By machining the parts to close tolerances, the fit between them at final assembly is guaranteed. This critical feature of mass production underlies the very existence of modern industry and contributed significantly to the continued progress of the Industrial Revolution in this country. By contrast, European manufacturers made no such advances in their production methods.

To gauge or assure the quality of the production department's machining accuracy required a new skill. Under Bourne, Singer factories established the beginnings of Quality Control departments. To ensure a close tolerance fit *the Singer Gauge* measured each part and the *assembling system* checked each machined part before mating. With these new tools and production testing methods, the company guaranteed that: "Singer parts always fit and they can be readily obtained at Singer shops located in every city in the world."[218] Besides his machinists, Bourne recognized the greater skill of American cabinet makers.[219] American forests also provided better woods for cabinet makers. By carrying over close-tolerance processes into his woodworking facilities, Bourne obtained the overall quality he wanted for his product line. He had his factories cut *in shape* and ship cabinet sections *in the white* for foreign assembly and surface finishing. Writing in 1895, Bourne noted the company produced about 694,000 sewing machine cabinets annually. At one time, the Singer Company supported the largest woodworking factories in the world in Arkansas, Illinois and in South Bend, Indiana.

Problems

Shortly, after attaining the presidency, Frederick Bourne embarked on a European tour of his facilities. The incoming president's world tour had become a company tradition. In England, he personally appraised the poor performance of the local central office. The British government had begun taxing all of the corporation's profits that transited through that central European office, whether the profits originated in England or not. While most believed that this unfair taxation had strained profits, Bourne's inspection revealed the lackluster performance by his agent-in-charge contributed heavily to the company's weak performance.

For a time, Bourne troubled himself with how to deal with the man in whom the company had placed so much confidence and trust. When he learned his married agent was living with a local woman, Bourne quickly discharged the troublesome agent.[220] Bourne's actions were no doubt spurred by his own moral and religious convictions. To the religious Bourne, the company's representatives must remain above reproach. To combat the English tax problem, Bourne returned central control of European operations to his New York City corporate offices.

The Bourne presidency signaled the end of the old guard. The Singer empire had become too large to hang decision-making processes on local preference or on a headquarters man's experience and personal acquaintance with a distant foreign agent. Besides centralizing operations out of his corporate offices, Bourne continued adding teeth to the standardization of company policy and operations. Edward Clark had first hinted at tighter controls, and McKenzie had actually made inroads into centralizing operational control. By 1891, Bourne completed his review of accepted company practices. As a result, he introduced bureaucratic forms and policies designed to give upper management control over his first line of supervision and their normal day-to-day operations.

Now, agents sent weekly reports to Bourne's corporate headquarters. These all-inclusive reports included passages summarizing local and national events that might impact Singer Company business. He further controlled agents by bringing in the "hire book." These booklets, which were assigned to each purchaser, provided serialized and colored coupons to accompany each payment that required agents to validate with a numbered stamp.[221] The new modern corporation had arrived. The days of conducting business using the old-fashioned corner store culture no longer existed within the Singer conglomeration.

In 1892, the year in which Grover Cleveland was elected to the U.S. Presidency, Bourne continued his European inspection tour by visiting Russia. He reportedly saw little hope in developing the Russian marketplace.[222] Bourne's analysis proved greatly off target. Perhaps, the new company president hesitated to proceed in Russia where 22 various competitive sewing machine makers enjoyed a strong market share. Moreover, Russia severely challenged the modern corporation by offering little or no communications for disseminating corporate controls or operational edicts. This vast country lacked even the rudiments of a transportation system or acceptable roadways for product distribution. However, Bourne's southern Europe agent-in-charge, George Neidlinger, believed otherwise.

Immediately, upon meeting Bourne, the excitable Neidlinger besieged Bourne to try to make inroads into Russia. This young man, who began Singer employment as a water boy in the Mott Street Plant, had by age 22 begun forming the company's overseas empire from the Hamburg office. Neidlinger's efforts had proved remarkable, and the young man enjoyed a great deal of respect and support in the front office. Notwithstanding Bourne's negativism, Neidlinger's Russian effort resulted in the establishment of forty-four retail stores answering to four Singer branch offices in the short space of three years. These facilities suddenly accounted for almost 50 percent of all sewing machines sold in Russia. Enough cannot be said of the energetic Neidlinger, who represented the Singer Company in all of Turkey, southern Europe and now in Russia.

In 1895 alone, Neidlinger's sales organization delivered 68,788 machines.[223] In 1896, Neidlinger had convinced visiting Singer Vice President Douglas Alexander to establish a full manufacturing subsidiary in Russia. Neidlinger's analysis made note of Russia's high import tariffs and high shipping costs associated with the great geographical distances. As a result of this meeting, Singer began manufacturing its heavy stands in Russia a year later. Singer became the first sewing machine maker to manufacture any part of the sewing machine in Russia.[224]

Within a few years, the president's report showed that Kompaniya Singer had grown into its third largest manufacturing facility. Later in 1902, as Kompaniya Singer continued expanding, President Bourne built a new six story headquarters in St. Petersburg. Besides the modern Otis elevators and novel steam heaters to keep its roof and gutters free of winter snow and ice, the new 1.5 million ruble headquarters made history by becoming Russia's first steel-girder building. It was also the first Russian structure to feature malleable bronze ornamentation.[225]

The SSMC Russian headquarters represented only a small architectural aside: Bourne was then planning construction and development of the tallest building New Yorkers had ever seen. The structural knowledge required for this feat would bring building technology to a new frontier in the skyscraper wars.

Bourne's Legacy

Bourne's major accomplishment rests in a successful company expansion in the face of an emerging European economic nationalism. This unfair European mercantilism showed itself in protective tariffs and trade policies coming it seemed, in a haphazard, uncontrollable daily basis. Many multinationals of the time had not withstood this challenge. F. G. Bourne also created a strong bureaucratic control, a solid chain of command centralized in his corporate offices. Bourne reacted to the unpredictable foreign and domestic political machinations of his time by introducing safeguards over internal policies. He chose to no longer publicly debate commerce department issues the company found itself at variance with. Branch managers were instructed to keep abreast of ongoing legislative debates in their regions while refraining from possible action without discussions with corporate management first.

Bourne closed his facilities to the prying eyes of the public and even to his own shareholders. His company reports, which consisted of lists of unidentified numbers, became difficult to decipher even for shareholders. To obtain an annual report, shareholders had to apply in person at corporate headquarters. Beginning with Bourne, the company no longer published its annual reports and did not resume their mailing to shareholders until 1949.[226]

Bourne's policy created a closed-door, tight-lipped security that soon characterized the company. Secrecy was enforced at all levels. Upper management no longer discussed or explained policy to lower level managers. Admittance to all Singer facilities remained closed to all non-employees. Even its own agents dared not attempt a visit to Singer manufacturing facilities. Bourne feared that reports of the company's internal machinations might influence public editorializing. In these uncertain political times, especially when both foreign and domestic tariff-making decisions remained so important, every little tidbit of information became an opportunity for editorial twisting. Now, even customary government requests for employment figures and the like were cursorily discarded. These issues have been well covered in Robert Bruce Davies' fascinating account, *Peacefully Working to Conquer the World: Singer Sewing Machines in Foreign Markets, 1854-1920.*[227]

Early Retirement: Another Farewell

At the 1905 shareholders' meeting, the 54-year-old Frederick Bourne stepped down from the president's office. Bourne lived in a $500,000 home in Oakdale, Long Island, NY. Unlike his predecessor, Bourne enjoyed organ music and installed one in his mansion. Friends recall he employed a black valet who attended him at all times. He loved the sea, was an able sailor and was eventually named commodore at the New York Yacht Club.

He once directed the New England Society of New York, a fundamentalist religious group advocating puritanism as expressed in the teachings of our first pilgrim settlers. The New England Society erected "The Pilgrim," a well-known Central Park statue of a Puritan standing under his wide-brimmed hat with his musket at parade rest. The Pilgrims, who had sailed to American because of their opposition to the teachings of the Church of England, called for a more radical expression of pure religion. They became known as Puritans, English Protestants, or followers of John Wycliffe. Puritans led exemplary, self-effacing, ascetic lives with limited outlets for recreation and with little appreciation for works of art. These religious fundamentalists self-promoted their sturdy independence, Spartan discipline, thriftiness, clear-headed intellectuality, personal initiative and defiant moral uprightness. Puritans, who trusted all to God while simultaneously disallowing commentary on His works, became famous for their narrow-thinking. One wonders how Bourne reconciled his restrictive inner belief system with his extensive and costly support of science and pursuit of invention. Perhaps, Bourne best exemplified the spirit of teamwork and cooperation that the early Pilgrims brought to their chosen land. Frederick Bourne succeeded, much like president McKenzie before him, in melding together a cohesive Singer family.

Frederick Bourne developed into a distinguished business man and urbane capitalist holding many important directorships and presidencies of several major concerns such as the Atlas Portland Cement Company and the Knickerbocker Safe Deposit Company. He served as director or corporate board member of the following companies: Long Island Railroad Company, Long Island Motor Parkway, Manhattan Company, City and Suburban

Homes Company, Babcock & Wilcox, Weber Piano and Pianola Company, and the Aeolian Company. He owned and operated his own business, Bourne & Co. Ltd., of New Jersey. Bourne also left us a distinct and precise overview of his industry that disclosed his own unique business philosophy. A close reading of his 1895 study, which Depew reprinted in his *One Hundred Years of American Commerce*, reveals the personality of a true renaissance man. His evident grasp of the historical antecedents of his industry, his well-crafted logic, and his personal remembrances deliver a believable and penetrating insight into the Singer Company and the sewing industry at the turn of the century.

On leaving Singer, Frederick Bourne retired to an active sport-filled life. He enjoyed breeding horses and maintained memberships at a yacht club and a dozen sporting organizations catering to the well-to-do.[228] He was a trustee of the New Theater. Besides his many interests, he remained a Singer Company director until his death 14 years after his early retirement.

According to Davies, "Bourne worked to create a strong sense of community of interest throughout the Singer organization."[229] Bourne also brought about a structured chain of command responsive to a centralized authority. He imposed structure and scientific method to an antiquated factory system. Thanks to F. G. Bourne, the complexities associated with the monstrous conglomerate had been reigned in through the standardization of normal operations and policies emanating from a central control point, corporate offices in New York City. Not to be forgotten is his continuation of equitable dealings with all concerned whether employee or customer. In 1904, he instituted a company-wide insurance program.

When Frederick Bourne retired, company assets approached $90 million and employment leveled off at 30,000 factory employees and an estimated 60,000 others engaged in various capacities in globally dispersed branch offices. One estimate has Singer company production levels at three million machines a year.[230] Now, thanks to advances in the sewing industry, consumers enjoyed well-sewn, long-lasting, ready-to-wear clothing at a lower cost than he or she could purchase in fabric alone. F. G. Bourne passed away on 19 March 1919. He was 68-years-old and left an estate of $25,000,000. During his 16-year-long term, the Singer Company had grown into a powerful, centrally controlled corporation as modern as any of today.

"Growing old is nothing but a bad habit which a busy man does not have time to form." — Andre Marois.

Chapter Seven

The Sir Douglas Alexander Era (1905-1949)
More Executive Panache

The mammoth conglomerate, still heady from the successes of the Bourne presidency, now expected to continue amassing prosperity at a never before seen rate. America's Open Door policy, which guaranteed impartial and equitable global trade, continued to prove felicitous for SSMC's global operations. Moreover, the world seemed at peace. The endings of the Boxer Rebellion, of the Spanish American War and now of the Russo-Japanese War seemed to have finally delivered a settled world community with little remaining heart for more warring. During this relaxed time, the U.S. grew into a great industrial giant and into a world political power.

Theodore Roosevelt, the recipient of the 1906 Nobel Peace Prize, was then beginning his second term as president and peace and prosperity appeared solidly at hand. And in the midst of good times, the Singer Company's monopoly over its industry seemed unbreakable. Its great financial assets and militarily-precise operations appeared to have secured the company an enviable and perhaps even unassailable standing in the world of conglomerates. The company had become the paragon of American know-how and ingenuity. The SSMC appeared as solid as some great landmark whose continued existence no one could possibly doubt. To observers, not even the sudden departure of its youthful and progressive president would sway the well-provisioned, cash-rich company from its predestined course.

However, even as the company fell in behind its new president, great calamities poised to surround the conglomerate of plenty. First would come the Financial Panic of 1907, the first great war, the Depression of '29, the second catastrophic world war, the rise of global labor unrest and the coming of labor unions, accompanied by devastating employee strikes, and lastly, this new president would be tested by the loss of half of his company's entire assets.

The New President

When Frederick Bourne unexpectedly chose early retirement, the passing of power within the president's office transpired uneventfully. Bourne had openly groomed the capable British-born attorney, Douglas Alexander, to assume his presidency. He had brought his right hand man along by slowly entrusting his protege with increasing responsibilities. When the still youthful F. G. Bourne announced his early retirement at the 1905 shareholders' meeting, it came as a surprise. When in his farewell address, he recommended Douglas Alexander, who most recently served as the company's secretary, to succeed him, there was little dissent. Bourne and Alexander had enjoyed a close working relationship for nearly 12 years. Company shareholders understood that the one-time Canadian barrister had for all intents and purposes assumed control of the company's day-to-day operations.

Through this planned succession, Bourne believed he ensured the uninterrupted continuation of his major policies as well as the company's good fortune. It seemed the new president need only make minor adjustments to Bourne's well-honed, almost self-guiding bureaucratic workings in order to further tighten the screws of the company's monopolistic control over its industry. But would this presumptive plan with its guileless expectations suffice to buttress the conglomerate against the battering that was to come? Had destiny chosen another able industrial leader? Or had the great conglomerate developed its own undeniable persona that must follow precedence at any cost?

The new president, Douglas Alexander, was born on July 4, 1864 in England. As a child, he migrated with his family to Hamilton in the Canadian province of Ontario. The elder Alexander had boldly dragged his large family into this primal wilderness. He was a botanist who expected to parley and work his science on a low-cost, large tract of Canadian farmland into financial independence. Unfortunately, the rough Canadian land proved too unyielding, and the elder Alexander, ever the realist, found employment in the local custom office.

In this city environment, one of Alexander's sons, Douglas, thrived. As an adolescent, Douglas Alexander enjoyed his work as a clerk in a law office. With this early foundation and practical experience, the young immigrant soon began studies at the Law Society of Upper Canada. In 1886, at 22 years of age he became a Solicitor.[231] After practicing law for several years, he, like Edward Clark before him, relocated his practice to New York City. Besides taking a step that his great predecessor, Edward Clark, had taken, Alexander would follow a path similar to his immediate predecessor at Singer, the great F. G. Bourne.

When the workday came to a close, Douglas Alexander's favorite pastime, in those days of barber shop quartet popularity, was singing. Fortunately, Alexander sang with the Mendelson Glee Club, a popular choral group patronized by Alfred Corning Clark. Soon the young lawyer, like Frederick Bourne before him, began attending Alfred Clark's singing soirees, and the two men became good friends. When Alfred proposed that Douglas apply his professional skills in the employ of his great conglomerate, the Canadian solicitor demurred. He was, he related, contemplating a full time career as an opera singer. As author Kobler relates, Alfred Clark ended the younger man's ambition for an operatic career with a single remark: "Think of your legs in tights, Douglas."[232]

The 27-year-old Alexander joined the Singer Company in 1891 as a secretary in the corporate offices. A year later, he married the vivacious Helen Hamilton Gillespie. This union produced two sons and a daughter. By 1896, his business acuity earned him a position on the board of directors and a promotion to vice president. In September 1905, at a mere 41 years of age, he became the Singer Company's president. President Alexander would head SSMC until his death on May 22, 1949, for a total of 44 years. In all, his employment at Singer, which began during Benjamin Harrison's presidency and carried into President Truman's, spanned a total of 58 years. But this long-tenured future could not be foreseen. When Douglas Alexander sat down in the president's chair, he expected only to make occasional adjustments to his predecessor's established policy.

However, in the same year that the new Singer president took power, world events transpired to quickly end the honeymoon period of the carefully orchestrated transition. From his corporate offices, Douglas Alexander recognized the strengthening of worldwide political unrest and economic uncertainty. The corporate world's arch enemies of socialism and labor unions began attracting growing numbers. Besides political posturing, actual military conflicts produced great concern in the conglomerate's boardroom.

Alexander had come to corporate power just as the Russo-Japanese War ended, after Japan destroyed the Russian fleet. The conglomerate had an enormous financial stake in Russia and had just completed a large investment in Japan when hostilities broke out. In that same year and amidst all the turmoil, the Bloody Sunday uprising erupted in St. Petersburg. This violent unrest brought about supportive labor strikes throughout the Russian countryside. These labor battles ended with the first time formation of a Union of Soviet Workers. The Russian economic turbulence and political unrest seemed to be spreading up all over the globe. In Dublin, the Sinn Fein political party came into being. On Crete, Greeks revolted against the Turks. Norway broke away from its historic Swedish rulers and set up its own constitutional monarchy.

Nor did the US did escape this global unrest. In this country, Eugene Debs formed the Industrial Workers of America. In 1906, Upton Sinclair published *The Jungle*, a best-selling novel that fueled labor union fires while exposing the ills of Chicago's meat-packing industry. U.S. troops occupied Cuba. A new international law forbade women to work on the night shift. Besides these warning signs, Alexander felt the added blow of a world economic crisis, the Financial Panic of 1907. In that year, the stock market collapsed and banks around the country depleted their reserves until finally closing their doors. Only J. P. Morgan's transfer of $100 million in gold from Europe ended the run on the banks. Congress investigated banking and currency systems and eventually passed the Federal Reserve Act.

Unemployment soared alongside grossly inflated food prices. In this same year, Alexander used his company's enormous cash reserves to acquire his major competitor in the commercial marketplace, Wheeler & Wilson. After this timely acquisition, the Singer Company now offered both brands of sewing machines out of its branch offices and sales centers.

The new Singer Company president further showed his backbone when challenged by the company's first major strike. For the SSMC, this strike had no historical precedent. When 10,500 Clydesbank employees went on strike and closed that facility entirely,[233] Alexander first accelerated productivity of his other manufacturing facilities and then redirected the increased output where most needed. At this time, sewing machine sales were exploding in Russia. On the eighteenth day of the strike, Alexander enticed his Clydebank employees back to work with the promise to deal fairly with the issues. A few weeks after their return, Alexander fired 400 of them and placed the remainder on a low-paying, abbreviated work week. It was not merely coincidence that most of the fired workers belonged to a local socialist labor union. However, the new president had shown an ability to stand his ground.

But labor's dissent had just begun. The difficult political and economic times produced waves of dissatisfaction that leveled public condemnation on the free-wheeling corporations. Nevertheless, the Singer Company pushed forward seemingly unaffected by the widespread turbulence and continued the business of growing its mighty business. By 1913, Alexander reported sales increases to 2.5 million sewing machines annually. The huge Podolsk manufacturing plant in Russia produced a third of this enormous output. Singer machines now shipped into every corner of the globe. Its hand-cranked machines sold briskly in Japan, China, Tibet, Indo-China, South America, North Africa, throughout Europe, Scandinavia and, of course, in Russia. In 1912, 200 of Singer's India branch offices reported annual sales totaling 67,750 machines.

During these years of political turmoil leading to World War I, the Singer Company enjoyed enormous sales increases. President Alexander fortified his manufacturing facilities to meet the unprecedented demand. To reduce production costs, he *diversified* his operations by taking on manufacturing of products the company usually contracted for. Besides another new facility in Prussia, he opened a cabinetmaking factory in St. Johns, Quebec, and a woodworking plant in Truman, Arkansas.

In 1912, Woodrow Wilson's presidential campaign promised to further reduce foreign trade tariffs. In one of his campaign speeches, he noted that Singer sold sewing machines in Mexico for $18 while Americans paid $30 for the same machine.[234] Wilson's opponents pointed out that lowered tariffs ignored lower foreign wages and manufacturing costs. Low tariffs permitted the Singer Company to flood American markets with cheap imports if it wanted to. Fortunately, the final version of the new tariff law reduced its tax only by five percent. But the debate signaled the advent of coming political controls over the corporate world.

In 1912, a textile workers' strike in Lawrence, Massachusetts, overcame manufacturers attempt at wage reduction following the enactment of the first minimum wage laws. Around the country, new laws governing factory working conditions, hours and wages now challenged manufacturers accustomed to having their way with workers. In 1913, 150,000 New York City garment workers struck and won concessions for a shorter work day, better wages, and the right to unionize. In the fall of that year, Congress passed the Underwood Tariff Act that reduced import duties and placed sewing machines on the free list. Some politicians predicted that Singer would ship its lower-cost, foreign-made machines into the states.[235] Perhaps, only continuing high demand in European and Russian sewing machine markets prevented this from happening. The Singer Company seemed to weather these events with little concern, but it was about to experience the biggest financial loss ever experienced by any company.

Bolsheviks

In 1917, the Bolsheviks came to power in Russia. A year later, the Council of People's Commissars nationalized Singer company assets. Many Singer executives stayed behind to enable their American employees to flee the country. Unfortunately, the revolutionists seized many of these dedicated executives and exiled them to Siberia. Others were summarily shot dead by kangaroo-style people's courts.

On the financial side, the great conglomerate lost a third of its assets, an estimated $115,000,000. Nevertheless, the company's great cash reserves generously spared shareholders by giving them a $6,000,000 profit for the year. Statistics from a few years before, in 1914, reveal that the company's Russian organization employed 27,439 people. At one time, the company employed 25,000 Russian salesmen alone. Singer's Russian facilities produced 110,000 machines during 1900 and production ran ahead by a factor of eight just before the communist takeover. Well-constructed modern manufacturing facilities along with carefully trained employees producing nearly a million sewing machines a year were lost in a fortnight.

Singer's 66-year-old presence in Russia had slipped away. Most of its Russian factories were state-of-the-art facilities less than 15-years-old. Alexander had accorded his Russian workers the same even hand he held out to all company employees. His Podolsk employees worked the same 58 and one-half hour long work week as their counterparts in Elizabethport. The workday began at 7 am, broke for a 90 minute lunch, and ended with a final whistle at 6:30 p.m. When Douglas Alexander came to power, he responded to labor unrest by reducing the workweek and made Saturday a half day. At Podolsk, the company trained unskilled Russians to manufacture interchangeable parts to small tolerances of one thousandth of an inch. It had not taken the Russian workers long to arrive at the same productivity and quality levels of their American counterparts in Elizabeth. At its peak, Russian sales surpassed domestic American sales. The Singer Company estimated it lost a full third of its production capabilities when the Bolsheviks took over. In another historical footnote, when the Russian army invaded Germany in 1945, they stripped all the machinery from the Singer Company's Wittenberg factory. And although both events happened nearly three decades apart, president Alexander presided helplessly over both of these grand thefts.

World War I

When the Great War broke out in 1914, it placed severe demands on Singer's foreign employees. A significant portion of its workforce were loss to the draft. As hostilities expanded, demand for sewing machines plummeted. The difficulties in world travel and shipping and distribution of sewing machines or their replacement parts became insurmountable problems. Reduced availability further reduced demand.

A first consequence of the war forced Singer to reduce its huge Clydebank facility to a three-day workweek. As World War I dragged on and as European manufacturing facilities forcibly closed their doors, a dramatic demand for U.S. manufactured goods arose. A prewar output of American made goods of $24 billion rose to $62 billion by war's end in 1919. For the Singer Sewing Machine Company, which would no longer compete against powerful German sewing machine makers, the war eventually delivered up an economic boom. But Singer company management gave little thought to this future economic likelihood. Like any other dutiful citizen, the company now threw its entire production facilities into the war effort.

The Elizabethport facility reduced its sewing machine output to a bare minimum and began mass-producing 75 mm cannons for the Allies. What sense would it make not to keep their large production facilities operative? To allow its massive production machinery to slip into decay? Without hesitation, Alexander also turned his Clydebank factory, with its thousands of skilled machinists, over to the British war effort. Clydebank's ability to produce close-tolerance, precision-fit interchangeable parts delivered up a significant portion of the Allied's World War I munitions and armaments.

Within a year of signing British Defense Department contracts, Clydebank alone churned out 6,000 artillery shells a week. Over the course of the war, the Scotland facility would produce hand grenades, airplane structures and engines, tank and rifle repair parts, 360,000 horseshoes and over 3 million artillery shells of various calibers. Only well-trained, skilled machinists working in state-of-the-art facilities enabled this critical contribution to the Allied cause. It is noteworthy that during the war years, women workers comprised nearly 70 percent of Singer's Scottish factory's employees. One contemporary estimate noted that sewing manufacturers mass-produced 170 distinct products for Allied armies. The war served only to increase worldwide demand for Singer machines and afterwards, Singer company employment rose to a high of 87,000 employees.

After World War I, King George of England conferred the title of baronet on Alexander in recognition of Singer Mfg. Co. Ltd.'s wartime services. There's also a hint that Sir Alexander provided personal services to the King during this time as well. These whispers surfaced when various medals for heroism were mysteriously conferred on the new baronet: Belgium conferred the Order of the Crown and France made him a Knight in its Legion D'Honneur.

Alexander Redefines Sewing Machine Marketing

While war contracts helped keep its enormous production facilities operating, the company did not sit idly by waiting the end of the great conflict. During this first World War, president Alexander redoubled existing sales efforts in Australia, the Phillippines, Burma, China and India. Each of these distant countries offered cultural anomalies needing careful analysis and separate marketing and sales methodologies. For example, India's caste system, which eschewed capitalism, proved exceptionally difficult to deal with. In this case, Alexander personally gave Indian branch office managers permission to deviate from established company policies. Throughout his tenure, Alexander never hesitated in delegating authority to his carefully selected and groomed operatives.

After the war and throughout the 1920s, foreign sales accounted for three fourths of all Singer's sales. Domestically, Singer struggled with the challenge of midwestern mail order companies like Montgomery Ward and Sears, which sold millions of low-cost treadle machines throughout the U.S. Mail order sewing machines, which sold for less than $10 before the war, rediscovered a vigorous market in the farm belt states. Following World War I, mail order sewing machines prices rose to $20 per machine and still sold vigorously. This low selling price was a difficult obstacle to the Singer organization with its much greater overhead.

To bolster domestic sales, president Alexander decided on a new long-term marketing strategy and began delivering sewing machines to high schools. Most schools had no budget for sewing machines and so Alexander usually provided the machines at cost and sometimes for free. Beginning in 1922, the company also sent along an easy-to-follow training manual, *Machine Sewing*. In this way, the Singer Company began grooming a new generation of home sewers. Company studies revealed that women preferred purchasing sewing machines they were familiar with. The idea to reach into the schools had come from Alexander's personally recruited and recently installed sales division vice president, Milton Lightner. The insightful Lightner would later succeed president Alexander as the company's new corporate president. (Lightner's marketing was not lost on 1980s Apple Computer makers who placed their personal computers in public schools at all grade levels).

Alexander's tactic proved itself during the slow-selling Depression years. While other sewing machine makers faltered during this slow economy that dragged on throughout the early 1930s, Singer's domestic sales remained adequate. After all, what better way to save money than to repair and make one's own clothes? These difficult years also brought novel, hard-sell sales techniques. As writer William Ewers says in his *Sincere's History of the Sewing Machine,* "A salesman who survived that era, was worthy of the name."[236] And Singer salesmen became the fittest of the survivors. One of the non-surviving employees who complained of the great difficulty of learning the intricacies of the many Singer models, was Nobel prize laureate and playwright Eugene O'Neill, who worked briefly in the company's Buenos Aires office.[237]

Singer company history reports that its far-flung salesmen used all available means of transportation to bring its *great civilizer* into the world's most secluded areas. Singer salesmen were known to travel by camel, elephant and even ox cart. William Ewers also recalls that during the 1930s, the coming of the automobile further extended Singer salesmen's reach into farming and outlying regions.[238] Great touring cars saddled with racks of Singer machines and accessories became full-time and hands-on advertising vehicles. In America's hinterland, the Singer Company recognized that capable direct mail specialists like Montgomery Ward and the Sears, Roebuck company succeeded mostly in America's farm belt. To counteract the mail order houses during the 1930s, Alexander pioneered the traveling trade show. A husband and wife team hauled a trailer filled with Singer machines around the countryside. These modified machines operated off six-volt battery power. Alexander tasked all employees to accord his "canvas car" the greatest priority wherever it went. All local agents helped the tour team knock on every door in the district.

1928

The postwar years proved a time of great growth for America as industrialization continued on a grand scale. By 1928, an American population of 120 million people enjoyed the goods produced from over 10,000 operating manufacturing facilities. New York City was then a city of six million. In Lowell, Massachusetts, the textile industry boosted that city's population to 115,000. Textile industries exported 60 percent of their products. The Singer Company sold 75 percent of its sewing machines overseas to a broad-based market Europe, Asia, and

India. While foreign markets preferred hand-crank models, Americans preferred its basic foot-propelled models. Singer factories employed 27,000 people engaged in the manufacture of 3,000 models of commercial stitching machines.

1929

Remarkably, Singer's commercial sales remained steady even during the gloomiest of the Depression years. On 28 October, 1929, the world's economic markets suffered their greatest blow. U.S. securities alone decreased in value by $26 billion. The Singer Sewing Machine Company seemed little affected by the economic conflagration. During 1932, the worst Depression year of all, the company paid out dividends of eight dollars a share on earnings of $2.5 million. While most other company officers blamed the Depression for its slackened sales, Sir Alexander believed the drop off in American sales resulted not from poor marketing strategy, but more from the flappers, a new social trend that featured emancipated women. Flappers simply did want to sit in front of sewing machines all day. During the roaring twenties, the stereotypical homemaker disappeared from the American scene. In President Alexander's view, social unrest had claimed a generation of sewers.

In 1929, Singer purchased the Standard Sewing Machine Company. Standard's important product was its *Sewhandy*, a well-designed portable sewing machine. Singer incorporated the *Sewhandy's* design features, like it reversing function, into its most highly regarded sewing machine model of all, the Featherweight. In 1933, the Singer Company used the occasion of the Chicago World Fair to introduce the Featherweight Model 221. The model 221 became so popular that it remained in production for thirty-one years until 1964. The sales figures that accompanied the Featherweight's popularity seemed to prove out Singer's well-publicized slogan, "A machine in every home!" The self-contained Featherweight weighed 11 pounds and performed like more expensive commercial machines. American models came in one color, black. Usually, gold engraving adorned them. Construction was mostly alloyed metal alloyed including some aluminum.

The Featherweight came with six attachments and ran at 1,000 stitches per minute. Its attachments enabled it to pink, ruff, quilt, scallop and bind. After the company ended its production in 1964, unrelenting consumer demand caused production of the Featherweight to resume in 1968. And contrary to longstanding policy, the company even produced white-colored models for at least two years. Even today, the Internet, or Information Superhighway, maintains a worldwide communications mailing list for a dedicated group calling themselves *Featherweight Fanatics.*

All through the pre-World War II years, two thirds of Singer's sales, both foreign and domestic, consisted of non-electric powered machines. Even with rural electrification, many purists like Pennsylvania's Amish looked on treadle machines as more closely aligned to their belief system. Besides its flagship treadle machine, the company's product line remained extensive. To document all the company's product offerings required a 380 page catalog weighing 12 pounds. This catalog listed the entire product line of 3,000 special purpose and industrial grade sewing machines.

By the late 1940s, this extensive variety of sewing machines lent itself to diverse applications as binding telephone books, applique beads and embroidery. The company's largest machine, which easily seamed three-quarter inch thick conveyor belt ends together, weighed in at 950 pounds. Another sophisticated machine stitched camel hairs to produce a porous weave for use in a special oil-based strainer. This machine, which stitched the seams of gunpowder bags during the war, now found additional employment fusing together newly discovered materials like nylons and plastics used in hosiery, parachutes and rain gear. This unique machine relied on an electronic fusing process and did not use a thread and needle.[239]

WWII

During the war years of 1939-1945, SSMC ended sewing machine development while it turned its resources into producing wartime goods. When America entered World War II, Alexander ended domestic production except for products directly related to the military effort. Singer manufacturing facilities, including its precision machining capabilities, its skilled production workers, its very best machine design engineers, its experienced tool makers and machinists threw their skills into designing, developing and manufacturing technical instrumentation like bomb sights and precision-machined piece parts for use in firing mechanisms and gun triggers. No fewer than 50 different high tech weapons spilled out of Singer facilities. The company even mass-produced computers for the B-29 and enjoyed a reputation for engineering excellence.

Shortly after American troops engaged Field Marshall Rommel, the Desert Fox, in North Africa, the U.S. Army prevailed on the Singer Company to find a way to bind a felt air breathing filter to a protective face mask to prevent air leakage. The standard issue mask was entirely useless in the real world of wind-driven desert sand. Within 24 hours, the company's Bridgeport, Connecticut, engineers designed a special machine to tightly seam the irregular contours as well as reduce the respirator's assembly time by several hours. The company constructed three additional machines and invoiced the government a more than reasonable $350 for each machine. Within weeks, thousands of desert sand air filters were shipped to North Africa out of the Bridgeport production department facilities.[240]

The Aftermath of WWII Ends the Single Product Conglomerate

World War II levied a heavy toll on the Singer Company. Many of its facilities were lost or severely damaged by the intense fighting. Early in 1941, the German Luftwaffe destroyed 11 of Clydebank's sections while inflicting significant damage on 20 others. But in Germany proper, where many Germans believed Singer was a national company, two of its facilities, Dulken and Wursden, escaped critical damage and reopened within days after the fighting subsided. However, a third Wittenberg facility, located in the Russian-occupied zone on the banks of the Elbe, had been stripped of all its machinery. In all, the company wrote off $50,000,000 losses in its German operations alone.

Besides damaged or destroyed facilities and capital equipments, the company suffered greater losses of its well-trained workforce. A significant number of its career employees, who had been claimed by the draft, did not return to the Singer Company after war's end. Many of these returning sewing industry skilled tradesmen accepted higher-paying positions with their former employer's competitors. Company loyalty, once the byword of an unworldly prewar population, no longer held an attraction to a suddenly mobile and thoroughly modern American family intent on self-betterment in a short time. William Ewers quotes a Singer executive, "We raised a lot of puppies who came back to bite us."[241]

War's End Brings Sophisticated Competition

Besides loss of facilities and its trained workforce, the Singer Company staggered from the added blow of sophisticated foreign competition greatly enabled by one-sided trade laws. During the war years, decreased production by all sewing machine manufacturers produced a marketplace hungry for new machines and for replacement parts as well. Unfortunately for the Singer Company, just as this demand surfaced, labor problems surfaced.

A strike at its Elizabeth facility effectively ended domestic production. This further opened the door to foreign sewing machine makers whose low cost machines were welcomed by American homemakers. By war's end, many new advanced machines entered the marketplace: Pfaff introduced a unique automatic-cycling machine in 1947 and its zigzag machine a year later, Wilcox & Gibbs brought out its own speed demon, the Model 10A, and the Reece Company offered the speedy Reece S2 in 1949.[242] Especially successful were the novel and versatile zigzag machines brought by Pfaff in 1948 and later by Necchi. Zigzag machines such as Necchi's sewed buttons, buttonholes and decorative stitching without relying on a separate attachment.

These foreign manufacturers, whose machines delivered greater all-around utility than Singer machines, represented the opening salvo in the Singer Company's battle with foreign competitors. In some cases, other sewing machine makers had continued product developmental work during the war. The SSMC on the other hand, had patriotically turned its resources over to the war effort.

Japan

About this time, Japanese makers, whose prewar competition had been noteworthy, now roared into the American marketplace. Among these were Brother Industries of Nagoya, Japan, which had been producing industrial machines since 1928, and the Tokyo-Juki Industrial Machine Company, which opened its doors in 1945. Tokyo-Juki's workforce consisted of machinists skilled in manufacturing carbines since 1938. The company's facilities, which were not bombed during the war, converted to sewing machine manufacturing with the occupation army's blessing on 25 October 1945.

During 1951, the Juki Company stunned the sewing machine marketplace, which had held the upstart Japanese makers in contempt by bringing out a breakthrough single-shaft rotary disc thread take-up.[243] Many manufacturers believed this method to be impossible to implement. Within a few years of this success, the Juki company gave its R&D department the go-ahead to develop commercial machines. No sector of the industry would be safe from the Juki company's onslaught.

By the 1950s, these and other competitors claimed a significant market share. Besides this sophisticated competition, Singer became the unwitting target of political price fixing. At the close of World War II, American politicians decided to establish a strong buffer zone to counteract the spreading communist influence in Asia. To avoid the expense of manning this political breakwater, American politicians decided to reconstruct Japan's economy. To this end the occupation army decided to support Japan's production of sewing machines. General MacArthur's reconstruction program resulted in an easing of trade laws that permitted low-cost Japanese sewing machines to flood the American marketplace.

Japanese machines offered more features at half the cost of Singer machines. With its production shackled by the

Elizabethport strike, the Singer Company watched helplessly as politically motivated competition made it seem that the great conglomerate could not survive. The Elizabethport strike not only reduced availability of Singer machines, it prevented the company from enhancing its product line to counter the sophistication of foreign competitors. As a result, Alexander scaled back his sales force. As his sewing machine sales declined, president Alexander bolstered his product line by introducing a variety of new products like vacuum cleaners into the company's many sales outlets. By moving away from its longstanding single product line, the Singer Sewing Machine Company entered a new operational pathway that would eventually redefine it. The diversification process had begun.

Summation Alexander's Problems

As America lowered its trade barriers, foreign countries flexed new nationalistic muscles. Unfair import duties, tariffs and corporate tax laws forced Singer into nationalizing its foreign assets. Not to do so would bring financial penalties too onerous to bear. Various legal maneuvers prevented Singer from extracting the bulk of its foreign profits without suffering unfair monetary penalties. During these difficult proceedings and litigations throughout his business empire, president Alexander refrained from engaging in political machinations even though the U.S. Congress's one-sided manipulation of the tariff laws must have greatly angered him.

Besides these unfair controls placed on its foreign marketing efforts, the company struggled with newfound internal problems. For the first time, work stoppages and strikes arrived with regularity. The troubles with labor relations had intensified since the New Deal law of 1935 and the Wagner Act that created the National Labor Relations Board. Besides the usual problems of increasing productivity while decreasing costs, Alexander battled the added challenge of the emerging voice of labor. The Singer Company management appears, in retrospect, to have been little bothered by what became no more than short-lived production losses. Perhaps the company's solvency permitted it to choke out these new firestorms as easily as it did its other financial setbacks. Besides financial downturns brought on by labor unrest and the growth of unions, the war cost Singer its substantial investments in Germany and Japan. The war stole its experienced personnel who generally returned from the war to work for better paying Singer company competitors. The war brought unfair trade laws into being and these in turn broke ground for a host of new, sophisticated competitors. And, finally the war changed the face of marketing. Old fashioned sales strategies no longer sufficed in the new communication age. After World War II, Alexander eliminated door-to-door canvassing and relied solely on the marketing efforts of his 1,200 retail outlets and the added appeal of a new and diverse product line. Under Alexander, the Singer Company became the first company in history whose advertising budget surpassed the million dollar mark.

Alexander's Accomplishments

Douglas Alexander first entered a factory system mostly defined by the Industrial Revolution. But Alexander had not relied on such fundamental methods. Instead, he developed scientific management in his production facilities known as the *Synchro-System*. This management method employed time and motion studies to simplify each worker's job. Even steps to candy and soft drink dispensers were kept to a minimum. The system devised work-flow diagrams to locate plant equipment in their most productive lineup.

At the end of Alexander's tenure, the company's domestic product line ranged from a child's sewing machine selling for $12.75 to an all-purpose deluxe model with a price tag of $310. However, the $149.50 Featherweight remained the company's mainstay. Alexander like his predecessor Bourne, quickly became noted for his fair business dealings and for concern with his employee's prosperity. Bourne's policy of ongoing training and internal promotion of company workmen continued.[244] Alexander also continued after-hours employee sports programs and the company's visionary pension plan. Sir Alexander continued Clark's original marketing strategy and furthered the company's foreign national commitment by increasing those investments. He

succeeded in broadening and reopening the marketplace for
Singer Sewing Machines in Canada, Mexico, Brazil, Italy,
France, Japan and Australia.

When the Depression hit, the company remained
profitable because of its foreign markets. Alexander, who earned
$100,000 a year while presiding over Singer, also began
diversifying his company. During his tenure, several companies
were acquired including Wheeler & Wilson, International
Securities Company in New Jersey, International Fidelity
Insurance Company, and the Poinsett Lumber Manufacturing
Company, a large cabinet factory in Pickens, S.C., which fed off
of 68,000 acres of South Carolina timberlands it also owned.
Under Alexander, the Singer Company expanded into
manufacture of surgical stitching machines, electrically powered
plastic laminating machines, clothes irons, speciality electrical
appliances, cooling fans, and vacuum cleaners made for Singer by
both Eureka and by Diehl Manufacturing. Besides vacuum
cleaners, a Diehl subsidiary in New Jersey, made fans and a
variety of electric motors including those for sewing machines.
Sir Alexander had given teeth to the diversification initiated by F.
G. Bourne.

When Sir Alexander died in 1949, the Singer Company
struggled to fill sales orders backlogged for more than twelve
months. These booming sales allowed the company to deliver
double-digit dividends to its stockholders. The Singer
Manufacturing Company, with a main plant constructed back in
1872 in Elizabethport, N.J., was then the largest commercial and
domestic sewing machine manufacturer in the world. In
Elizabethport, 7,000 employees manufactured 2,500 different
domestic and commercial sewing machine models. Before his
death, Alexander had drawn up plans for doubling the number of
his sewing centers and sales outlets.

Through aggressive marketing, Alexander kept a leg up
on a very credible main competitor, the 70-year-old White
Sewing Machine Company of Cleveland, Ohio. By 1947, the
White Company's facilities produced and sold 300,000 sewing
machines. Unlike the Singer Company, which sold its machines
only through its sales and service centers, White distributed its

product line including the White Rotary in department stores. White also manufactured Kenmore sewing machines for distribution through Sear's department stores. In 1947, White Sewing Machine, which had originated sewing instruction courses, boasted that it supported 185 teaching facilities that alone furnished the company with annual revenues near $10 million. Not to be outdone by the White Company's successful instruction methods, Alexander, working through his personal assistant Milton Lightner, had also introduced similar creative sewing instruction classes in all of his 1,000 service centers in 1929. Douglas Alexander deserves credit for surviving the very sophisticated competition from the White Company.

Personal Farewell

This great capitalist leader, Douglas Alexander, made his home in Stamford, Connecticut. He commuted to the Singer building first by train and then by New York City's subway. He maintained an in-town residence at One West 72nd street. Alexander maintained memberships at exclusive golf clubs near both of his residences. He was an active and athletic man who enjoyed golfing, tennis and horseback riding. Besides athletics, Alexander's after hours interests included photography and music. Sir Alexander's athleticism and esthetic appreciation belies the lifestyle of an energetic and creative man. He was widowed in 1923 and spent the remainder of his life living with his son and daughter. Like his predecessors in the president's chair, Douglas Alexander was a Renaissance man, a truly progressive and modern intellectual.

Under Alexander the company had weathered two world wars, competition from four dozen sewing machine makers, a depression, several recessions, and reached a point in 1941 when analysts averred that the sewing machine market was saturated. Alexander must be remembered for having kept the great corporation solvent during the country's most difficult years of labor unrest. Sir Alexander is also remembered for completing the Singer Building, a original skyscraper located at 149 Broadway. On its 1908 completion, it was the tallest building in the world.

Where once there had been four dozen competitors, the end of Alexander's presidency recognized but four individual American sewing machine manufacturers. Of these four, perhaps only two could challenge Singer's dominance in the sewing machine home appliance market. In the commercial sector, the company went up against one commercial competitor, the Union Special Machine Company of Chicago. Throughout his 44 years as Singer Company president, Alexander's steady helmsman ship kept the company on course in unsettled seas. During his tenure, Singer employees developed into pure company men: men who carried a missionary zeal into their employment: men who believed they were helping raise the standard of living around the entire globe.

When asked about his company's success Sir Alexander replied, "All we do is make the machine, take it out and sell it, collect the money, then send it back to make another machine."

"Secretive almost to the point of silence is the great Singer Manufacturing Company." – *Fortune* magazine 1934

Chapter Eight

The Milton Clarkson Lightner Era (1949-1958)
Refined Management Perseveres

During 1927, Sir Douglas asked Milton Clarkson Lightner, a partner in a law firm representing SSMC, to accept a vice presidency in his sales department. President Alexander admired the youthful attorney who had successfully represented the Singer Company through long and difficult litigations. For Lightner, moving to Singer meant a distinct career change and likely end to his successful law practice. Nevertheless, in 1928 Lightner became a Singer Company director working on equal footing with Sir Douglas. The elder industrialist entrusted all of the company's domestic affairs to his new protégée and now concentrated on his foreign operations.

Over the years, the close working relationship that developed between the two men culminated with Lightner succeeding his mentor as the corporate president of both the Singer Manufacturing and its then distinct the Singer Sewing Machine Company in 1949.

Another Great Retail Leader Arrives

Milton C. Lightner was born on April 11, 1890 in Detroit, Michigan. He matriculated at the University of Michigan in 1910 and moved on to Harvard Law School, graduating in 1913. During 1914, the year in which the first Great War erupted, Lightner joined the New York National Guard. Two years later, his guard unit traveled to the Mexican Border to chase after Pancho (nee Doroteo Arango) Villa. On March 9, 1916, Pancho Villa and 400 of his daring revolutionaries had crossed into Columbus, New Mexico, where the unwelcome raiders set most of the town afire and slaughtering 16 American citizens. This flagrant violation of U.S. sovereignty outraged all Americans while simultaneously raising Mexican national pride. Many Mexicans believed Villa had exacted an act of vengeance against the American colonial-like control over their unpopular government.

While many Mexicans perceived Pancho Villa as a hero, most American businessmen believed differently. U.S. businesses like the Singer Company held large financial investments in Mexico. As a result, America's big business interests closely followed the well-reported pursuit of the elusive bandit. Pancho Villa had succeeded in bringing down the unpopular government of the ruthless Mexican President, Porfirio Diaz. President Diaz's attempts at bringing prosperity to his country had relied solely on soliciting foreign investment. Because of this practice, Diaz had ingratiated himself with his many American businessmen investors. In fact, the Mexican president regularly consulted with high-level Singer executives.[245]

Singer Company executives and employees enjoyed a prestigious standing in Mexico's high political and social circles. No doubt, Lightner's involvement in the pursuit of Villa, which saw several months of unsuccessful chasing after the Villa gang all over Mexico's countryside, endeared him to Sir Alexander. When World War I broke out, Lightner joined the regular U.S. Army and served through the remaining war years as a supply officer. After his 1917 demobilization he returned to the practice of law and finally settled down after marrying Margaret Griffin. In 1924, he became a partner in the firm of VerPlanck, Prince,

Burlingame and Lightner. Three years later, he made his final career move by signing on with the Singer Company as Vice President in its Sales Division then located in New Jersey.

The Strike of '49: Lightner's Baptism by Fire

On May 22, 1949, Sir Douglas Alexander died. Alexander's last days had not been pleasant ones for the ailing president or for his management team. No one suffered more than the Singer Company's longest-serving corporate president when Singer employees, who had voted in the United Electrical Workers Union, struck his manufacturing facilities. Sir Douglas felt betrayed by workers whom he believed he had treated well. During his last few weeks on earth, both his Elizabeth and Bridgeport plants went on strike.

On May 2, 1949, 7,000 members of the Local 401 of the United Electrical, Radio and Machine Workers Union struck the Elizabeth plant. Four days later, Local 227 of this same union struck at the Bridgeport plant. Workers accused the company of seniority rights violations and work speed-ups. Besides the cessation of these alleged workplace abuses, the strikers additionally demanded a "substantial" wage increase of $500 per year and 40 hours pay for a 35-hour-long workweek. The strikers central issue challenged the fairness of company-designed work "standards." The company relied on standards to gage and to reward superior production efforts.[246] This bonus system was not unlike the piece-work incentive plans in use by most manufacturers of the day. To avoid physical confrontations, the company ordered its 2,000 supervisory and nonunion workers like engineers and office workers not to cross the picket lines.

When Milton C. Lightner succeeded to the corporate president's office, he was thrust into the limelight as the central figure in what was on that day the very worst strike in all of U.S. labor history. Like Alexander, Lightner undoubtedly felt the company treated its employees well and that the strike resulted not from SSMC's unfairness but from the prevailing general labor unrest then assailing all of industry. But now the entire world waited to see how the Singer Company would deal with this unprecedented labor strike.

The new president decided to stand firm. But the strikers, who answered to their own strong-willed leadership, also decided to hold firm. Weeks and then months slipped by without a sign of progress toward resolving the conflict. As the impasse lingered into late summer, Elizabeth merchants began feeling the pinch of loss revenues. The Singer Company payroll, which averaged $500,000 per week, had not reached the community's infrastructure for many months. The *New York Times* reported that "Grocers, butchers and bakers are carrying thousands of individuals on their books."[247] One grocer said all his sales consisted of canned beans.

However, when strikers learned that at least two of their union organizers were active Communists Party members, the strike began losing momentum. As a result of the 1948 Berlin blockade by Russia and the recent conviction of 11 Communist Party leaders in conspiring to overthrow the U.S. government among many widely-reported left-wing political activities, the socialist movement in America was losing favor. For SSMC workers, the revelation of their union's leftist links soon broke the impasse. The resulting agreement favored the company and workers gained little on the major issues they had struck for. On October 2, local bargaining with the company's Bridgeport plant strikers ended in an agreement. Local 227 of the United Electrical, Radio and Machine Workers, CIO, representing 1,500 Connecticut employees gained raises of 4 to 6 cents per hour, various enhancements to hospital and pension plans and an additional vacation week beyond the customary two weeks awarded to those with 15 years service. Workers were also promised continued payment of normal bonus wages even when their machines were idled through down time.[248]

But even though the Bridgeport plant resumed operations, the Elizabeth strikers appeared to be standing firm. Then, in late October, conditions in Elizabeth worsened when news that Communists agitators also infiltrated their union. Now, even local clerics urged strikers to rid themselves of the communist influence. The Catholic Church recent emendation of its bylaws made it possible to excommunicate communists agitators. Some Catholic priests warned of the added hardships promised by the coming of winter and they further urged their church goers, who were also union members, to elect new union leaders willing to negotiate fairly. These events: the political revelations, the coaxing by the religious community, the company's reported $275 million cash reserves and Lightner's uncompromising stand soon led to successful mediation. When the strike ended in mid-December, Lightner rewarded his returning employees earning less than $60 per week with a Christmas bonus of $25.

It should be noted that throughout the strike both Sir Alexander and then Lightner had continued funding the company's hospitalization program. Years later, Milton Lightner would note with satisfaction that it was his employees who had divested themselves or the Communists in its ranks.

The Singer strikes represent only a small sidelight of the great labor struggles of the time. Labor problems would persist; the war had returned a work force believing it deserved more. Moreover, this new labor force was unafraid to make its demands known. For the next few years, the Singer Company found itself dealing with labor issues on a continuing basis. For example, on July 6, 1951, the St. John, Quebec, factory went on strike. At this same time, Elizabeth employees threatened to strike again. Modern times had raised the workforce's consciousness and added an element of complexity to the worker-management relationship.

The Problems of Postwar Modernism

After WWII, Milton Lightner recognized that besides more complex labor relations, the emergence of newly devised international trade barriers would grow into limiting if not insurmountable economic barricades. Lightner, a capable corporate lawyer always cognizant of the ever changing ways of conducting business, recognized that the emerging world economic order of modernism would effectively end business as usual. The Singer Company would no longer control its destiny in traditional ways. It would no longer devise new strategies to dominate competitors through aggressive marketing or by clever sales pitches that captured the imagination of its marketplace. Its sales personnel now competed among other well-trained sales professionals, many who had grown up within Singer's ranks. Moreover, its single product was no longer the only practical sewing machine on the market. Added to quality competition and sophisticated market competitiveness came the new limiting factors of sophisticated trade and tariff laws. These laws had come about in war-devastated countries who found themselves saddled with shortages of all kinds. These economically recovering countries enacted strict trade laws designed to keep precious capital resources within their own borders. Unrestrictive U.S. trade laws designed to help foreign powers recover, actually supplied direct support to the Singer Company's competition. Like ungrateful parents, Washington bureaucrats failed its greatest exporter of capital equipment, one of its more ardent corporate supporters and a preeminent symbol of corporate American business.

Zigzag Machines

Besides world events and the changing business climate perhaps no single factor hurt the Singer Company's sewing machine market share during the post war boom years than its earlier decision to not market zigzag machines for domestic use. Singer executives had somehow concluded that U.S. homemakers would not be attracted to the relatively more complex operating but lowcost zigzag sewing machines. Unfortunately for Singer management, European manufacturers of such machines could hardly keep up with American purchase orders.[249] Besides the novelty and added utility the zigzag offered, European producers were aided by reduced tariffs brought in with the Marshall Plan designed to help rebuild Europe.

The popularity of zigzag machines arose mostly out of their ability to embroider. Zigzag sewing machines, which had been commonplace in industrial settings since 1905, allow their needle to move both laterally and longitudinally thereby allowing for zigzag patterns, for smooth arcs or curves and for straight-line stitching as well. Because zigzag machines provided for automatic-making of button holes, for sewing on the buttons, and for producing creative designs, they greatly enhanced the sewing capabilities of home seamstresses. The zigzag's relative user-friendliness permitted little-skilled home sewers to zigzag complex patterns and clever designs. The first zigzag sewing machine suitable for domestic users was developed by a Switzerland-based company, Gegauf, during 1943. The Swiss machine employed a free-swinging arm that could alternate directions.[250] The first zigzag to reach American shores was the Nechhi zigzag machine that first shipped from Pavia, Italy, in 1947. A Swiss-made machine, the *Elna,* soon followed. The Elna was a green-colored novelty that shipped with a single zigzag attachment permitting sewing of buttons, buttonholes, and decorative stitching. These zigzag machines were quickly followed in 1948 by several German makers including Adler, Anker and Pfaff. The Viking sewing machine, made by Sweden's Husqvarna, a gun manufacturer who had begun building sewing machines in 1880, entered the competition soon afterwards. Numerous foreign makers of inexpensive zigzag sewing machines enabled by America's relaxed trade laws and MacArthur's Japan policy now flooded the American market.

Japan

Japan eventually became the world's largest sewing machine manufacturer thanks to its ability to cheaply produce zigzag machines. Japanese makers, who had brought 50 years of sewing machine manufacturing experience, began world-wide marketing of their lower-priced models after World War II — and discovered an avaricious U.S. market. Japanese producers enjoyed the advantages of favorable trade and tariff laws, low-cost labor and, since their machines were generally distributed by large department store chains, equally negligible shipping and distribution cost.

These factors alone brought about enormous competitive advantages. In their drive for acceptance and to overcome postwar prejudice, several Japanese manufacturers fooled American buyers by painting the required "Made In Japan" logo with fast-fading paint. Japanese machines often sported symbols that closely resembled Singer's trademark red "S." Besides infringing on Singer trademarks, the Japanese also infringed on the trademarks of Packard, Crosley, Bendix and other American sewing machine makers.[251]

U.S. policy, which hoped to quickly rebuild Japan's economy and self-defense forces so that it could act as an effective buffer against the spread of communism in Asia, chose the Japanese sewing machine industry as one of the key industries to revive. The Singer Company, which initiated many patent infringement suits against Japanese makers, could do little but watch as its former apprentice snatched its hard-won business away. American policymakers chose not to remember that the Singer Company's war losses in capital outlay, its pre-war years of product marketing and heavy investment in worker and management training outlay into Japan. During the 1930s, Singer had maintained close to 800 branch offices staffed by 5,000 employees in Japan. Singer had given Japan its unique and thoroughly modern methods for operating large scale business. In return, Japan dissolved all ties to the Singer establishment during the course of the second Sino-Japanese War, 1937-1945. When these hostilities threatened, Japanese nationalists forced Singer to liquidate its Japanese assets at deep discount. When war eventually broke-out, Singer recalled all of the company's Japanese staff members. Only the general agent in charge chose to remain at his desk and he was sent to a detention camp. He was only freed through a prisoner exchange after twelve months of imprisonment.

After the war, Japan and MacArthur's policy makers did not allow the Singer Company to reestablish itself. By denying the Singer Company a license to import its machines into the country, Japan kept the door open for an estimated 500 of its own sewing machine manufacturers to jump into the void left by Singer. Though Japan would later reimburse Singer for its war losses, it would never repay the company for the more important gift of its operational expertise and trained labor force. As a result in 1952, Japan became the global leader in sewing machine exports by shipping more than a million machines in a year's time.[252]

By early 1950, the Japanese sewing industry, which the Singer Company had struggled so hard to establish over six decades, now prospered. In the postwar years, a third of the Japanese population put aside its kimonos in favor of western dress. After World War II many others besides the Japanese discovered sewing. By the mid 1950s, sewing experienced an unexpected surge in global popularity. After all, in a time when jobs were few and when manufactured clothing appeared relatively expensive, home sewing remained a sure way to save money.

In America, nearly every homemaker owned a sewing machine. As a result, even as foreign competitors made many inroads into the booming sewing industry, the Singer Company somehow prospered as well. The end of World War II brought about a more-closely engaged world economy. In the face of intense domestic and offshore competition the Singer Company managed a magnificent expansion. During these years, Singer's worldwide employment remained near 85,000.

Italian and German Competition

Early in 1950, the *New York Times* reported on the wide availability of low-cost import sewing machines. Popular among these were the $69.95 Tru-Sew from the Sigma Company of Italy, which sewed both forward and backward, and a zigzag machine from the Anker Company of Germany that also made buttonholes and sewed buttons on as well. The Pfaff company's Kaiserslautern plant in West Germany, which by 1951 had revived only 35 percent of its war-damaged facilities, still provided employment to 5,000 workers. However, Pfaff's American sales soon surpassed 2,000 machines per month and the company predicted its US exports would quickly double by the following year. Pfaff also boasted that its South American sales equaled that of all American competitors combined.[253]

Singer management recognized that its one time dominance in the southern hemisphere had been deeply cut into. During 1952, Pfaff, which grossed $1,800,000 during its first year in the U.S. domestic market three years earlier, reported revenues of $20,000,000, or more than double its 1951 revenues of $9,4000,000. The company pointed to its attachment-free "Dial-A-Stitch" feature as the main force behind its success.[254] In response to the Singer Company's well-publicized milestone advertising budget, Pfaff predicted it would also spend $1,000,000 for direct advertising in the U.S. during 1952. By 1954, Pfaff manufactured its five millionth sewing machine. In addition to Japanese and German competition, a single Swedish firm proved to be an effective competitor. During 1952, Sweden's Husqvarna shipped 6,000 sewing machine heads, the critical part of the sewing machine (as the engine is to the automobile), into the U.S. and 5,000 more heads to Canada for a total value of $6,500,000. At this time, Husqvarna's worldwide sewing machine revenues reached $30,000,000.[255]

Domestic Competition and Other Factors

To compound Singer's foreign competition problems, high-quality, lower-priced American-made machines also filtered into their once-secure market place. Quality domestic manufacturers like National, Free and the White Sewing Machine Corporation emerged as viable competitors. During the 1950s, Singer reported losing half its sewing machine market. By the end of this decade the low-price Elna alone had matured and offered fully automatic operation through recursive control over the fabric. A Japanese-maker, Brother, also followed Elna with a similar product.

By 1955, Brother became Japan's largest sewing machine maker. The Singer Company accused Brother of copyright infringement and entered into bitter negotiations with the Japanese upstart company.[256] By the mid 1950s, Brother began exporting numerous household products into this country including: clothes irons, knitting machines, juice blenders and fans.[257]

Fortunately, Lightner's domestic sales, which were supported by the lion's share of an estimated 52 million home sewers, remained steady. Lightner hoped to retain this large customer base by focusing on education or training in the use of its products. During the postwar years, Singer continued supplying its machine-buying customers with free training, including advanced sewing classes. This marketing strategy seemed to work, and Lightner felt comfortable enough to open a fourteenth manufacturing facility in Anderson, South Carolina, and a Distribution and Service Center in Charlotte, North Carolina, in 1952.[258] Also in the mid 1950s, he opened a fifteenth facility in Campinas, Brazil.

Essentially, even with former president Alexander's introduction of a varied product line, the sewing machine remained the company's sole main product; but now it sold only one-third of all sewing machines made. The Singer Company no longer dominated its marketplace. Because of its singular commitment to its flagship product, the company faced a substantial downsizing. But even a slight dismantling of its major manufacturing facilities would send its production costs spiraling upwards. The corporation's board of directors and shareholders voiced little concern over these important matters since company profits, thanks to its large cash reserve, remained stable.

In 1952, the U.S. sewing industry grossed $225,000,000 and domestic manufacturers enjoyed a 21.5 percent rise in machine sales. But even in the face of this booming market, Singer's performance continued to lag behind its competitors. The biggest piece of this pie went to foreign zigzag makers. In 1953, Pfaff alone supported 1,600 US-based dealers.[259] But Nechhi and Elna zigzag machines enjoyed even greater popularity in this country. Enhancements to an Elna machine, the Supermatic, permitted it to perform zigzag functions without troublesome attachments. To promote its new model, "the first fully automatic zigzag machine," Elna invested close to $1,000,000 on advertising its novel product.[260] By 1956, Nechhi-Elna sales claimed 17 percent of the U.S. market.[261]

Newly elected president Lightner, still struggling with labor relations, finally brought out a domestic zigzag model. But, even the introduction of "The Slant-O-Matic" did not boost Singer's domestic sales. Among its domestic competitors, the White Company rose to prominence during the postwar boom years. White succeeded by attracting former Singer salesmen and experienced managers, offering them higher wages and better sales commissions. The White Company also manufactured machines for the Sears department store chain under the Kenmore name brand. Quite unexpectedly, however, the White

Company lost its promising foothold in the industry in 1957 by losing the Sears account to two Japanese sewing machine makers.[262] Two years earlier, the White Company president had warned during a House Ways and Means Committee hearing that planned tariff cuts would "seriously injure his company."[263] Milton Lightner had once voiced these same concerns as well. And now these tariff cuts bore fruit.

As seen, the 1950s brought intense competition within the sewing industry. Additionally, with the coming of plastics and synthetic fabrics presented an entire new set of technical design problems. High-speed sewing often melted these new, light fabrics. The Singer Company met this challenge by developing bonding machines. In prior years, the company's development of such a product would have allowed it to regain its market; but now its many competitors also produced bonding machines. Difficult times for the sewing machine industry had become an understated fact of doing business.

Lightner's Legacy

President Lightner first made his mark while heading up the sales division. When in 1929, Singer felt pressure from a competitor whose basic instructional sewing classes succeeded in increasing its market share, Lightner emulated this tactic. But, Lightner took it one step further by introducing advanced sewing classes out of Singer Sewing Centers. Over the next 20 years, 600 Singer sewing service centers trained 400,000 housewives. Lightner also devised the scheme of offering Singer sewing machines to high schools and colleges at low or sometimes no cost. By the late 1950s, over three million young women a year were learning how to sew in home economics classrooms. And most often, they trained on Singer machines.

During the 1930s, Lightner also sparked the sales division with a new tool: when automobiles proved to be reliable transportation, Lightner provided his salesmen with company cars. With this new found mobility, well-trained and aggressive company salesmen extended their reach into rural areas.

President Lightner came to power during an era of great historical change. These forces of change no longer submitted to elegant enhancements of the customary ways of conducting business. During his brief time at the conglomerate's helm, during the post World War II years, society and its industry grew in complexity. New fabrics, new plastics and synthetic materials, lighter metals and alloys, electronic miniaturization, worker sophistication and specialization, mechanization in the assembly line, and the continuing onslaught of automation evidenced in the growing implementation of computer controls all impacted business as usual. And these represented but few of the many signposts that heralded the coming of modernity. This complexity changed the American business model for all time. This complexity demanded government intervention to place controls on its peoples, who would strike and destroy the great industrial centers, and to place controls on its industry, which would exercise old-fashioned, oligarchical policies over his workforce as it had throughout the Industrial Revolution. Industry, whose traditional control had rested with a handful of owner/operators and sometimes robber barons, now fell into the diverse hands of stockholders. This increased public ownership of the means of production necessitated the need for checks and balances and led to the demise of laissez-faire politics.

It must be remembered that it was Lightner who had always been the power behind the power, the man charged with controlling the Singer Company's domestic arena. It was he who withstood unaccustomed labor-management issues through its most difficult years. And through these difficult times, the Singer Company continued to see itself not as some autocratic power-levying monster, but as a great and benevolent monarchy. It is to Lightner's great credit that he recognized the unstoppable forces of modernity and wisely chose to not throw his remaining resources into salvaging a business methodology that no longer applied. The odds at maintaining the Singer Company's monopoly in the face of government intervention were too great. To maintain his large conglomerate, to avoid downsizing, Milton Lightner chose diversification.

Diversification

Milton Lightner devoted his work life struggling with a newly arriving, unstoppable and highly competitive sewing machine market. Under Lightner's stewardship, the Singer Company product line, which had largely limited itself to design and production of industrial and domestic sewing machines, continued the diversification strategy begun by his predecessor. For example, Singer's heavy presence in Mexico included the manufacture of washing machines, furniture and other small appliances. With Lightner in control, the company maintained its lumber operations in Canada and in the U.S. South and it also began making material handling equipment, floor polishers, commercial electric motors, fans, servomechanisms and other electronic devices.

A Personal Farewell

President Lightner, under whom the annual advertising budget surpassed one million dollars, remained as low-key as his predecessors had. This powerful corporate leader choose anonymity at a time when others basked in the newly discovered limelight of national television and radio advertising. During Lightner's presidency, modernity surfaced. Perhaps, Lightner recognized this fateful arrival when he replaced the company's flagship skyscraper flagpole with an aircraft warning beacon. Now, office boys no longer hoisted pennants signaling "Bon Voyage" or "Welcome Home" to globe-trotting Singer executives as they embarked or disembarked on and off of transoceanic liners. Such relaxed travel was no longer feasible in the fast-paced, incipient global community. [264]

Under Lightner, the Singer building evolved into an enormous complex linking two other office buildings housing, besides SSMC corporate offices, no fewer than 156 other business lessees. The building's 32nd through 37th floors held the company's executive offices. Lower echelon employees referred to these high reaches as "The Tower." Mr. Lightner rarely strayed from the Tower during working hours. At midday, he lunched lightly with his fellow executives and sometimes invited an up-and-coming employee to join with his select power elite.

Lightner also forbade liquor anywhere in the Tower. He capped his own Singer salary at $150,000 a full third more than President Truman's salary.

Lightner's publicity shyness contributed to maintaining the tradition of company secrecy. In this regard, the company's financial solvency also helped. Since Isaac Singer's stroll into Edward Clark's office, the company had never again groveled before financiers for loans. Since the company did not trade its shares publicly, it exempted itself from Securities and Exchange Commission rules. More constrained corporations, whose shares where not privately held, grudgingly placed all their financial facts and figures into the public domain. During Lightner's presidency, the company's shareholders never numbered more than 4,000, and only a handful of these lay claim to controlling interests. On the whole, the public and the financial community knew little of the company's inner workings.

In his personal life, Mr. Lightner enjoyed bass fishing in Canada, weekend golfing and gardening. He was six feet tall and prone to humor. He was a well-known family man, active in community affairs in his hometown of forty years, Ridgewood, New Jersey. The Lightner family also chose an unostentatious lifestyle. Mr. Lightner's wife was a Wellesley collegemate of Madame Chiang Kai-Shek. Madame Kai-Shek and her famous husband regularly visited with the Lightners whenever in this country. In 1957, commenting on the ongoing Cold War, *Time* magazine quoted Mr. Lightner: "To be militarily strong, to give proper aid to our allies, we must have a strong economy here at home."[265] Mr. Lightner once shared the speaker's podium with Vice President Richard Nixon at a National Association of Manufacturers function early in December of 1957.[266]

When he stepped down from SSMC's presidency in 1958, Lightner accepted a one-year term as president of the National Association of Manufacturers, the most powerful manufacturers union of all times. This organization boasted of 21,000 member companies representing 85 percent of all American production of goods and services. It was fitting that this amalgam of business complexity selected this great business leader as their titular head. On the day after his appointment, Mr. Lightner, who prided himself on the enviable relations enjoyed between Singer management and its workforce, was elected chairman of the board of the Singer Company. Lightner once said, "In my day every young man knew where the Singer Building was, and if he didn't, he made it his business to find out."

President Lightner, a lifelong Republican, nevertheless criticized President Eisenhower for not applying anti-trust principles against unions. As a result of his experience, Lightner felt the government should reform its corporate tax code and prevent trade unions from demanding large wage increases. He also felt that industry as a whole needed to be more progressive in developing new products and more effective sales techniques. Under Milton C. Lightner the Singer Company had met modernity and survived. But as Lightner stepped down, more complex and the most difficult days of all awaited the next great conglomerate's chief.

"A man with ability and the desire to accomplish something new can do anything."[267]   — Donald Kircher

Chapter Nine

The Donald Peter Kircher Era (1958-1975)[268]
A Vision for the Information Age

When Milton Lightner left the Singer Sewing Machine Company's president's office, he was only the sixth man to do so. Besides Lightner, two former presidents had been lawyers, Clark and Sir Douglas Alexander. Lawyers had presided over SSMC for two out of every three years of its more than hundred years of existence. And now another lawyer, Donald P. Kircher, the company's seventh president, would sit in the president's chair. Once again, the great conglomerate had somehow attracted a world-class business leader. Donald Peter Kircher would become another Singer company president who would leave a legacy as one of industry's most innovative leaders. Like Edward Clark before him, Donald Kircher made his mark by meeting the fast pace of modern technology head on.

Sometime during his thirtieth year with the company, Milton Lightner decided to relinquish day-to-day control over company operations. In late 1957, he recommended that his protégée Donald Peter Kircher succeed him. Another carefully devised presidential transition occurred on January 1, 1958 when attorney Donald Kircher assumed command of *The First Conglomerate*. On that day, the Singer Company prevailed as the last remaining American maker of sewing machines. The onslaught of foreign competitors and their innovative, low-cost zigzag machines had delivered the death knell to all other American sewing machine makers except the Singer Company.

Donald P. Kircher Brings an Inevitable Philosophy to a Venerable Conglomerate
On his 1948 arrival at the Singer Company, Donald P. Kircher reported to the president's office as Milton Lightner's personal assistant. Just as Sir Douglas Alexander had drawn Lightner away from a law practice, Lightner personally recruited the capable Kircher away from a prestigious New York law firm. Within a short time, the elder Lightner began relying on his younger associate's fresh insights into the ever-changing nuances of modern corporate law. And as hoped, Kircher's acumen in his speciality soon brought resolution to thorny legal issues, both foreign and domestic, that had long troubled the company. The legal maneuvering required to withstand the pressures of ever-changing foreign trade laws, laws often targeted to Singer installations, had become mind-boggling. A master of commercial foreign intrigue had been needed; some great intellect, some great chess grandmaster capable of simultaneous play against a global army of equally masterful opponents. For Milton Lightner that grandmaster proved to be Donald Kircher.

Background For Change
Kircher's remarkable insight and expertise in corporate law enabled him to correctly assess international business trends and keep his company in tune with the changing world economic order. Lightner also appreciated the younger man's grasp of emerging world affairs. Kircher, an army veteran of the European theater, understood postwar Euro-politics and the implications of the developing cold war between east and west. For example, he could lay bare the roots of emerging economic globalism engendered by the Marshall Plan and its ultimate meaning for the

Singer Company's widespread foreign interests. As the industrialized nations rebuilt their manufacturing infrastructure, Singer's foreign sales, which had surged afer the war, must begin to decline. And indeed, during Lightner's stewardship, the company witnessed not only a return of foreign competition – it found this competition intense not only here in the states but throughout the globe as well. So comprehensive was this competition that industry observers studying the sewing machine's worldwide import and export figures predicted the end of the Singer Company monopoly. Kircher recognized that unfair Japanese competition had forced all other U.S. sewing machine makers out of business.[269] Additionally, by the mid 1950s, the sewing machine market appeared saturated. Only the most dedicated company man or profit-hungry shareholder ignored or disbelieved in this inevitability of coming change. Diversification had to be the only answer.

In response to Kircher's cautious but real world prognostications, Lightner began putting more teeth into diversifying the company's product line. For example, Lightner continued contracting for the Department of Defense after war's end. Lightner also initiated the company's emergence as a large pulp and paper manufacturer. During Lightner's watch, the company bought up woodlands and wood manufacturing facilities that eventually reduced the company's cabinetmaking costs. To Lightner, continued diversification seemed unavoidable. How could the conglomerate's massive size and workforce be maintained after the victimization of its main product line through overwhelming, unfair, external political manipulation? Because of the continuing unfair politicization of his base means of competing, Lightner recognized his declining sales must continue to fall. Reduced sales and reduced overall demand for a giant, one-dimensional manufacturer's single product line must bring its own unique problems. For example, could a facility designed to produce 10,000 sewing machines a week economically manufacture 1,000 machines every week? Could a factory built to accommodate thousands of workers operate efficiently with a downsized workforce of hundreds? Was it profitable to lease smaller facilities, to relocate plant equipments and further downsize by salvaging mere pennies on a dollar through divestment of wholly owned capital assets like manufacturing facilities and retail outlets and training centers? Lightner knew one fact remained unassailable, the company's descent into declining revenues would never sustain a sales and product support force estimated at 81,000. On the other hand, however, Lightner recognized that his great conglomerate owned tremendous assets, employed a capable workforce deployed throughout a tightly-knit retail network, all of which was driven by a business structure perfectly prepared to service the needs of a booming postwar economy.

Donald Kircher fully supported Lightner's efforts at introducing a more varied product line. Soon, a close working relationship developed between the two attorneys. After two years in the president's office, Lightner transferred Kircher to his legal department as assistant to the vice president. In 1952, a 37-year-old Kircher earned a promotion to full vice president in this same department. In June of 1954, Kircher's intellect brought widespread recognition throughout the company and earned his entrance into the close-knit and select group comprising the board of directors.[270] In a mere six years, Donald Kircher proved himself as a unique and key corporate affairs manager. His reward was his entry into the great conglomerate's inner circle. In 1958, at 43 years of age, Kircher succeeded his mentor to the company's most important position, the president's chair.

In their pursuit of diversification, Kircher shared Lightner's vision of the importance of the office equipment division. Both men realized that some form of modernization, some method of automation, must come along to keep company records of payrolls, inventories and sales. Manual entries had become too unresponsive. Ordinary sales transactions and records had become complex. The associated inventory controls even more complex. Electronic databasing had taken control over both the airlines and the banking industries. Now the entire retail industry recognized that their means and methods for conducting business on a large scale must shift, must adapt to the changing times. An old, mid-1950s, super-secret first generation computer project, the Bizmac, had proven that computers were well-suited to all commercial ventures including all those related to day-to-day retail operations. To this end, Kircher enlisted Sam Harvey, one of Bizmac's developers, to computerize his conglomerate's worldwide operations. Within a relatively short space of time, a complex network of Point of Sale (PoS) terminals linked to intermediary and then mainframe computers solved SSMC's bookkeeping problems.

Besides the inevitable modernization of the office, both Kircher and Lightner anticipated the coming explosion in the new field of electronics. Both men recognized that a fast-paced, machine-oriented way of conducting business loomed in the offing. The new machines relied on electronic controls. In those heady days, newspapers eagerly reported on overnight technological breakthroughs accompanied by corresponding business successes. Many of these accounts came out of the airlines and banking industries which were fully committed to the emerging EDP technologies. Now, with Kircher at the helm, and with Lightner as chairman of the board, the Singer Company seemed on its traditional course of anticipating Automation's next mutation. But this time, the new technology would not be put to the sole enhancement of a single product line.

The great conglomerate began quiet but surefooted moves to ensure its future. If the company must diversify, why wouldn't it pursue a selective expansion into those industries the emerging technologies must rely on? And in areas that had close links to the company's existing product mix? Diversification must not be foolhardy or accomplished for its own sake. While both men looked forward to the coming challenges of modernism: neither man could have foreseen that the company's most difficult era had arrived.

Kircher's Problems

In 1958, as Milton Lightner stepped aside, 40 million Americans owned sewing machines. The sewing industry marketplace reported revenues surpassing $1 billion per year. This astronomical figure represented real money in the noninflationary business climate of the 1950s. A third of these gross revenues came from actual sales, another third from the sale of textile fabrics, and the remainder from sales of patterns, thread, needles, and miscellaneous accessories. The Singer Company continued to grab the lion's share of these revenues; but low-priced foreign-made machines had established solid inroads. Even as far back as 1952, German, Italian, Swedish, Swiss and Japanese imports had accounted for $50,000,000 of U.S. domestic sewing machine sales. Three years earlier, this figure had been negligible.[271] During the four years prior to Kircher's presidency, the Nechhi-Elna company alone experienced 130 percent growth in its U.S. domestic sales. Moreover, the new foreign upstarts blossomed because of unwitting governmental allies whose politically motivated tariffs tamed the Singer monopoly. The Singer Company, which once enjoyed a de facto global monopoly, now suffered serious competition both domestically and globally. No sector in the great Singer empire went unchallenged. The challenge from so many creditable competitors was systematically reducing Singer's share of the pie.

As a result, and mostly due to the unrelenting invasion of low cost Japanese machines – machines that sold for less than Singer could manufacture them – the new Singer president took bold and drastic steps by cutting prices across his entire product line throughout 1958. For example, Singer's Economy model dropped from $119.95 to $89.50. Kircher accomplished the price reduction by importing machines from his own foreign plants which produced at significantly lower cost than his domestic plants. Kircher maintained this tactic all through his first year in the corporate president's chair. In response, business writers gloated over the conglomerate's difficulties while neglecting to study how foreign makers produced so cheaply using low-paid labor with the added bonus of unfair tariff and trade laws. Instead, they overlooked basic research and editorialized about an aging Singer Corporation incapable of standing up to credible competition. In their assessment of all American corporations' inability to compete with foreign makers, the critics failed to recognize the coming of the Information Age and its handmaiden of global competition that had already changed the business model for all time. Milton Lightner had foreseen these changes: Donald Kircher would have to deal with them.

The Age of Critics Arrives

Besides the great problems of modernity now confronting the company, Donald Kircher's accession to the president's chair met with a new, unpredicted sign of the times – the added problem of a loud, critical group of shareholders. In 1958, the company realized $12 million profits on gross sales near one-half billion dollars. This figure represented another $2 million decline more than the prior year. Stockholders were unhappy with niggardly four percent earnings, or less than half of what General Motors investors earned during the same time period. Business writers and economic analysts railed at the company's seeming decline. After all, it had been a long while since Singer had returned earnings near $50 per share. To these critics, the change of personnel in Singer's office of the president seemed long overdue. Some said the company's near half billion dollars in capital assets would have returned more profits if this sum had simply been invested in government bonds.

Milton Lightner had momentarily quieted the profit mongers in 1957 by selling off 37,000 acres of Arkansas woodlands to bring in nearly $3 million in profit. In 1959, to quiet his own critics and to obtain much needed capitalization to modernize his facilities, Donald Kircher decided to register with the Securities and Exchange Commission. For the first time in its history, the company would offer its shares publicly. Kircher also decided to issue a financial statement for the first time in the Singer Company's one hundred plus years of operations.[272] Kircher had thrown the company's closed doors wide open. These doors widened in 1964 when Frederick Ambrose Clark, grandson to founder Edward Clark, died leaving 600,000 shares of Singer stock, about $53 million, to be sold publicly.[273] These events effectively ended the company's control by a small vested group. The Singer Company's chairman and president, who had always held court over this small select group, now became little different than other corporate leaders at other publicly traded corporations. This fact seemed to matter little. Now in its 113th year of operation, the company still operated profitably while managing respectable increases to shareholders' quarterly profits from 50 cents to 55 cents per share.

The Task: How To Turn it Around

Donald Kircher, like his predecessor became intent at somehow returning the company to its former levels of profitability. To do so required maintaining the massive conglomerate's size. This would be no slight task. Kircher would somehow have to better his mentor, somehow better a Milton Lightner who had created growth and turned magnificent profits during 30 long, difficult years plagued by financial depression and world wars. But this same Milton Lightner, who had deftly guided the company's domestic policies through these difficult times of global business downturn, had not been able to reverse the company's economic slide in the face of the new external limiting factors of tariff-enabled foreign competition, of competition from an estimated 300 sewing machine manufacturers and of out-of-control operating expenses brought on by new high costs of advertising, shipping, distribution and wages. Lightner had selected Kircher as the company's best chance at reclaiming the company's traditional sewing machine market and at continuing the needed diversification of the great conglomerate.

Kircher set his sights on increasing sales and pulling more profits out of each of those sales. He brought in Alfred di Scipio to head his sales and marketing departments. Mr. di Scipio, who had emerged as notable executive at the ITT Corporation, a company whose own diversification program appeared legendary even in those days, changed Singer's stagnated sales program to one more in line with the great social changes associated with postwar America. With di Scipio's arrival, the company began marketing itself not as a simple sewing machine maker but as an entire way of life for the new homemaker. The company introduced more streamlined and pastel-colored machines. It also sold bold, colorful fabrics out of its own and other retail centers like the new shopping malls that recently began dotting the landscape.[274] Kircher reinvigorated Singer's merchandising and marketing departments by directing di Scipio to mount an aggressive and lively sales policy. In 1963, Kircher broke all previous marketing expenditures by placing more than $8 million in advertising.

Donald Kircher introduced change on every front. Like Frederick Bourne before him, he reinvigorated the company by hiring younger, ambitious executives from outside the company. Kircher also decided to bolster areas where the company had prior successes. For example, he reentered the home appliance market by once again stocking his 25,000 retail outlets – 1,300 in the U.S. – with home vacuum cleaners. The new company president also concentrated on reducing redundant operations by downsizing wherever he could.

To counter the new onslaught of one-sided trade barriers, he constructed eleven new manufacturing facilities in foreign lands within four years' time. Nearly a century before, Edward Clark had taken up a similar strategy to overcome similar domestic problems brought on by the Civil War. Kircher and his directorial board believed that the company's strength remained where it traditionally had, in its foreign operations. This commitment to its foreign operations was not a minor one. For example, in August of 1959, Kircher invested $1.3 million to construct a new sewing machine manufacturing plant in Istanbul, Turkey.[275] Additionally, he sought out additional markets by falling back on the company's historic policy of expanding into developing countries. He opened new facilities in the Phillippines, Australia and in Mexico.

In 1959, Kircher succeeded in purchasing the Japanese-based Pine Sewing Machine Company. This acquisition required five years of legal maneuvering.[276] In response to the public uproar, a national media event in Japan, the Japanese government cooked up laws to prevent The Singer Company from exporting any of its Japanese profits. In America, there was no uproar. There were only newspaper reports of how the U.S. courts would handle the problem of steadfastly supporting its foreign ally. How could Japan defend itself from encroachment by nearby communism if it were not economically sound? Politicians subscribed to the domino theory of rapid communism expansion.

They reasoned that a strong Japan, which America could hardly expect to defend at so great a distance, would act as an island buffer against the Communist tide.

More Diversification

Besides introducing a new social awareness to Singer, besides bringing in new vigorous management, besides expanding his global facilities, besides reinvigorating his home appliance product line, besides modernizing his sales and marketing departments and introducing new third world markets, Kircher, like his more recent predecessors, also invested heavily into R&D to setup another parallel path whereby his company would open itself up to modern technology. Kircher began diversifying his company through select acquisitions of new technology companies capable of injecting their expertise into enhancing Singer's existing product line. The only weapon against the onslaught of new competitor technologies was a farsighted R&D effort. Kircher's solution was to buy the technology he needed. As a plus, the acquired companies would added their own product line to Singer's narrow offerings.

In this major policy shift, Kircher did not act autonomously: he delegated the diversification program to a management team that made the actual purchasing decisions.[277] Kircher's diversification program represented a bold step and decision to no longer rely on a single product as a major source of income. Critics charged that the company was grasping at straws by giving up on its main product. But Donald Kircher had carefully outlined his expansion plans to fellow board members and, at least for the moment, enjoyed their support.

Kircher's diversification program began by converting the Metric Division, which was located in Bridgeport, Connecticut, from a sewing machine manufacturing plant into a research, design and production facility for electronic instrumentation. He effected this changeover by acquiring and merging together other related technology companies along with their experienced key personnel. Other acquisitions at this time included: two knitting machine companies, a carpet manufacturing company and a manufacturer of audio equipment.

On 17 July 1962, Singer agreed to purchase Panoramic Electronics, Inc., of Yonkers, NY, a maker of spectrum analyzers. In 1963, Kircher acquired Empire Devices, Inc., of Amsterdam, NY, a prime manufacturer of microwave devices and electrical and electronic test and measuring equipments.

In July of 1963, Kircher made his boldest move of all by acquiring the company's longtime manufacturing and alliance partner, Friden, Inc, for $175,000,000. Friden became the heart of Singer's office equipment division. Friden's 9,500 employees were skilled in the manufacture of: desktop calculating and adding machines, ticketographs, mail room sorting equipment, miscellaneous office machines and equipment and data processing machines. Kircher's team believed that this established company, while still the leader in the office equipment field, was in dire need of modernization. The acquisition team believed such an invigoration of Friden's complacency would quickly deliver up untapped profits. Kircher noted that like his sewing machines, Friden's sales relied on having its products demonstrated and followed up with suitable training. Singer's own sales force also employed a similar operational structure and Kircher expected the expansion into office equipment to be a natural one. Other Singer divisions also made sewing machine cabinets profitably and now Kircher expected to expand to this related product line by beginning manufacture of office furniture. He increased Friden's research capabilities and introduced electronic technology to its typewriterlike desktop calculators. Kircher believed these gear-driven, electro-mechanical number crunchers were nearing obsolescence. He upgraded Friden's kludgey business and engineering machines into sophisticated, compact solid state calculators offering an infinite range of new capabilities. Kircher understood that the big black typewriter-key-driven boxes and their associated mechanical clamor would soon be a distant memory.

With the new Singer bosses at the helm, the stagnant Friden company developed state-of-the-art data processing and photocopying machines.[278] In response, Singer's recently acquired Friden division soon doubled its sales volume. With this newfound profitability of this large acquisition, The Singer

Company's 1963 sales revenues rose to $630,000,000. Thirty million of these dollars went to furnish ecstatic shareholders with a profit of $3.29 per share. By 1964, Singer sales neared the billion dollar mark. Shareholders' squealed gleefully as their profits climb to $4.29 per share.

Kircher continued in a carefully orchestrated diversification of his company. In 1964, Kircher acquired the Empire Electric Corporation, Lakeville, Indiana, and Wirekraft, Inc., Rolling Prairie, Indiana. In 1968, Singer acquired the General Precision Equipment Corporation, a widely diversified company with a large gas meter manufacturing facility. General Precision also produced numerous electronic products for the defense and aerospace industries. This acquisition greatly increased Singer's sales revenues. Singer also bought 35 percent, about $17 million, of all Packard-Bell company stocks. In 1966, Kircher purchased Packard-Bell Electronics Corporation outright for $44 million cash.

By the early 1960s, the Singer Company emerged as this country's fifth largest electrical and electronic test equipment manufacturer. For example, it produced Craftsman power tools for the Sears department stores. Kircher continued company policy of owning the building and grounds of all its branch offices and sewing centers. Kircher's acquisitions would prove to be the key industries that would flourish during the boom years of the approaching Information Age. Within the short space of ten years, Kircher's innovations had reversed the conglomerate's declining revenues.

Enter the Defense Industry

The Singer Company now had a strong foothold in the fast growing electronics field. One of Donald Kircher's first acquisitions, Haller, Raymond & Brown, HRB, a respected research facility located in State College, Pennsylvania, established the company's presence in the military defense research field. HRB produced infrared cameras for the military and was a forerunner in electronics information storage and retrieval technologies. Kircher and his management team expected HRB to introduce sophisticated automation to its own production equipments and significantly reduce Singer's manufacturing costs. HRB also contracted about $3 million worth of military research on an annual basis. With the HRB foothold, Singer created its Military Products Division with an office in Washington, D. C.

An example of the Singer Company's new found expertise that evolved during the Kircher years arises out of a four-day-long trade show the company put on in Moscow during 1973. Spurred by the Soviets recent $8 billion deal with Armand Hammer's Occidental Petroleum Company, many American companies including Westinghouse, Bechtel, IBM and others began Russian solicitations in hopes of capturing an expected explosion in the Soviet market for sophisticated office machines. During this trade show, Singer's PoS system attracted the greatest interest. The Soviets expressed interest in developing a centralized computer database to electronically link all of their far flung empire. Other Singer company products of interest to the Russians included TALAR, a microwave landing system designed by Singer engineers for small airports, and a radar navigation system.[279] This sales promotion resulted in a $20 million trade deal that initiated various Singer technological enterprises in Russia.

Modern Facilities

Besides keeping his company's main product line competitive in the face of heavily weighted foreign mercantile warfare, Kircher, with Lightner's boardroom support, began a company facelift. The critics railed: the new *reorganization* would accomplish little but further erode company profits. Kircher simply ignored his detractors. The president's office issued policy changes that echoed Kircher's understanding of the changing world of international commerce. His first step in preparing for the significant workplace changes that would befall all of industry became the modernization of his company's manufacturing facilities, both here and abroad. Mostly, he retooled his aging facilities by investing in expensive state-of-the-art, often electronic-based capital equipment. In time, the newly automated production machinery, which produced more with less labor, would deliver a great return on investment. For example, the company's $12 million refurbishment of its Slant-O-Matic production line within its Elizabeth plant reduced manufacturing cost for that model by 30 percent. Kircher refurbished all his manufacturing centers, branch offices and sales centers here and overseas in Scotland, France, Brazil, and in West Germany. These efforts of new production machinery and new workflow automation guaranteed the continuance of the company's longstanding tradition of producing high-quality products.

Earlier, in 1961, Kircher moved corporate headquarters from 149 Broadway to 30 Rockefeller Plaza. Kircher made the move only after responding to a two-year-long ergonomic study. The lengthy study concluded that his existing, congested offices spaces were no longer suitable for the work of modern corporate executives. With reluctance, Kircher agreed to move to the larger, more modern office surroundings. The Singer Company skyscraper on Broadway had contained its executive offices since 1908. To many, the move represented the ignoble, heartless passing of a great era.

Results of Kircher's Policies

During the first five years of his presidency, Kircher doubled the company's previous sales figures to an annual average of $1.2 billion. But the surge of cheap Japanese machines also found steady growth since Kircher's first days in office. In 1960, Japan exported three-quarters of a million Japanese sewing machines a year to America. By the mid 1960s, Japan annually sold one million of its cheaply made and low-priced sewing machines to thrift-conscious Americans. During these years, Brother Industries Ltd. blossomed into the largest of Japanese sewing machine makers. For the Japanese, their success as sewing machine manufacturers led to other US government-facilitated exports of electronics, cameras and cars. By the 1970s Japanese sewing machine exports to the United States, which still enjoyed loosened trade restrictions, reached 1.5 million machines a year. Even in the face of this substantial, unethical competition Kircher somehow found a way to stand his ground.

During his presidency, Kircher doubled his company's sewing machine sales by emphasizing quality. Foreign makers could not match the versatility, reliability and strong construction of Singer sewing machines. The Singer Company's 1960 introduction of its *Touch and Sew* model especially cemented its hold on the quality market and managed to stabilize the company's domestic business. Besides the ongoing popularity of the Touch and Sew, new technology impacted the Singer line with the introduction of the "Photo-Line Tracing Unit." This 1963 innovation, which became the talk of the industry, employed electronic programming and photo-sensing to duplicate line art with stitching.

Besides implementing novel technology, Kircher added to his slow-rebounding revenues by offering companion sales products and other non-sewing-related merchandise into his product line. Alongside sewing machine attachments and sewing accessories came fabrics and dress patterns and other products including: vacuum cleaners, washing machines, refrigerators, stereo entertainment centers, record albums, typewriters and other consumer electronics and gadgetry that ironically often originated from Japan. During the 1960s, the company experimented with mail order after purchasing the third largest mail order firm in Germany, Schwab A. G. The new acquisition grossed $8 million during its first year of operations under the Singer banner.

The great behemoth that was the Singer Company responded to Kircher's innovative and invigorated management by regaining its status as market leader by claiming 40 percent of worldwide sewing machine sales. Kircher had recovered eight percent of the company's original sewing machine market share during his first five years alone. His policy of diversifying the company's interests paid off as well: Singer sales doubled and surpassed a billion dollars at a time when no more than 60 US corporations surpassed this benchmark. Under Kircher, Singer grew from a one-dimensional company reliant on a single and highly competitive product into a large, modern and diversified conglomerate. Kircher's acquisitions, which had all been targeted by his management team, eventually leveled off at 22 companies.

Each acquisition was itself a proven and key producer in its industrial specialization. Under Kircher, the Singer Company became noted for the worldwide manufacture and distribution of high fidelity and stereophonic entertainment systems, calculators, photocopying machines, electronic PoS cash registers, computer systems and for its widespread investment in real estate. In less than ten years, Donald Kircher maneuvered the once single product appliance maker into a major space-age electronics and defense department supplier producing, for example, antisubmarine warfare weapons control systems, flight simulators and high quality internal guidance and radar systems.

In recognition of his great achievement, Kircher was elected chairman of the board in 1968: Donald Kircher had become the controlling figure of the world's most respected conglomerate, a very powerful man surrounded by a dedicated corps of career-designated employees. His successful reorganization and restructuring garnered colossal sales figures. Unfortunately, this great turnaround would not suffice; the barking media dogs only temporarily restrained themselves while awaiting new opportunities to resume their sniping. Stockholders, looking over lowered earnings, waited to benefit from this company hype. Unfortunately for Kircher, the bottom line still remained bogged down in the ongoing recession. No amount of promised future profitability could surmount the new age philosophy of *nowism*.

Roiling Waters

Unfortunately, the Singer Company would never benefit from Kircher's careful and well-timed restructuring. It would never enjoy the fruits of these great labors. As the worldwide recession crept along, Kircher's acquisitions slowed in their profitability. By the early 1970s, Kircher had reduced Singer's dependence on its sewing machine product line to 35 percent of its total sales revenues of $1.9 billion dollars. Forty percent of these profits continued to accrue from foreign sales. But all was not well.

Shareholders publicly lamented the loss of their great customary dividends. Many felt that regardless of the bad economic times Kircher's presidency should have returned the company to its former monopolistic prominence long before now. It mattered little that Kircher's acquisition loans labored under unpredictable and unforeseen interest rates of nearly twenty percent. Kircher's guarantee of a large *future* profit once the recession ended fell on deaf ears.

In 1974, the company reported an astonishing $2.6 billion in sales. However, market analysts pointed first to the company's high debt of $1.1 billion held at double digit interest rates, and the to the worldwide glut in office equipment, to the decline in defense and aerospace activities, and finally to the company's reported $10.1 million loss for the year. Many on the board of directors felt that, while the company prospered in a following sea, Kircher should have found a way to ride the waves of turbulence. Singer's board of directors felt that it was time for them to take action. Under Kircher, the board of directors had changed face from a select group descended from the company's founders to a group of unrelated outsiders. Once again, change was needed. And would quickly arrive.

At the start of his appointment, Singer's board of directors had looked on Kircher's reputation as a tireless and uncompromising manager as the kind of tough leadership skills needed to restore the company's foundering profits. Now, these same strengths were perceived as unforgiving character flaws. Kircher, many said, was imperious and autocratic. As remembered by one of Kircher's business equipment division corporate managers, Sam Harvey, "Everybody called him the *boss*. When you sat with him, you could feel the power of his personality. You didn't try to bluff him. If you had thought it out, were prepared, and stood your ground, he respected you. He respected well-organized opinions. He believed in an intellectual aristocracy. But if you bluffed him or tried to bamboozle him, you were gone."[280] *Forbes* magazine once reported, "Kircher ran Singer with a high hand, but he listened when he had to."[281]

But in 1975, Donald Kircher became hospitalized with a stomach problem: diverticulitis. Surgery eliminated ten inches of his intestinal tract. Kircher's operation kept him bedridden for 11 weeks. He remained infirm, working a few hours each day. Co-workers made note of his obvious pain and understood his return to his sick bed at 2 p.m. every day. Before completely recovering from this first surgery, Kircher's spinal disk acted up and again placed the once athletic Kircher into full time bed rest. Doctors scheduled more surgery. Mr. Kircher also suffered from arthritis and phlebitis that also required surgery.

Believing the boss' illness to be of long duration, four board members reluctantly led the charge to replace their once great captain. In their discussions, board members emphasized their president's failing health and the need for strong leadership during the ongoing financial recession. The whispers filtering through financial page editorials no doubt brought concern over the company's long term debt. Like the editorializing financial analysts, board members criticized Kircher for investing in 'fad' industries and for pouring money into them long after their faddishness faded. Moreover, they believed his acquisitions had not been well thought out; his expansion of the company had diluted the company's stock.

The interest on the company's debt during a time of skyrocketing interests rates ranged in the hundreds of millions; and, most importantly, shareholders' earnings had fallen to a miserly ten cents per share. A year before, shareholders seem satisfied with a return of 65 cents per share. In 1974, company losses amounted to $10.1 million, But now in 1975 overall losses lessened to $3.7 million. These facts coupled with the report that sales revenues had hit the roof left shareholders wondering why their returns had not increased. How could there not be an enormous dividend trickling out of this great profit? Kircher reported the need for the reduced dividend because of "the deepening economic recession which affects several major areas of our business and the previously announced problems in the business machines division."[282] All companies in this product line like SCM Corporation, Victor Comptometer, Litton and Underwood-Olivetti, had all been unprepared to compete against the sudden incursion of inexpensive Japanese electronic calculators.

The only one area of his new acquisitions showing promise was the office equipment division. Kircher had reason to hope since his PoS contract with Sears still had five years left to run and the J. C. Penney Company had recently contracted to buy 10,000 PoS registers and 10,000 computers to network them. About this time in 1973, the Woolworth company also contracted for $35 million worth of 10,000 PoS registers and networking computers. But these sales, which required a great deal of groundwork, did not bring immediate profits.

Again Kircher pointed to favorable future trends, but he also realistically alluded to overall unfavorable performances from the company's home furniture, climate control, and industrial sewing and knitting divisions. This president's report elicited a noisy outpouring of dissent during the annual stockholders meeting. At this meeting, nearly 800 longtime company investors loudly expressed their dissatisfaction with Kircher's management. Kircher, they said, angered many and sometimes forced key employees out. They disliked his waiting policy. How could the company land some future profit if it went bankrupt before then? The company needed to make money now. Company management had lost sight of how to return a profit as it had during the Depression of '29. This public outcry also moved the board of directors toward their decision to remove their CEO.

Kircher, who was homebound while recuperating from his operation, was unable to defend himself. Many in the president's office, like Sam Harvey, believed that if the boss, whose debating skills were unmatched, had been well enough to defend himself, the company would have remained on course. Unfortunately, shareholders and board members alike appeared disinterested in trading immediate profits in return for future, long-term staying power. Both groups had forgotten their enthusiastic approval of Kircher's 1959 fifteen-page-long grand scheme for diversifying the company. As these negative rumblings lay on the table, and after board members visited the bed-ridden Kircher, the board passed a motion to engage a professional recruiter to search for Kircher's replacement. Within a few weeks, the headhunter located an acceptable candidate who quickly replaced the ailing Kircher.

Donald Kircher had assembled a close knit workforce. Most of these career employees respected "the boss" and felt that the Singer Company's Board of Directors decision to replace Kircher sounded the company's death knell. Years later, Sam Harvey would say, "Just when the ship entered rough waters, its owners took away its most able captain. All of us in corporate headquarters knew then, this great company was in a lot more trouble than anyone realized. Mr. Kircher was the best retailer we had ever know. We knew he couldn't be replaced."[283]

Kircher's illnesses left the conglomerate without direction. The company's cash flow declined further with lagging profits brought as double-digit interest rates rose. Such rates had never before seen in all of modern economic history. The office equipment division, known as Singer Business Machines, also developed unforseen problems. The R&D expenses associated with redesigning the old Friden mechanical marvels into modern electronic calculators had proved too costly. Moreover, the new electronic office products had obsoleted Friden's main product line of electro-mechanical calculators. Friden's profits, which like its parent company traditionally relied on a single main product, all but disappeared.

During 1974, Kircher shut down Friden's electro-mechanical facilities entirely. Singer and Friden ended their manufacture of dated accounting and billing machines. This write-off cost Singer $30 million. Compounding this loss was the fact that the office division's new minicomputers, which replaced the old-fashioned and manually operated office calculators, were expensive. Prices ranged from a low of $30,000 to a high of $150,000. These costly state-of-the-art first generation computers demanded an even more costly sales force trained in their use. IBM's entry into the business computer field did not help the Singer Business Machine Division's sales. Even the PoS electronic cash register, that Kircher had forced Friden management to develop, delivered more problems than profits. An estimated $60 million was lost by the PoS division between 1970 and 1974. Friden's long time management, which believed that only the Singer Company would ever have use for such a sophisticated, databasing cash drawer, apparently made a half-willed effort with this project. The proliferation of solid state office equipment gadgetry only compounded the division's confusion and problems. Friden managers complained that Kircher rarely consulted with them while making major decisions that expanded their operations into new fields.[284] The Singer-Friden PoS register, which once controlled that market, quickly loss market share as well-heeled competitors like NCR and Litton entered the field. The Friden acquisition had proved costly. Beyond the office equipment division's initial purchase price of 2.2 million in common shares, Kircher borrowed $150 million during 1974 to keep it afloat.

The General Precision Equipment purchase also proved costly. This company, which specialized in avionic products, also flipped into an economic tailspin as the recession forced reductions in defense spending. The 1972 housing slump also slowed usual company profits from its heating, air conditioning and home building divisions. The recession forced the company to shut down most of its furniture manufacturing and upholstering plants entirely. A poorly timed acquisition of a European mechanical calculator manufacturer ended abruptly with its doors closing when cheap electronic calculators flooded the market. The decision to place home entertainment electronics into its retail centers also proved misguided as the company learned that its mostly women customer base generally never purchased hi-fi equipment. These failures resulted in a $39 million write-off during 1974.[285]

However, though the company's profit and debt burdens were onerous, some have argued that the beginning of the end occurred, not because of the economic downturn, but because of the company's traditional close-mouthed philosophy. President Kircher, like the great company he had inherited, had remained publicity-shy. Kircher customarily refused media requests for interviews and usually needed cornering for any comment at all. Had Kircher accorded the media dogs an occasional interview or group luncheon, they may have understood his perspective and treated him more kindly. Before him, Lightner had also sidestepped the little-informed but highly critical media. Both men placed little value on groundless, ill-formed public speculation. Yet, in a world of declining values nothing arises more important than the *appearance* of great corporate control in the front office. The critics chose to overlook the simple truth that Singer remained the most solvent conglomerate in existence.

During 1973, it had reported its most profitable year of $2.5 billion in sales with $94.5 million in profits. But the company's poor profit showing that began in 1974 incited the business media. The media naysayers enjoyed the persecution brought on by their negative prognostications concerning the Singer Company's failing fortunes. And years later, long after Kircher's departure, they gleefully reported that this *once cash rich conglomerate* had squandered its fortune. Board members pointed to 1974's $10 million loss and reflected that the company's last dip into red ink happened way back in 1917. Beginning with this loss, the directors began a financial analysis of their company. Board members overlooked the fact that their stock in the company was now worth three times what is was when Kircher took over. However, the continuing economic recession and declining profits finalized the Board of Directors decision to search for a successor to the future-looking Donald P. Kircher.

The Saddest Farewell of All

Donald Kircher, like Frederick Bourne before him, had pushed research and development to its limits bringing new, highly competitive products into the company's product line. One could argue that his introduction of electronics into business equipments accelerated the modernization of American business. And like Bourne, Kircher reinvigorated his company by assembling a team of outsiders within his corporate inner circle and within key management areas. Kircher had also raised the company's profitability to unheard of levels by creating a multidimensional conglomerate producing multibillion dollar sales. He had turned his company around in the face of sophisticated opposition. Donald Kircher had been undone by negative criticism; not by hard number analysis. His company's earnings and posted tax credits hinted of untold prosperity. Oldtime Singer hands like Sam Harvey believe that had the conglomerate held onto its foundation in base information technologies, the Singer Company would have surged in profitability when the space age exploded. Sam Harvey should know. His own Business Research Institute, which grew out of his Bizmac and later Singer executive service experience, became a successful player in Information Age computer networking.

After his ignominious removal from office, Kircher retired to his 132-acre summer estate in Kingwood Township, New Jersey. He once said to a close friend, "When I had the job, people came around here all the time. Now, these same people, who I treated as my close friends and confidants, never come around."[286] Besides his presidency and chairmanship of the Singer Company, Kircher served on several important corporate boards such as that of the Morgan Guarantee Trust Company, the Bristol-Myers Company, the Lehman Corporation and the Metropolitan Life Insurance Company. He was also Director-General of the Cable Corporation.

This once powerful man remained at 63 years-old youthful, athletic with a forward-thinking business acumen and expertise still at its zenith. Now, this visionary industrialist faced the most debilitating and demoralizing experience of being turned out early to pasture. And, in this morose retirement, this once proud man met his untimely and tragic fate.

Who was Donald Kircher? He was an engineer's son. A St. Paul native, Kircher had graduated from the University of Minnesota and then gone on to Columbia University Law School. His Columbia classmates remember him for his imposing personal bearing and an intellectual prowess that ostensibly benefitted from a photographic memory. For example, while everyone struggled to complete a three-hour-long New York State bar exam, Kircher astounded even his classmates by completing the exam in half the allotted time. Donald Kircher was a lifelong reader. He especially enjoyed studying and researching technology. He read scientific text manuals extensively.

In 1939, he gained a position with the New York law firm of Winthrop, Stimson, Putnam, and Roberts. As World War II progressed, Kircher continued to feel duty bound until, in 1941, he volunteered for the U.S. Army. While he should have held a high commission, General MacArthur had expressly excluded business leaders from high-ranking staff or managerial positions in his army. Nevertheless, Donald Kircher served with distinction as one of General Patton's medium tank company commanders. Some say Kircher ran the Singer Company in the same authoritarian manner that General Patton, whom Kircher greatly admired, ran his Third Army. In the European theater, Lt. Kircher earned many military decorations including at least one for heroism under fire. He was wounded twice. His military record lists a Silver Star with Oak Leaf Clusters, a Bronze Star, a Purple Heart with Oak Leaf Clusters, Chevalier, Order of Leopold, and Croix de Guerre (Belgium).

After World War II, Kircher regained his position in the law firm. He made his mark by simultaneously guiding and enabling one corporation's restructuring while handling that company's high-visibility fraud case. The resolution of the complex litigation rested on Kircher's ability to restructure his client corporation to the satisfaction of all the complainants. In 1948, one of his firm's clients, the Singer Company, recruited him. Singer company president Milton Lightner personally made the overtures to the successful lawyer. Within ten years' time, Kircher succeeded Lightner as president; and, in ten more years, at the age of fifty-three, Kircher became the Singer company chairman of the board as well.

When in New York, Kircher lived in a 53 East 80th Street apartment. However, he much preferred life with his family on his large New Jersey estate. Those who knew Donald Kircher knew a quiet, affable, deep thinker. A conservative, reserved man careful of maintaining proper protocols. A spry, athletic man who enjoyed grooming and riding his horses to the hounds. He was recognized as a bold, hard-paced disciplinarian known for his ability to handle pressure with steadfast elegance. Kircher's complex, highly organized personality flowered alongside that of his greatly admired wife, Lois Kircher. Mrs. Kircher, in complete contrast to her serious-minded husband, always flowed with an ebullient, light, airy and fun-loving disposition. Acquaintances often enjoyed the playful contrasts and resulting balance between these two opposing personalities.

These two opposites had married in 1965 in Kircher's fiftieth year. To Kircher's amazement, the couple was quickly blessed with a son and a daughter. According to close friends and associates, the hard-driving Kircher, who carried an oversized, work-stuffed briefcase home every night, always regretted waiting so long for the contentment he found in family life. Until his fiftieth year, Donald Kircher had always allowed his important career to take precedence over any personal life.

While often criticized for his uncompromising management style, Donald Kircher, who believed that a manager must control his company the way General Patton controlled his army, was nevertheless a compassionate man. Don Kircher had provided for his wife's family for many years. He employed his father-in-law as a caretaker on his estate, and he showed compassion in also providing for his wife's mentally troubled brother, Charles J. Moeller, Jr. Charles Moeller was the complete opposite of his sister, Lois. Charles had remained unemployed for several years following an apparent debilitating automobile accident. Besides the resulting physical disability, Charles developed a vitriolic, disagreeable personality. Even though the unstable Moeller often vilified him with an unrelenting barrage of verbal abuse, Kircher continued to provide for the troubled man by supporting him in his guest house. This accommodation, which had promised to be temporary, persisted for many years. After leaving Singer, Kircher eventually tired of his brother-in-law's limitless stream of abusive, always critical ranting and raving. This tiresome verbal assault, which was coupled with the man's refusal to help out on the estate at all, eventually prompted Kircher to ask the ingrate to leave.

The 52-year-old Moeller then moved in with his father who also lived on the Kircher estate in a separate caretaker's cottage. On a Saturday night, Moeller told his father he was returning a clothes iron to the main house. The elder Moeller believed his son intended to borrow money from his sister, Lois. However, instead of obtaining the handout, Moeller had a heated argument with his longtime benefactor, Don Kircher. The argument ended with Kircher's demand that Moeller remove himself and his belongings from the estate. Moeller left in an rage. However, he soon returned with a .32 caliber handgun an shot the defenseless Kircher twice in the chest.

Donald Kircher, the great corporate leader, war hero and compassionate family man who accomplished so much for so many, fell silently dead in his own driveway – in full view of his loving wife and two young children. On return to the elder Moeller's caretakers quarters, Charles Moeller, Jr., told his father, "I done something I shouldn't have done."[287] This was the tragic end of one of America's legendary industrialists.

And, perhaps due to this unspeakable tragedy, this most successful, innovative, far-seeing corporate leader of all time has been forgotten by history. One of the world's great capitalists has slipped into oblivion without a deserved farewell. No more telling footnote can be added than that of Sam Harvey's: "In the ten years time I worked for him, I never witnessed, or heard of, or even heard the mention of his ever doing anything unethical. His business dealings never got the company in trouble – legal or otherwise. Ours was a smooth, well-run company that benefitted from many dedicated and long term employees. And we were a profitable operation. We were the most cash-rich company in the world. Companies today could learn a lot from a man like that."[288]

Kircher had maintained the tradition started by the company's real founder, Edward Clark. He had even followed Clark's master plan as it might have surfaced in a modern world. And like Edward Clark before him, Donald Kircher had recognized that technology acting as the handmaiden to manufacturing eventually returned fabulous corporate profits when also grounded in the highest moral principles. Don Kircher had built a conglomerate whose name earned worldwide recognition second only to Coca Cola.

"Things do change. The only question is that since things are deteriorating so quickly, will society and man's habits change quickly enough?" – Isaac Asimov

Chapter Ten

The Joseph Bernard Flavin Era (1975-1987)
Simplifying the Future

After month's of agonizing over the company's falling stock values and their CEO's failing health, Singer's Board of Directors replaced Donald Kircher. To succeed their ailing president, they chose a 47-year-old avid skier and golfer, Joseph Flavin.[289] More than any of the candidates they considered, Mr. Flavin's exceptional corporate financial accounting experience, his expertise in foreign trade, his obvious energy and enthusiasm, proved convincing to Singer's Corporate Board members. The company's directors needed someone to shore up the overall value of Singer company shares – someone to rein in Kircher's high-flying extravagance. The efficient finance expert Joseph Flavin offered the right temperament and corporate background required for the monumental task of steering the great conglomerate out of an increasingly nebulous futurism and back into sure-footed profitability.

Flavin's selection came after very little deliberation. A headhunter's telephone call, one of many directed toward dozens of capable executives, had delivered the original proposal to the unsuspecting Flavin. Recognizing that the Singer Company operated mostly as an international company within his area of expertise, Mr. Flavin was quickly attracted to this enormous challenge. Within weeks of the headhunter's fishing expedition, Joseph Flavin became the venerable 124-year-old company's new president, its new chairman of the board and its new overall director. This new Singer CEO, perhaps America's most capable finance man of the time, would quickly accomplish everything board members hired him to do.

Career

Joseph Flavin, was born on October 16, 1928. He earned his undergraduate degree at the University of Massachusetts and then went on for a Master of Science degree at Columbia University's Graduate School of Business in New York City. He rose rapidly in the business world by quickly distinguishing himself as a capable executive manager at both IBM and Xerox Corporations. During the years of 1953-1965, Joseph Flavin, as IBM's number three man, headed that conglomerate's World Trade Corporation. In 1965, he earned a key promotion to company controller. Moving to the Xerox Corporation in 1967, Flavin filled successive positions of increasing responsibilities as controller, vice president, manager Corporate Services, senior vice president Finance and Planning, and by 1972, executive vice president and president of International Operations. These rapid promotions marked Mr. Flavin as an enormously capable young executive, as a great rising star in the business world.

A Return to Fundamental Operations

Joseph Flavin was a realist who believed that profits needed posting on today's balance sheet and not in some indeterminate, future promise. In this regard, he mirrored the business acumen of his times. Doubtless, both Flavin and his board felt that the precise timing and the method of Kircher's promise of coming riches was anybody's guess. Unfortunately for the Singer Company, Kircher's vision evolved into a drawn-out waiting game always filling with expensive red ink.

Joseph Flavin must have wondered if rescuing the conglomerate was attainable at all? On assuming his new offices, Flavin conferred with the press saying the company was *basically sound* but beleaguered with problems. During the interview process, he forwarned Singer's board of directors, "There might be some dramatic write-offs."[290] This proved to be an understatement. On entering office, Flavin first requested financial statements from each of Singer's 24 divisions. With this information in hand, he led a marathon 9 ½ -hour-long strategy session with his board members. A later director's board meeting, which also lasted nearly a full day, resulted in an agreement to pursue an unheard of write-off campaign that would become the largest corporate loss in all of business history – a staggering $451.9 million.[291] Flavin and Singer's directors had concluded that only a wholesale divestiture of the company's cash-draining divisions would restore the old profitability.

The new president first set about establishing a firm financial footing to operate from. To bring in ready cash, Flavin sold the company's entire accounts receivable. The GE Credit Corporation picked up all Singer retail sewing centers' charge accounts for $88 million. For Flavin's turn-around to work, there was apparently no time for nitpicking credit authorizations that engaged so much of a Singer field worker's time. Flavin knew that many of his credit customers, especially those in the third world's hinterland, were slow paying. Slow-paying clients were completely inimical to Flavin's charter requiring him to turn a fast profit.

After unloading his accounts receivable, Flavin continued downsizing by essentially giving away the company's marginally profitable subsidiaries such as: its Graphics System Division and Tele-Signal product line, a telecommunication company, a computer company, a printing company, a home construction company, a parts and service business, a troubled 2,000 employee Italian appliance manufacturing facility and the West German mail order firm. Flavin also *spun-off* its sewing machine division: *The Singer Company would no longer make sewing machines.*

The now completely separate sewing machine division became the Singer Sewing Machine Company, SSMC, Inc. This spin off provided shareholders with a special dividend that boosted their stock value by 20 percent. To accelerate this transition, Flavin directed Singer's global network of company-owned sales and service centers to either close or attempt to succeed independently. The parent company would no longer support them. Flavin's downsized company now concentrated on certain key high-technology divisions, all linked to the defense industry. These included its electronic warfare command systems, its navigation and guidance systems and its profitable flight simulator division.[292]

De-Diversifying Leaves a Salty Taste

The rapid divestment of these subsidiaries stunned many high echelon Singer company executives. These executives felt that these company's acquisitions had not been haphazardly made by the Kircher team. In their view, those newly acquired companies that did not immediately enter the balance sheet's plus column but only treaded water as part of a careful orchestration and melding of base industries primed for the coming Information Age, for the new age of automation and electronics. These longtime company executives understood the path their conglomerate was taking. Secret internal studies had predicted the future of the industrialized world. And now, even as the rapid industrialization enabled by electronic miniaturization descended upon them, corporate seemed to be throwing the towel in. But this futurism, this hoping, was exactly the course that the directors headed by Flavin were intent on swaying.

Oldtimers watched with disbelief as a decade of subtle maneuvering suddenly flew out the window. The irony in this sudden turn of events was that the divestment came at the hands of an outsider backed by another group of directors – themselves outsiders – that Kircher had personally recruited to reinvigorate his struggling empire. Singer's old hands frowned on these outsiders who did not relate to the surefooted inner workings of the great conglomerate.

However, Mr. Flavin, like his predecessor, accomplished precisely what Singer's board of directors hired him to do. Back in 1958, Kircher had decried the venerable company's inefficient and complacent management that stood aside as modernism marched along. Now, at the end of Kircher's term, Flavin was the new outsider with little regard for well-entrenched corporate executives holding a vision glazed over by some pie-in-the-sky futurism. Flavin's actions pleased the board and Singer shareholders even more. In a few weeks time, Flavin's write-off campaign all but eliminated the company's revolving credit debits of $400 million owed to a consortium of 29 banks. These deficit-cutting measures reduced Singer company's real world assets by fifty percent. Kircher had borrowed the money in order to modernize and diversify his company. At the time, diversifying seemed a foresightful business endeavor that appeared to emulate International Telephone & Telegraph Corporation's capable CEO, Harold Geneen, and his track record of successful diversification. Unlike the haphazard Geneen acquisitions, which acquired dozens of companies only according to their ability to add to ITT's growing coffers,[293] an in-depth Harvard Business School study praised the Singer Company and promoted it as a model for diversification. But the Singer Company's diversification, which developed a high debt burden during the unexpected and long lasting economic slump that hit so suddenly during the early 1970s, appeared to stockholders to be too expensive.

To many insiders, it seemed that Flavin's downsizing had but one goal of actually closing the company. As one disgruntled employee said, "Upper management made sure they'd show a profit, even if they have to give away half of it." Perhaps the biggest blow came when Flavin spun off all sewing machine operations into a separate and self-contained industrial firm. Although the new Singer Sewing Machine Company remained in the control of Singer shareholders, it no longer had any affiliation with its parent company. Flavin had ended a 135-year-old legacy. To an inquiring *Forbes* magazine journalist Flavin said, "I believe in being a diverse company; But not a financial conglomerate where only the numbers hang the company together."[294] The resulting *Forbes* article sounded a favorable note: "With a solid, multibillion-dollar sales base, substantial tax credits and a respectable flow of earnings, Flavin definitely has something to work with. But it will take time to get Singer's balance sheet back in shape. You can't undo a decade of mismanagement in a single year."[295]

Singer Company shareholders continued their uproar for higher dividends. The fact that America's deep business recession showed no sign of diminishing made not a bit of difference to profit-taking stockholders. In these troubled financial times, the profit motive had become the only measure of a company's worth. The corporation's staying power and positioning for future economic growth paled against the expectations of a large and immediate return on investment.

In 1976, Flavin finally made good on his original promise to divest the company of Kircher's prized PoS computer division by selling it outright. The Singer Business Machine division, which Donald Kircher had so long nurtured and supported, was now gone. Although the office equipment division had become a steady drain on profits, board members, who had struggled with Donald Kircher for so many years over the explosive future value of the office division's leading edge technology, looked the other way as Kircher's expensive, prized project was sold. One must assume that Joseph Flavin, who had made his mark with two competing office equipment manufacturers, IBM and Xerox Corporations, understood the ultimate need for this divestment. Doubtless Flavin believed the Singer PoS product and its associated Bizmac offspring would not stack up well up against either of his two former employers' industry-leading electronic data processing computer product lines. Perhaps, the proof of Joseph Flavin's hard work was in the bottom line: during 1976 the Singer Company posted $38.4 million in earnings. This figure represented close to a 200 percent increase over 1975 profits.

Goodbye to the Big Apple

Later that year, in October, Flavin assured a nervous New York State Commerce Board inquiry that he made no plans to relocate his corporate offices out of state. Flavin, through his spokesman, added that he was in fact *satisfied* with New York City. Moreover, the spokesman additionally promised to report to the Commerce Board of any changes in its future plans. Commerce Board members had recently witnessed a sharp decrease in their tax revenues: no fewer than 30 corporations, perhaps pushed by ever-diminishing profits, had crept out of the Big Apple during a five-year period. When rumors of an approaching Singer Corporation relocation began traveling around the business luncheon circuit, the Commerce Board became interested.

During 1977, the widely diversified Singer company enjoyed sales of $2,285 billion and ranked 109th on *Fortune* magazine's list of top 500 U.S. corporations. And then in June 1978, without a hint of warning, Flavin handed New York State officials the financial bombshell they suspected by announcing the move of his corporate headquarters from its longtime and traditional *30 Rock*, 30 Rockefeller Plaza, Manhattan location, to Stamford, Connecticut. Singer employees were only accorded a few minutes of advance notice before the public disclosure of the surprise relocation. A Singer spokesman reported to the *New York Times* on 14 June 1978 that the company had closely studied the merits of various relocation possibilities including that of remaining in New York City. The newspaper article reported: "Although (the Singer spokesman) noted that Mr. Flavin, the chairman, and several other senior executives live in Connecticut, he said, 'Mr. Flavin bent over backwards to make this decision in as objective fashion as could be done.'"[296]

Chairman Flavin used the opportunity of the relocation to bring in his own management team. He replaced 80 out of the company's top 200 and most experienced executives. Many of these career employees openly criticized the changing company policy and the damaging downsizing. Many felt that Flavin had torn the conglomerate's sustaining inner fabric. These critics forgot that Donald Kircher had also cleaned house, but perhaps not in such a dramatic fashion.

During the early 1980s, the company rebounded as its marine and aerospace sales produced $36,000,000 in profits alone. Most of this substantial profit gain related to the company's technological lead in making simulators for both aircraft and space shuttle flight training. An indication of the Singer Company's expertise in this field comes out of the fact that it supplied much of the electronic instrumentation that filled NASA's Apollo lunar modules.

However, in 1979, ongoing downsizing efforts in Europe brought the company's oldest plant in Clydebank, Scotland, to a sudden close. This $130 million write-off further reduced Singer's hold on its core product, the sewing machine. As the 1980s progressed, Singer sewing machine profits continued dwindling. Ongoing pressure from low-priced Japanese machines and from European manufacturers like Bermina, Viking and Pfaff finally threw the giant sewing machine company against the ropes. Financial analysts as well as company management attributed the ongoing losses to encroachment from this low-end sewing machine market. A secret trending analysis warned of a final disappearance of the sewing machine market for all high-priced – and therefore American machines – entirely. This report merely echoed Lightner and Kircher's two-decade-old findings.

The 1980s marketplace had become one of computers, color televisions, home appliances and hi-fi stereos. Under Kircher, Singer had developed a strong presence in all these wildly expanding segments of the consumer marketplace. Critics lamented Singer's directors and shareholders for their premature decision to abandon the world's hottest consumer growth sectors.

Farewell

By 1987, the Singer Company, which no longer included its sewing machine product, survived as a $2 billion a year defense contractor producing flight simulators, electronic warfare and navigation systems for both aircraft and ships. It also manufactured sophisticated guidance electronics used in Trident missile systems. During the year, a report of a $20 million loss quickly drove its stock value downward. Before president Flavin could shore up this sudden downturn, he unexpectedly died at age 58. With his passing, Mr. Flavin's vision died; no one stepped forward to carry on the great financier's work.

"Private enterprise is ceasing to be free enterprise."
– Franklin Delano Roosevelt

Chapter Eleven

The Paul A. Bilzerian Era (1987-1989)
Junking the Conglomerate

After Joseph Flavin's death, the Singer Company suddenly found itself without direction. Where was Flavin's downsizing taking it and what should be the company's next move? Its problems were many. The company still struggled with an onerous debt load requiring payments of $500,000 per day. Singer had become a major defense contractor and now its profits slowed as defense spending went into a slump. Besides lackluster business, Singer stock had steadily declined after its July announcement of a $20 million loss due to unexpected R&D expenses in its aerospace divisions. Lastly, Joseph Flavin's public downsizing efforts in this difficult business climate had alerted the finance community that Singer was in trouble. Many corporate raiders now targeted the conglomerate as ripe for a takeover that could be easily paid for by select selling off of Singer's many profitable divisions.

Paul A. Bilzerian, a Florida-based corporate raider, was the Singer company's main admirer. The Florida investor with several other high-flying financiers had long coveted the Singer Company for eventual takeover. In fact, Bilzerian had attempted four previous hostile takeovers. It was widely reported that Bilzerian had earned no less than $50 million from other failed takeover attempts of other companies. Never giving up on his latest target, Bilzerian bided his time by hoarding Singer Company stock and quietly attracting investors from the banking industry. The ongoing disarray caused by Flavin's death now coupled with a sudden stock market instability gave the circling raider the opening he had hoped for.

On Black Monday, during the severe 1987 downturn in the stock market, which plummeted 508 points in a single day of trading,[297] corporate raider Paul A. Bilzerian purchased the Singer Company for $50 per share – $15 less than the going market value. Bilzerian managed to leverage a $1.1 billion buyout on a day when the market took the largest one day plunge in its history since 1914.[298] Bilzerian reportedly lined up the deal after four sleepless days of telephone solicitation to various investors and managed the buyout with $505 million of junk financing.

Paul Bilzerian and his backers knew of the company's existing debt load $500,000 per day interest payment. They had planned to sell Singer's flight simulator and defense divisions to pay off the heavy Singer loans and their own loans obtained for the raid. Unfortunately for 38-year-old Bilzerian, the rapid, across-the-board economic downturn, the weakened dollar, and the defense industry's downsizing greatly reduced his new acquisition's usual profit flow and worth. As a result, the conglomerate found itself in a new race for cash that made Paul Bilzerian appear hare-like against Joseph Flavin's turtle-like restructuring.

Within months of acquiring the Singer Company, Paul Bilzerian began liquidating his new assets for needed cash. Three hundred buyers, 200 of whom were foreign investors attracted by the weak American dollar, quickly expressed interest in owning Singer's many divisions. Eight of Singer's twelve divisions became cheap acquisitions for other avaricious conglomerates.

CAE Industries Ltd. bought the Link Flight Simulation Division for a bargain $550 million. The British Plessey Company purchased Singer's Electronic Systems Division for $310 million and the Japanese Ryobi Ltd. company purchased the power tools division for $325 million. West Germany's Ruhrgas A.G. bought Singer's American Meter Division for $132 million. General Instrument Corporation purchased Dalmo Victor, which made radar warning devices for Singer, for $175 million. HRB Singer went to the Hadson Corporation for $145 million and the Career Systems Development Division went for $20 million. Foreigners purchased three out of five of Singer's defense divisions. Besides selling off his major division, Bilzerian further reduced his operating expenses by radically downsizing the company's experienced workforce.[299]

Reportedly, this wholesale divestment, which took only four months to accomplish, brought in $2 billion which was more than enough to pay off the financier's junk financing. *Business Week* reported the Singer Company's debt load had leveled off at $1,825,000,000. The bulk of this financing was owed to a bank consortium led by Security Pacific and Bank of Nova Scotia.[300] The sell-off brought in plenty of money to pay everyone off and still return fabulous profits in a fortnight.

Bilzerian's reduced Singer holdings now consisted of five companies: Link Industrial, Kearfott Guidance and Navigation Systems, Link Miles and Librascope. Additionally, he still owned a 40 percent joint venture stake in Mitsubishi Precision and 1.9 million shares of SSMC, the Singer Sewing Machine Company spun off by Flavin in 1986. However, Paul Bilzerian's apparently successful financial moves nevertheless challenged the pared-down company with even more difficulties. Bilzerian's anti-business reputation and his well-known history for pursuing quick profits also limited his efforts at managing his remaining assets. Soon the troubled company became sluggish, like some supertanker unable to make headway.

During 1988, Bilzerian's pared-down conglomerate strained under S.E.C. and U.S. attorney Rudolf Giulliani's investigations. Giulliani inquired into suspected Bilzerian improprieties that may have taken place during the takeover. The

Singer Company itself was mired under numerous lawsuits from former employees over their pension rights and benefits and from buyers claiming they had overpaid for the divisions they had purchased. The Justice Department also sought triple compensation of $231,000,000 worth of alleged Defense Department contract overcharges. Finally, Singer stockholders became frustrated with Bilzerian's financial dealings and with the knowledge that their new owner had never successfully operated a business.

The end came when the Securities and Exchange Commission indicted Paul Bilzerian for violations unrelated to his Singer holdings. The S.E.C.'s successful prosecution of Bilzerian for stock market crimes, securities fraud, conspiring to commit tax fraud and for filing false financial disclosures to the S.E.C. forced the deal maker and the Singer Company into bankruptcy. In 1989, Paul Bilzerian was fined $1,500,000 and sentenced to a four year prison term. This term was later reduced to 20 months. On his release, Paul Bilzerian worked for a small Utah-based software marketing company as a consultant.

Farewell

Paul A. Bilzerian, like many former company leaders, was a hard-driving perfectionist. He was an intense man who often worked into the late night hours even at the expense of family life.[301] Nevertheless, it is known that he often flew home to Tampa in his private jet to coach his little league team. He often made this trip just to be present for his team's practice meetings.[302] He maintained close friendships with former college classmates and enjoyed golf and skiing. His design for his new Tampa, Florida, home included space for tennis courts, two swimming pools, and a basketball court.

Mr. Bilzerian, a native of Worcester, Massachusetts, was known as something of a rebel and was quoted by *Fortune* magazine, "I used to think that businessmen are money grubbing and greedy and need to be controlled."[303] Mr. Bilzerian reportedly left high school after being told he could not wear blue jeans to class. In 1968, in a sudden turnaround and to his great credit, Mr. Bilzerian easily passed a high-school equivalency exam, enlisted in the U.S. Army and made it through Officer Candidate School. As a Signal Corps officer Mr. Bilzerian volunteered for service in Viet Nam where he served for twelve months.

After his war-time service, Mr. Bilzerian went on to study Political Science at Stanford University where he was regarded as a serious student. In 1975, he entered Harvard's Business School where he earned an MBA. On graduation, he landed a job in the mergers and acquisition department of a forest products company, the Crown Zellerbach Corporation. He worked there for a year.

In 1978, he married Ms. Terri Steffen, a former Stanford classmate. The couple managed to buy a Florida radio station. Unfortunately, this venture ended in bankruptcy. Undaunted by this failed business experience, Paul Bilzerian moved on to earn a fortune through buying and selling Florida real estate. Soon his Biocoastal Financial Corporation claimed assets in excess of $200 million.

And What of SSMC's Future?

The SSMC barely existed after Bilzerian's machinations. At no time in its long history has the sewing machine maker's future looked so grim. Paul A. Bilzerian's raid on the Singer Company included a valuable lesson for preferred shareholders who learned that even their preferred stocks are not always a safe investment. Bilzerian's raid, his downsizing of the company for cash, and the bankruptcy of Biocoastal Corporation, which the Singer Corporation was renamed, reduced the value of the company's preferred stock to a small fraction of its previous worth.

After three years of litigation, shareholders were awarded a $3 million settlement – before attorney fees. The remainder was left to compensate 8,000 holders of 1.4 million preferred shares for their losses. How did these great financial losses affect the Singer Sewing Machine Company? Somehow SSMC stayed alive perhaps only because of its capable CEO, William F. Andrews. Andrews and his dedicated workforce stood tall while its controlling corporate parent crumbled to dust around them.

Notwithstanding these efforts, *The First Conglomerate* now appeared to have been reduced to a small, failing sewing machine manufacturer. Perhaps, only the company's longstanding reputation for quality products and its well-recognized trademark kept it from closing its doors. But how much longer could it survive on good will?

"We came in with a new focus." – James Ting

Chapter Twelve

The James H. Ting Era (1989-   )
Reinvesting the Future: Destiny Roused

In an attempt to head off personal bankruptcy, Paul
Bilzerian sold his 26.7 percent interest in the SSMC to a 38-year-
old Hong Kong businessman and computer maker, James H.
Ting. To James Ting, the company's financial problems seemed
superficial. The company's recent leaders had not appreciated the
value of 42,000 Singer retail outlets with locations in 100
countries, its experienced sales force, and perhaps most
importantly, its world-recognized Singer brand name trademark.
The Singer Company was still respected and known for fair play,
good value, and high-quality merchandise.

In Mr. Ting's view, Singer management undervalued the
company's growth potential in the emerging third world. "If
Singer had focused on its business and not ventured into
aerospace, it would have been a $10 billion company today. We
(Semi-Tech Global) came in with a new focus."[304] Nevertheless,
just as with Bilzerian management the company remained barely
profitable netting less than $20,000,000 during Ting's first two
years.[305]

The Past Comes Alive

However, James Ting intended to create the largest conglomerate of all times. Soon, the company began a miraculous turnaround. Once again, world markets clamored for Singer sewing machines. As in former times, the SSMC found new foreign markets. Profits poured in from less developed countries like China, Vietnam and many Latin America countries. Ting, like I. M. Singer and Edward Clark before him, had spurred foreign market growth by reintroducing easy financing.[306]

Within two years, this strategy produced a 44 percent increase in the SSMC's annual revenues that topped a quarter-billion dollars. In two more years, Singer sewing machine sales edged over a billion dollars in a single year while earning nearly a $100 million in profit. The company now reported more annual profit than it ever had throughout its long history. Most of these growth revenues came, as Mr. Ting had forecast, out of the company's Latin American and Asian markets.

Mr. Ting reintroduced and reinvigorated the company's historical methods of conducting business. When its U.S. market declined, it looked to new foreign marketplaces and it revived its efforts at reaching into developing countries. As in its historical past, it empowered local management and it resumed offering easy consumer credit; it also diversified its product line. Mr. Ting, like Lightner and Kircher before him, believed in large scale diversification. In 1991 for example, Ting's parent corporation, Semi-Tech Global (STG), acquired Japanese electronic manufacturer, Sansui. As a result, SSMC outlets began selling electronics, televisions, and refrigerators. However, unlike in the past, the SSMC no longer maintained its own production facilities. Instead, it outsourced its manufacturing needs to low-operating-cost countries like Brazil and Taiwan.

After acquiring the German sewing machine maker, Pfaff, on November 6, 1997, the Singer Sewing Machine Company once again became the largest sewing machine company in the world. Pfaff specialized in high-end industrial machines while the Singer product line had targeted low and mid-range sewing machines. As Mr. Ting said, "The acquisition is a fine example of synergy. The business of Pfaff and Singer are complementary.

Pfaff specializes in high-end industrial sewing machines; Singer manufactures mainly low-end to mid-range industrial models. Our consumer lines also complement each other. Pfaff will now be able to take advantage of Singer's greatest strength, marketing and distributing in developing markets." The Pfaff acquisition added 185 company-owned stores and 4,200 mass merchants and dealers to the Singer conglomerate.

Diversification Returns

In 1998, the Singer Sewing Machine Company again became the leading manufacturer, marketer and distributor of consumer sewing machines by claiming 40.2 percent of the world's entire sewing machine sales. The company's sewing machine product line consisted mostly of straight stitch, artisan (a light industrial zigzag machine), and electronic domestic zigzag machines. Zigzag machines became the company's main sewing machine product. The company continued to market a diverse product line of consumer electronics including: televisions, video cassette recorders, stereos, compact disc players, portable audio cassette players, and home appliances such as refrigerators, gas ranges, water filters, washing machines, dishwashers, dryers, ironing and pressing products, juicers and blenders, power tools and home furnishings such as bedroom, dining room, occasional and ready-to-assemble furniture.

The SSMC is today located in 140 countries around the world where it operates 1,500 retail centers. More than 18,000 canvassers and an estimated 54,300 independent retailers and mass merchants continue to market the Singer sewing machine.

James H. Ting

No measure of the SSMC's success is complete without taking note of its new leader, James H. Ting. Mr. Ting was born in China, raised in Hong Kong, and attended college in Canada. He is another dedicated, perhaps work-obsessed capitalist, who has, at 44 years of age, not found time for a family of his own. Mr. Ting made his mark during the high-flying 1980s computer market. Ting manufactured computers in Hong Kong and then shipped them to avaricious Canadian and American markets.

When the computer marketplace took a nosedive in the late 1980s, Ting's renamed company, International Semi-Tech Microelectronics, Ltd., dipped close to bankruptcy and barely survived as a $20 million company. But, now 20 years since he founded his company, James Ting's parent holding company, Semi-Tech Corporation (STC), has grown from its initial $100,000 in assets to a company valued at $2.8 billion today.

Mr. Ting's continuing diversification of his company and his frequent public stock offerings have worked to consistently move his parent Semi-Tech Corporation into becoming an enormous conglomerate. The 1989 Singer Company $240 million acquisition proved a milestone by pushing STC's assets over the one billion dollar mark. A 1991 public stock offering increased the SSMC stock by 130 percent over a three year period. In 1995, Singer's worldwide sewing machine market share rose to 41 percent. Its closest competitor, the Brother sewing machine company, claimed only 10 percent of all sewing machines sold around the world. At the same time, the SSMC's Japanese market, which its affiliate Singer Nikko controls, produced diversified product annual sales that topped $100 million.

The SSMC has learned to segment its market. Its low-end models target beginner and budget-minded buyers; its mid-priced machines add more easy-to-use features; and its high-end models, which target its experienced customers, offer all features such as a low-noise magnetic bobbin system, built-in accessory storage and automatic tensioning. The company manufactures its mid-range machines in Brazil and all its other models in Taiwan.

As in the old days, Singer salesmen continue to entice existing customers into trading up to more feature-rich and advanced machines. Its salesmen especially push its latest electronic models that create sophisticated patterns from computer files. For example, Singer's model SJ-1, Scanner and Sew, can reproduce a pattern scanned out of a magazine.

Besides sewing machines, the SSMC's diverse durable goods product line, which it markets through its own distribution system, now comprises 47 percent of all its sales. The Singer Company's diverse product line is ironically reminiscent of the Kircher days. Its many retail outlets offer, beside sewing machines, a varied product line including electronics such as televisions, stereos, various audio products, cordless power tools, ironing and other pressing tools, vapocleaners (a combination steam and vacuum cleaner) and small appliances such as blenders. Its Akai subsidiary makes VCR's and audio and video equipments. Sansui produces high-end audio equipment. Its Kong Wah Chinese company makes low cost televisions. It has also found success in manufacturing home furnishings and ready-to-assemble furniture out of its cabinet-making factories. Singer furniture products sell well in the Middle East, the Carribean and Thailand. Nineteen ninety six furniture sales brought in $90 million.

The Singer Company also sells, in another throw back to the Kircher years, $150 million a year of major appliances like refrigerators, washing machines, dryers, dishwashers and kitchen ranges. Its new line of water filters expects to produce an added $60 million in annual sales. Such products, from its low cost faucet-mount to its large 30,000 gallon capacity water filter systems, have great appeal in underdeveloped countries where municipal water treatment plants remain too expensive for local government. Besides these specific examples, SSMC's continues to acquire qualifying companies and subsidiaries that fit with the new conglomerate's complete product line. Structured diversification, which Donald Kircher emphasized, has returned bringing handsome profits.

Conclusion

Under James Ting, the Singer Company remains the only sewing machine company that does not manufacture solely for wholesale distribution. The SSMC continues to ship directly from 15 manufacturing facilities to its end users. Singer sewing manufacturing goes on in Viet Nam, the Philippines, Thailand, Sri Lanka, Brazil, Hong Kong and Mexico. Three Mexican plants make furniture, washing machines and other small appliances. Thailand's 303 Singer stores provide the company's largest market with $300 million in sales. In Sri Lanka, the company added a 15,000 square foot mega-retail store to its existing chain of 81 retail stores. The company's distribution network has nearly doubled in the last few years and now reaches 79,000 points of sale. The U.S. and Canada provide 18,000 sales locations. Its largest U.S. customer is Wal-Mart. It continues to expand in Brazil, Portugal, Mexico, Thailand, India, Bangladesh, North Africa, South Africa, and Pakistan.

In many developing countries, The Singer Company remains the only source of credit or installment buying. In Mexico, for example, credit or installment buying remains relatively rare excepting the Singer Company. As in its historical past, offering credit brings a sales advantage that competitors once again refuse to offer. The company reports that installment buying in poorer countries accounts for a third of its sales. Remarkably, only 2 out of 100 of its credit customers default on loans. The Singer Company is essentially participating in the rising living standards of Latin America, Africa, South Africa, India, China and all Asia. Asia is the fastest growing region in the world and the Singer Company has an established presence and foresees unlimited opportunity.

According to Mr. Ting, when new markets open to commerce, the usual first purchase is a sewing machine purchased through his company's installment plan. As emerging markets mature, the company's sales of durable goods show regular increases. From 1990 through 1995, Singer's emerging markets earnings rose 72 percent.

During the 1990s, Mr. Ting, like his fabled predecessors, was again challenged by a worldwide recession, volatile currency devaluations, foreign exchange rate fluctuations and worldwide inflation. For example, in Mexico, soaring interest rates reduced the SSMC's 1994 earnings by $15 million. Recent financial crises in Asian and European markets have also challenged Ting's presidency. During these recent market jitters, African and Middle East revenues have increased while U.S. and Canadian revenues have remained steady.

James Ting has also relied on his R&D departments to bring out new products. In 1995 alone, his R&D brought out three new zigzag models. Through R&D, the company has recently developed two new product lines of novel power tools and water purifiers. Like all his predecessors, Ting recognizes that the company's competitive edge rests largely with ongoing R&D.

Under James Ting, the Singer Sewing Machine Company has resumed its place alongside the world's conglomerates. Once again, hard-working and competent Singer men and women travel the world's trade routes. And once again, *The First Conglomerate* has reclaimed its people and rediscovered its proven byways. This great company, this great spiritual entity, has returned to the course set by its distinguished historical leadership.

Endnotes

1. Bourne, Frederick G., "American Sewing-Machines," reprinted in *1795 1895: One Hundred Years of American Commerce*, ed. by Depew, Chauncey M., LL. D., Greenwood Press Publishers, New York, 1968, p.535.
2. Singer Company, *The Singer SewingMachine: America's Chief Contribution to Civilization*," New York, Singer Co., 1911, p.3.
3. Kobler, John. "Mr. Singer's Money Machine," *Saturday Evening Post*, 28 July 1951, v224, no. 4, p. 104.
4. Cooper, Grace Rogers, *History of the Sewing Machine*, Smithsonian Institution, Bulletin 254, Washington, D.C., 1968.
   This work contains numerous photos of old sewing machines and a detailed chronology of sewing machine development.
5. "The Story of the Sewing Machine. Its Invention - Improvements - Social, Industrial and Commercial Importance," *New York Times*, January 7, 1860, 2:2.
6. Godfrey, Frank P. *An International History of the Sewing Machine*, Robert Hale Limited, 1982, p. 18.
7. "Home-Sewing Booms Singer," *Business Week*, August 14, 1 948, p.75
8. ibid., p.75.
9. ibid., pp.75-76.
10. ibid., p.75.
11. Davies, Robert Bruce. *Peacefully Working to Conquer the World: Singer Sewing Machines in Foreign Markets*, New York City, Arno Press, 1976, p.103.
12. ibid., p.154 and also Brandon, Ruth. *A Capitalist Romance*, New York: J. B. Lippincott Company, 1977, p.167.
13. Birmingham, Stephen, *Life at the Dakota: New York's Most Unusual Address*, New York, Random House, 1979, p.23.
4. Lyon, Peter, "Isaac Singer and His Wonderful Sewing Machine," in *Great Stories of American Businessmen*, New York, American Heritage Publishing Co., Inc., 1954, pp.147.
15. Ibid., p.27.
16. Davies, p.31.
17. Lyon, p.146.
18. Kobler, John, *Saturday Evening Post*, July 14, 1951, v224, no.2, p.22.
19. Eastley, Charles M. *The Singer Saga*, Brauton & Devon England: Merlin Books Ltd., 1983, p.11.
20. Ibid., p. 10.
21. Ibid., p.11.
22. Ibid., p.11.
23. Brandon, p.33.
24. Ibid., p.33.
25. Scott, John, *Genius Rewarded: or The Story of the Sewing Machine*, New York, John J. Gaulon, Printer, No.20 Vesey Street, 1880, p.19.
26. Brandon, p.50.
27. Singer Company, *The Singer Sewing Machine: America 's Chief Contribution to Civilization*, New York, Singer Co., 1911, pp.6-7.
28. article reprinted in Singer Company, p.9.
29. "Archives Picture Sewing Progress," *New York Times*, July 2, 1951, 15:2.
30. Scott, p.10.
31. Singer Company, p.4.
32. Bourne, p.534.
33. Brandon, p.52.
34. Kaempffert, Waldemar, ed. *A Popular History of American Invention*, New York, Charles Scribner's Sons, 1924, vol.11, p.389.
35. *The Singer Sewing Machine*, The Singer Company 1911, p.7.

36. See Eastley for Singer's collusion with his wife's attorney, pp.26-33.
37. Lyon, p.150.
38. Eastley, p.39.
39. Brandon, p.197-8.
40. Eastley, pp.26, 30, 33.
41. *New York Daily Tribune*, December 28, 1875, in Davies, p.9.
42. Birmingham, p.29.
43. Brandon, p.212; Eastley p.36.
44. Groner, Alex. In *American Business & Industry*, American Heritage Publishing Co, Inc., New York, p.131.
45. Brandon, p.12.
46. Lyons, p.147.
47. , "The Story of the Sewing-Machine," *New York Times* January 7, 1860,2:2.
48. Davies thesis, introduction, p.1.
49. Cooper, p.164.
50. Kaempffert, pp. 320-321.
51. ibid., p.322.
52. Clark, Victor S. *History of Manufactures in the United States*, Carnegie Institute of Washington, 1929, p.400.
53. ibid., p.322.
54. Clark, p. 438-439, and Ward, 3. T. *The Factory System*, Barnes & Noble, New York, 19--, Vol.1, p.65.
55. Kaempffert, p.322.
56. Kaempffert, Waldemar, ed. *A Popular History of American Invention*, New York, Charles Scribner's Sons, 1924, vol.11, p.322.
57. "The Story of the Sewing Machine," *New York Times*, 7 January 1860, 2:2.
58. Godfrey p.19 and English, W. *The Textile Industry*, Longmans, Green and Co. Ltd., London and Harlow, 1969. p.211.
59. Plummer, John. "The Sewing Machine; Its Industrial and Social Results," in *The British almanac of the Society for the Diffusion of Useful Knowledge for the Year...*, London: Charles Knight, 1877, p.96.
60. Davies, p.21.
61. Kaemppfert, p.404.
62. Cooper, p.40.
63. Iles, George. *Leading American Inventors*, New York, Henry Holt and Company, 1912, p. 341.
64. Plummer, John. pp.95-115.
65. Kaempffert, p.404.
66. Ewers, William, Baylor, H.W., *Sincere 's History of the Sewing Machine*, Sincere Press, Phoenix, Arizona, p.7-8.
67. Iles, p.338.
68. Godfrey, p.25, includes James Henderson as fellow patent owner.
69. Cooper, p.6.
70. Ibid., p. 137-138, Plummer p.97 and Godfrey pp. 321-33.
71. Kaempffert, p.378.
72. ibid., p.378.
73. Plummer, p.97.
74. ibid., p.379.
75. Kaempffert, p.379.
76. Bourne, p.525.
77. Brandon, p.9.
78. Kaempffert, p.381.
79. ibid., p.381.
80. Brandon, p.59.
81. Scott, p.12.
82. ibid., p.59, and Lyon p.148.
83. Brian Bunch and Alexander Heilemans, *The Timetables of Technology*, Simon & Schuster, New York, 1993, p.247.

84. Kaempffert, pp. 381-3 89, and Plummer, pp.95-i 00.
85. Scott, p.10.
86. Bourne, p.525.
87. Scott, p.16.
88. Kaempffert, p.381.
89. Kaempffert, p.381.
90. Kaempffert, p.382.
91.Parton, James. *Famous Men: Triumphs of Enterprise, Ingenuity, and Public Spirit*, New York, James Miller, Publisher, 1880, c. 1874, p.139.
92. Kaempffert, p.383.
93. Kaempffert, p.383.
94. lies, p.345.
95. Parton, *History of the Sewing Machine*, p.146.
96. ibid., p.142.
97. Kaempffert, p.383.
98. Iles, p.346.
99. ibid., p.351.
100. Godfrey, p.48.
101. ibid., p.352.
102. Bourne, p.526.
103. Davies, Robert Bruce. *The International Operations of the Singer Manufacturing Company, 1854-1895*, Doctoral thesis at the University of Wisconsin, 1967, p.73.
104. Iles, p.355.
105. Parton, *Famous Men*, p.155.
106. ibid., p.155.
107. Scott, p.16.
108. Ibid., p.14.
109. Iles, p.357.
110. Parton, *Famous Men*, p.157.
111. Ibid., *Famous Men*, p.160.
112. Brandon, p.95.
113. Iles, p.363.
114. Ibid., p.368.
115. Ibid., p.368.
116. Cooper, pp.24-25.
117. Godfrey, p.46.
118. Kaempffert, pp.391-392.
119. Cooper, p.26.
120. Bourne, pp.526-527.
121. ibid., pp.392-393.
122. Davies thesis, p.17.
123. Lyon, p.150.
124. Davies thesis, p.17.
125. Ibid., p.22.
126. Singer Company, *The Singer Sewing Machine*, 1911, p.12.
127. Birmingham, p.24, and Lyon p.152.
128. Brandon, p.84.
129. Singer Company, 1911 publication, p.12.
130. Ibid., p.18.
131. Lyon, p.153.
132. Bourne, p.529.
133. Davies, p.19.
134. Birmingham, p.27.
135. Cooper, p.47.
136. Davies, p.16.
137. Bourne, p.529.
138. Clark, p.401.
139. Godftey, p.20.

140. Davies thesis, p.74.
141. Davies thesis, pp.36-38.
142. Cartensen, Fred V. *American Enterprise in Foreign Markets: Studies of Singer and International Harvester in Imperial Russia*, University of North Carolina Press, Chapel Hill and London, 1984, p.5.
143. Davies thesis, p.75.
144. Bourne, p.535.
145. Davies, p.44.
146. Davies thesis, p.200.
147. Wilkins, p.37.
148.See Brandon, pp.97-99, Davies, pp.22-27, Godfrey, pp.79-82, and Cooper, pp.41-42, for discussions of the "Sewing Machine Combination."
149. Boume, p.528. Frederick Bourne is the only source who has recorded Orlando Potter's presidency of the Grover & Baker Sewing Machine Company.
150. Lyon, p.152.
151. Bourne, p.530.
152. Cooper, p.41.
153. Carstensen, p.14.
154. Groner, p.133.
155. Bourne, p.535.
156. Clark, p.521.
157. The Singer Company, *The Singer Sewing Machine*, p.29.
158. Lyon p.146, Davies, p.31-32 and Davies thesis, p.47.
159. Davies thesis, p.28.
160. ibid., p.48.
161. Brandon, p.181, and Davies thesis, p.48.
162. Davies, p.33. Note that Hopper's selection is viewed differently by Brandon, p.181.
163. Brandon, p.181.
164. Kobler, John. *Saturday Evening Post*, July 28, 1951, v 224, no.4, p.25.
165. Davies, p.35.
166. Davies thesis, p.81.
167. Ibid., p.64.
168. Davies, p.34.
169. Lyon, Peter. "Isaac Singer and His Wonderful Sewing Machine," in *Great Stories of American Businessmen*, New York, American Heritage Publishing Co., Inc., 1954, pp.146.
170. Quoted in Brandon, p.87.
171. Birmingham, p.26.
172. Kobler, p.103.
173. Singer Company 1911, p.22.
174. Davies, p.55.
175. Ibid., p.150.
176. Bourne, p.529.
177. Davies, pp.280-281.
178. Godfrey, p.262.
179. Brandon, p.172.
180. Davies thesis, p.51.
181. Ibid., p.51.
182. Ibid., p.121.
183. Ibid., p.122.
184. Wilkins, Mira. *The Emergence of Multinational Enterprise: American Business Abroad from the Colonial Era to 1914*, Cambridge, MA: Harvard University Press, 1970, p.43.
185. Wilkins, p.45.
186. ibid., p.34.
187. Scott, p.29.
188. Davies, p.185.
189. Davies thesis, p.276.
190. Wilkins, p.68.
191. Carstensen, p.32.

192. Davies thesis, p.65.
193. Davies, p.57.
194. Plummer, p.103.
195. Davies thesis, p.54.
196. Kobler, part IV, p.104.
197. Davies, p.76.
198. Wilkins, p.43.
199. Ibid., p.46.
200. Davies, p.78.
201. Davies, p.83.
202. See Davies pp.92-110, Davies thesis pp.272-299, and Carstensen pp.33-36.
203. Davies thesis, p.273 and Peacefully Working to Conquer the World p.90.
204. Wilkins, p.70.
205. Ibid., p.71.
206. Ibid., p.72-73.
207. Davies, pp.92-94.
208. Ibid., p.100.
209. Vpp.98-99.
210. See Bourne discussion pp.531-534.
211. Bourne, p.533.
212. Ibid., p.533.
213. Ibid., p.531.
214. Davies, p.107.
215. Godfrey, p.137.
216. Singer Company, p.24.
217. Ibid., p.28 and Bourne p.535.
218. ibid., p.29.
219. Bourne, p.535.
220. Davies thesis, p.283.
221. Cartensen, pp.65-6.
222. Ibid., p.33.
223. ibid., p.33.
224. ibid., p.35.
225. Ibid., pp.56-7.
226. "Singer's Surprises," *New York Times*, 21 May 1959, 44:2.
227. Davies, pp.93-141.
228. Davies thesis, p.274
229. Davies, p.109.
230. Ibid., p.143.
231. Kobler, *Saturday Evening Post*, July 28, 1951, v224, no.4, p.105.
232. ibid., p.105.
233. Davies p.151.
234. Ibid., p.160.
235. Ibid., pp. 162-3.
236. Sincere, p.186.
237. Kobler, III, p.114.
238. Ewers, p.174.
239. Kobler, John. *Saturday Evening Post*, 7 July 1951, v224, no.1, pp. 17-19+.
240. ibid., p.87.
241. ibid., p.203.
242. Godfrey, p.167.
243. ibid., p.170.
244. Davies, p.150.
245. Kobler, John. *Saturday Evening Post*, July 21, 1951, v224, no., pp.112.
246. "7,000 go on Strike at Singer Factory," *New York Times*, May 3, 1949, 21:3.
247. "City Feels Impact of Singer Strike," *New York Times*, May 3, 1949, 21:3.
248. "Bridgeport Union Ends Singer Strike," *New York Times*, October 3, 1949, 10:1.
249. "Sewing Machines Face Record Sales," *New York Times*, December 10, 1952, 56:5.

250. Godfrey, p.165.
251. "Japan Spurs Sales of Sewing Machine," *New York Times*, September 9, 1951, 11:1.
252. "Japanese Mark Set In Sewing Machines," *New York Times*, January 15, 1953, 36:8.
253. "Pfaff Unit Output Surpasses Pre-War," *New York Times*, August 8, 1951, 39:5.
254. "Pfaff To Push Sale of Sewing Machine, " *New York Times*, August 7, 1952, 25:2.
255. "Swedish Concern Plans Drive Here, "*New York Times*, May 29, 1952, 21:3.
256. "Brother v. Singer," *New York Times*, March 30 1955, 41:4.
257. "Japanese To Push Appliances Here," *New York Times*, March 24, 1955, 45:2.
258. "Singer to Build Charlotte Plant," *New York Times*, May 22, 1952, 46:2.
259. "Pfaff Unit Output Surpasses Pre-War," *New York Times*, August 8, 1951, 39:5.
260. "New Stitching Device Out," *New York Times*, January 7, 1953, 23:5.
261. "Miscellany, Nechhi-Elna Sales" *New York Times*, July 10, 1956, 42:3.
262. "Sears Turns to Japan For Sewing Machines," *New York Times*, June 19, 1957, 49:3.
263. "More Industries Score Tariff Cuts," *New York Times*, February 4, 1955, 8:3.
264. ibid., p.88.
265. *Time*, 16 December, 1957.
266. "Nixon Tells N. A. M. of Urgency To Counter a Soviet 'Offensive,'" *New York Times*, December 7,1957, 16:5.
267. Singer," *Forbes,* 15 October 1964, pp. 23.
268. Author's several interviews with Mr. Sam Harvey, who served in Mr. Kircher's corporate president's office for more than a decade, provides the background material for Mr. Kircher's life and accomplishments.
269. "Singer Plans Fight of Antitrust Suit," *New York Times*, December 24, 1959, 5:2.
270. "Singer Adds Two to Board," *New York Times*, June 24, 1954, 45:6.
271. "Sewing Machines Stage A Comeback," *New York Times*, February 24, 1952, III, 11:4.
272. "Singer's Surprises," *New York Times*, May 21, 1959, 44:2.
273. "Estate To Sell Stock In Singer," *New York Times*, April 25, 1964, 24:4.
274. "How the Directors Kept Singer Stitched Together, *Fortune*, December 1975, pp. 102.
275. "Singer Slates Turkish Plant," *New York Times*, 27 August 1959, 36:4.
276. "Japan Approves Deal: Singer Sewing Machine to Join with Company There," *New York Times*, October 8, 1959, 57:2.
277. Singer Company Special Report," *Forbes*, October 15, 1964, p.21.
278. "Faces Behind the Figures," *Forbes*, February 15, 1968, 101:56.
279. Smith, Hedrick. "Soviet Eases Visa Rule; Singer Co. Presses Plan," *New York Times,*April 14, 1973, 43:4.
280. Author's interview with Sam Harvey.
281. "For Reasons of Health," *Forbes*, May 15, 1976, 117:102-103.
282. "Singer's Dividend is Cut 40C to 10C," *New York Times*, February 14, 1975, 51:2.
283. ibid.
284. "How the Directors Kept Singer Stitched Together, *Fortune*, December 1975, pp.186.
285. "Why the Profits Vanished at Singer," *Business Week*, June 30, 1975, pp. 106-108.
290. "Faces Behind the Figures: Flavin of Singer," *Forbes*, January 25, 1977, 119:72:6.
291. "Flavin's Master Plan for Ailing Singer, *Business Week*, May 10, 1976, p.66.
292. North, Sterling. *New England Business*, "Singer Spins Off Its Homespun Roots for HighTech, Defense Concentration," vol.8, Iss: 7, April 21, 1986, pp.39-40.
293. Sampson, Anthony. *The Sovereign State of ITT*, Stein and Day, NY, 1973, p.298.
294. "Faces Behind the Figures: Flavin of Singer," *Forbes*, January 25, 1977, 119:72:6.
295. ibid.
296. Sterba, James P. "Singer Co. Is Moving to Stamford To Surprise of New York Officials," *New York Times*, June 14, 1978, II, 3:1
297. Engardio, Pete. *Business Week*, 23 November 1987, p: 62, 66.
298. Fierman, Jaclyn. "Boone's New Partner," *Fortune*, :89+, March 28, 1988.
299. Curtis, Carol. *CFO: The Magazine for Chief Financial Officers,* "Aftermath of an LBO (Leveraged Buyout)," vol.6, iss: 4, April 1990, pp.20-26.
300. Mitchell, Russell. *Business Week*, "Can Paul Bilzerian Fatten Singer for the Kill?" May 16, 1988, pp.43-44.
301. Byrnes, Nanette. "The Ting Dynasty?" *Financial World*, vol.163, May 10, 1994, p: 28-33.

302. Ibid., p.30.
296. Author's interview.
287. McNeil Jr., Donald G. "Ex Head of Singer Company Slain In Jersey; Brother-in-Law Is Held," *New York* Times, May 2, 1978, 28:1.
288. Author's interview.
289. "Xerox Officer to Head Singer," *New York Times*, November 11, 1975, 43:6.
290. "Faces Behind the Figures: Flavin of Singer," *Forbes*, January 25,1977, 119:72:6.
291. "Flavin's Master Plan for Ailing Singer, *Business Week*, May 10, 1976, p.66.
292. North, Sterling. *New England Business*, "Singer Spins Off Its Homespun Roots for High Tech, Defense Concentration," vol.8, Iss: 7, April 21, 1986, pp.39-40.
293. Sampson, p.298.
294. "Faces Behind the Figures: Flavin of Singer," *Forbes*, January 25, 1977, 119:72:6.
295. ibid.
296. Sterba, James P. "Singer Co. Is Moving to Stamford To Surprise of New York Officials," *New York Times*, June 14, 1978, II, 3:1
297. Engardio, Pete. *Business Week*, November 23, 1987, p: 62, 66.
298. Fierman, Jaclyn. "Boone's New Partner," *Fortune*, :89+, March 28, 1988.
299. Curtis, pp.20-26.
300. Mitchell, Russell. *Business Week*, "Can Paul Bilzerian Fatten Singer for the Kill?" May 16, 1988, pp.43-44.
301. Fierman, p. 92.
302. "Paul Bilzerian Still Don't Get No Respect, " *Business Week*, November 23, 1987, pp. 62-63.
303. Ibid.
304. Byrnes, Nanette. "The Ting Dynasty?" *Financial World*, vol. 163, May 10, 1994, pp. 28-33.
305. Ibid, p. 30.
306. Hawkins, Chuck; Lee, Dinah; King, Resa W. "Who is James Ting and What Will He Buy Next?" *Business Week*, February 13, 1989, p. 33.

Years of Singer Company Presidents

1851-1863	Edward S. Clark and Isaac M. Singer
1863-1876	Inslee A. Hopper
1876-1882	Edward S. Clark
1882-1889	George Ross McKenzie
1889-1905	Frederick Gilbert Bourne
1905-1949	Sir Douglas Alexander
1949-1958	Milton Clarkson Lightner
1958-1975	Donald Peter Kircher (d. 1978)
1975-1987	Joseph B. Flavin (d. 1987)
1987-	William Smead/William F. Andrews
1987-1988	Paul Bilzerian
1989-	James H. Ting, Chairman of the Board and Chief Executive Officer

Author's Working Timeline

1755	Charles F. Weisenthal patents two-pointed needle with centered eye.
1790	17 July, Thomas Saint patents a leather sewing machine.
	Oliver Evans invents an "automatic flour mill."
1792	Walter Hunt, sewing machine inventor, is born in New York.
1804	Glasgow's J. Duncan patents an embroidery machine.
1805	14 February, Parisian, J. Stone, patents a sewing machine.
1811	27 October, Isaac Merritt Singer is born.
	19 December, Edward S. Clark is born in Athens, New York.
1812	War of 1812 introduces the Industrial Revolution to America.
1818	John Knowles VT, first American sewing machine inventor.
1819	9 July, Elias Howe, Jr., sewing machine inventor is born.
1820	George Ross McKenzie is born in Kingussie, Scotland.
1821	Singer's mother, Ruth, abandons her son.
1823	A 12-year-old Singer leaves home.
1824	18 October, Allan B. Wilson, is born in Willet, N.Y.
1826	American Lye patents a sewing machine but records lost in 1936 Patent Office fire.
1828	Josue Heilmann patents a multi-needle embroidery machine.
1830	19-year-old Isaac Singer joins a traveling actor's troupe.
	Isaac Singer marries 15-year-old Catherine Maria Haley.
	30 June, B. Thimmonier, invents wood frame stitching machine.
	France feels effects of the Industrial Revolution for the first time.
	Edward Clark enters Ambrose Jordan's law office in Hudson, NY.
1831	First clothing factory opens in New York City.
1833	Edward S. Clark begins law practice in Poughkeepsie.
	Walter Hunt develops his "seaming and sewing" machine.
1834	Walter Hunt patents his sewing machine.
	Isaac Singer's first child, William, is born.
1835	Isaac Singer moves to New York City.
1836	In Baltimore, Isaac Singer meets 18-year-old Mary Ann Sponsler.
1837	Births of second son with Mary Ann Sponsler and a daughter with his legal wife.
	Edward Clark and Ambrose Jordan form a law partnership in NYC.
	Year of financial depression affecting the textile industries.
1839	28-year-old Isaac Singer joins his brother on Canal project.
	Isaac Singer patents a rock drilling machine earning $2,000.
	"The Merritt Players," Isaac Singer's traveling acting troupe.
1840	Voulettie Theresa Singer is delivered by Mary Ann Sponsler.
1841	Englishmen Newton and Archibold patent the eye-pointed needle.
	On 4 May, they receive patent for a sewing machine.
1842	21 February, John Greenough first U.S. sewing machine patent.
1843	4 March, Benjamin Bean receives 2nd U.S. sewing machine patent.
	27 December, George H. Corliss, third U.S. sewing machine patent.

27 December, George H. Corliss, third U.S. sewing machine patent.
Mary Ann Sponsler gives birth to a son, John Albert Singer.

1844   Fredericksburg, OH, Singer works in print shop carving typeface.
Isaac Singer patents a "Machine for Carving Wood and Metal"
I. M. Singer (Sponsler) family returns to New York City.
Mary Ann Sponsler delivers another daughter, Fannie Elizabeth.
American Walter Hunt invents a working sewing machine.

1846   Singer opens a wood type and sign-making shop in Pittsburg, PA..
Mary Ann Sponsler delivers another son, Joseph Singer.
10 September, Elias Howe, Jr., patents a two-thread, lockstitch
sewing machine.
December, Englishman W. Thomas steals Howe's patent and
obtains a British patent.
26-year-old Scottish immigrant, George Ross McKenzie, arrives.
5 February, Elias Howe sails to England.

1848   Thimmonier and Magnin open the first French sewing machine
manufacturing company that is destroyed by the French Revolution
leaving both men financially ruined.

1849   Singer moves back to NYC's east side neighborhood with new
patents for his enhanced typeface carving machine in hand. An
explosion at A. B. Taylor's destroys Singer's typeface carving
machine and the lives of 63 workmen.
Mary Ann Sponsler delivers another daughter, Mary Olive Singer.
George B. Zeiber, becomes Singer's new financial backer.
May, John Bachelder, patent no. 6,439 for a single-thread chain-
stitch sewing machine.
Englishman C. Morey patents a running stitch sewing machine.
April, Elias Howe returns penniless from England.

1850   12 November, Allan B. Wilson, patents the four motion feed.
Thimmonier awarded an American patent for his sewing machine.
In August, Zeiber/ Singer bring the type carving machine to Boston.
Zeiber, Phelps and Singer form a partnership.
Isaac Singer creates his first sewing machine.
10 December, Frederick R. Robinson patents a sewing machine.
December, Singer buys Phelps' share in his company for $4,000.00.
Mary Ann Sponsler delivers a son, Charles Alexander.
Isaac Singer introduces the treadle machine.

1851   12 February, Grover & Baker patent a sewing machine.
12 August, Singer patents his sewing machine (#8294) and begins
production in Boston.
12 August, Allan B. Wilson receives sewing machine patent(#8296).
Singer retains attorney Edward S. Clark. Clark accepts one-third of
Singer's company as compensation for his legal fees. I. M. Singer
& Company emerges (c. 1 January 1851).
William O. Grover, patents the double chain-stitch process.

George McKenzie enters Singer employment as a cabinetmaker.
Mary Walters gives birth to a daughter, Alice Eastwood (Merritt).

1851 Edward S. Clark oversees the Singer Company.
Brown, J. R. invents vernier caliper permitting fine measurement.

1852 Clark opens first branch offices in Boston, Philadelphia and NYC.
In March, I. M. Singer tricks George Zeiber into selling his third share for a pittance.
April 13, Singer patents a tension device.
Mary Ann Sponsler gives birth to Julia Ann who survives two years.
Mary McGonical provides a daughter named Ruth.
The *No. 1 Standard* goes on the market.

1853 Amasa B. Howe opens a sewing machine factory.
Grover & Baker open their sewing machine business.
I.M. Singer & Co. setup corporate offices and a manufacturing facility in New York City.
I. M. Singer & Co. renamed to the Singer Manufacturing Company.
The Singer Company issues 5,000 shares of stock.
23 March, contract signed with French agent, Charles Callebout.

1854 Elias Howe successfully sues the Singer Manufacturing Company for patent infringement. In May, an agreement is reached.
May 30, Singer patents a chain stitch machine.
The *No. 2 Standard* goes on the market.
Singer becomes world's largest sewing machine maker.
Edward Clark takes up residence in Cooperstown, NY
Charles Alexander, Singer's four-year-old son dies.

1855 The Singer company begins overseas expansion.
Singer awarded first prize at World's Fair in Paris.
Singer opens a branch office in Paris after sale of French patent to Charles Callebout.
October 9, Singer patents embroidering sewing machine.
September, the company ends selling of 'territorial sales rights.'
George McKenzie loans Singer $5,000 to keep the company afloat.

1856 The Sewing Machine Combination forms.
Singer introduces the first machine targeted to the domestic market.
James A. E. Gibbs patents an automatic chain-stitch machine.
A branch office opens in Glasgow, Scotland.
March 18, Singer patents a ruffler and tucker.
June 3, Singer patents a binder.
The *No. 3 Standard* goes on the market.
The *Turtle Back* goes on the market.
Grover & Baker produce first portable sewing machine encased in wood carrying case.
Mary Ann Sponsler delivers another daughter named Julia Ann.
Edward Clark initiates hire-purchase plan initiated.

1857 5 July, Barthelemy Thimmonier dies.

Mary Ann Sponsler delivers a daughter, Caroline Virginia.

Singer establishes headquarters and showroom at 458 Broadway.

1858   The Grasshopper arrives. The first lightweight domestic machine.

Branch office opens in Rio de Janiero, Brazil.

5 July 1857, Barthelemy Thimmonier sewing machine inventor dies.

1859   "Letter A" introduced. An improved domestic sewing machine.

Singer Company cuts its sewing machine prices to half.

April 8, Singer receives first of three patents for lock stitch vibrating shuttle machines.

Walter Hunt passes away.

Willcox & Gibbs opens its doors on Broadway, NYC.

1860   23 January, Singer succeeds in divorcing Catherine Haley.

7 August, Mary Ann Sponsler brings assault charges against Singer.

19 September, Isaac Singer moves to Europe.

1861   July, Singer returns to New York with Isabella Summerville.

Singer European sales surpass its American sales.

U.S. Civil War begins.

Alonzo Kimball becomes Singer's Glasgow, Scotland, agent.

Singer hires representative, W. E. Broderick, in London, England.

1862   London's International Industrial Exhibition.

Of 300,000 US sewing machines, 75,000 belong to homemakers.

Georg Pfaff invents an industrial machine to sew leather in Kaiserslautern, Germany.

1863   13 June, Singer marries Isabella Eugenie Summerville.

25 June, Isabella conceives the first of six Singer offspring, Adam Mortimer Singer.

6 June, Isaac Singer and Edward Clark dissolve their partnership.

Isaac Singer moves to Europe.

The Singer Manufacturing Company becomes a New York Corp.

A branch office opens in Hamburg, Germany. Frederick Neidlinger is the agent.

Inslee A. Hopper becomes the figurehead Singer company president.

McKenzie promoted to vice president and general manager.

1864   4 July, Sir Douglas Alexander is born.

1865   The Singer Company delivers the "New Family" sewing machine.

U.S. Civil War ends.

Isabella gives birth to a daughter, Winarette Eugenie Singer.

1866   December 11, Singer patents an oscillating shuttle sewing machine.

Denmark's H. P. Henricksen patents a glove-stitching machine.

Isabella Eugenie Boyer delivers a son, Washington Merritt Grant.

1867   Clark establishes the first overseas manufacturing facility in Glasgow, Scotland.

3 October, Elias Howe, Jr., dies in Brooklyn, NY.

Singer Company acquires the Union Buttonhole Company.

Singer sales begin dominating the sewing machine market.

The No. 1 Drop Feed, a modification of the New Family, arrives.
William Baker of Grover & Baker retires as a multi-millionaire.
Isabella Eugenie Boyer delivers Paris Eugenie Singer.

1868   Cabinet factory opened in South Bend, Indiana.
McKenzie hires Thomas J. Jones as a R&D technical expert.

1869   Electromagnetic-driven sewing machine patented by A. E. Dupas.
Isabella Eugenie Boyer delivers a daughter, Isabella Blanche.

1870   The Singer Manufacturing Company sets up sales and distribution
centers in England.
There are 69 American sewing machine manufacturers.
Isabella Eugenie Boyer delivers a son, Franklin Morse.
Trademark red "S" debuts.

1871   Solomon Jones patents an electromagnetically-driven stitching
machine.
Singer's Bridgton factory becomes the largest in Britain.

1872   Elizabethport, NJ, becomes the site of a large state-of-the-art
manufacturing facility.
Howe Machine Co. consolidates with Howe Sewing Machine Co.

1873   February, the Singer Company becomes a New Jersey Corporation.
Canadian manufacturing begins.

1874   Official opening of Elizabethport factory.

1875   23 July, England, I. M. Singer dies in Torquay, England.
Edward Clark replaces Hopper as The Singer Company President.
Willcox & Gibbs introduce a quiet machine with an automatic
tensioning device.

1876   Howe Sewing Machine Company closes down due to competition
from Singer and others.
White Sewing Machine Company opens its doors.

1877   The Sewing Machine Combination ends after all patents lapse.

1879   Oscillating Shuttle mechanism developed by The Singer Company.
Second manager added to branch offices.

1880   Reece Machinery produces a useful button hole machine.
There are 124 American sewing machine manufacturers.
The Singer Company dominates England's domestic market.
An Edison electric motor drives a sewing machine.

1881   "New Family Machine" introduces more automatic features.
Factory opens in Cairo, Illinois.
September, Inslee Hopper dies at age 44.
Canadian, John Reece, patents automatic eyelet and buttonhole
sewing machine.

1882   October, Edward S. Clark dies in Cooperstown, NY.
62-year-old George Ross McKenzie becomes company president.
Factory opens in Montreal, Quebec Province, Canada.
Factory opens in Floridsdorf, Autria.

1883   Factory opens in Kilbowie, Scotland.

Singer Company attempts to sell in Asia.

1884	Statue of Liberty, in Isabella Singer's likeness given to US.
1885	Griscon applies an electric motor to a domestic sewing machine.
	Singer introduces the first practical electric sewing machine.
1886	28 October, unveiling of the Statue of Liberty.
	22-year-old Douglas Alexander admitted to the Canadian bar.
	American Federation of Labor consolidates 25 trade unions.
1887	Philip Diehl patents a direct drive sewing machine.
1888	29 April, Allan B. Wilson dies.
1889	George Ross McKenzie retires.
	March, 32-year-old F.G. Bourne becomes the new president.
1890	Singer company claims an 80 percent worldwide market share.
	11 April, Milton C. Lightner is born.
1891	First use of electric motor to commercial stitching machines.
1892	6 January, retired Singer Company president McKenzie dies.
	Singer develops a commercial grade zigzag machine.
1895	7,000 patents now govern sewing machine manufacture.
1896	Douglas Alexander becomes a Singer Company director and travels to and sets up a Russian joint stock company.
1899	Willcox & Gibb introduce a rotary take up lockstitch machine.
1900	660,000 people employed in the sewing machine industry.
	Singer company producing 40 different sewing machine models.
	Introduction of the "The Singer 66."
	Kilbowie, Scotland, factory renamed to Clydebank.
1902	Factory opened in Podolsk, Russia.
	Bourne builds a six story headquarters in St. Petersburg.
	William Proctor dies.
	Pfaff introduces machine tolerancing system guaranteeing manufactured parts interchangeability
1904	New factories: Wittenberge, Prussia; St. John's, Quebec, Canada.
	December 10. Russian corporate headquarters opens with modern building. It is Russia's first steel girder structure.
	Singer Sewing Machine Company becomes the sales arm of the Singer Manufacturing Company.
1905	Frederick Bourne chooses early retirement but remains as director.
	Sir Douglas Alexander becomes Singer company president.
	Singer acquires Wheeler and Wilson Manufacturing Co.
	Zigzag machines find commercial uses.
1906	Singer Building construction begins in NYC.
1907	Factory opens in Bridgeport, Connecticut.
	Financial Panic of 1907.
1908	Singer produces the "Singer 66" or "Twentieth Century Machine."
1909	Factory in Floridsdorf, Austria, closes.
1910	Pfaff introduces group drive system for its commercial installations.
1912	Factory opens in Truman, Arkansas.

Singer India report sales of 63,750 machines.

1913   Singer's annual sales top 2.5 million machines. Clydebank alone
        ships 1,301,851.
        Lightner graduates from Harvard Law School.

1916   Pancho Villa pursued by U.S. Army with Lightner in Army ranks.

1917   Bolshevik uprising stops further Singer expansion in Russia.
        Podolsk plant nationalized.

1918   Diehl Manufacturing Company attaches an electric motor to the
        sewing machine.

1919   March 9, Frederick Bourne dies.
        Union Special Company introduces first "safety-stitch" machine.
        White Sewing Machine Co. emphasizes electric domestic machines.

1920   German makers, Haid & Neu, celebrate manufacture of their two
        millionth machine.

1921   Fred Lazarus., Jr., creates the Associated Merchandising Corp.
        Singer introduces the "Portable Electric," an electric-motor powered
        model 99K.

1924   White Sewing Machine Company acquires King Sewing Machine
        Company and through this acquisition continues to produce
        machines for the Sears department store chain.

1926   Opening of woodworking plant in Thurso, Quebec, Canada.

1927   Milton Lightner accepts a vice presidency in sales.
        First Singer sewing center opens in NYC.

1928   Brother Industries, Nagoya, Japan, begins manufacturing industrial
        sewing machines.
        Lightner leaves Sales to become VP and Director of Manufacturing

1929   Singer purchases the Standard Sewing Machine Company and its
        popular *Sewhandy* portable sewing machine eventually leads to
        development of Singer's Featherweight..
        Lightner begins advanced sewing classes in Singer Sewing Centers.
        Now, there are nine worldwide Singer manufacturing facilities
        employing 27,000 people producing over 3,000 models.

1930   Pfaff introduces class165 and class166 single and twin needle post
        bed machines.

1933   Singer introduces its *Featherweight* at the Chicago's World Fair.
        Singer factories open in Monsa, Italy, and Bounieres, France.

1936   Willcox & Gibb acquire Metropolitan Sewing Machine Company
        and its "Superlock."

1938   Gegauf, produces the first zigzag machine, the Bernina Class 117.
        15 December, Tokyo Juki Co. makes rifles for the Japanese military.

1940   Singer introduces gear drive rotary mechanism Class 201K.

1943   Gefauf, Swiss maker introduces a domestic, production model
        zigzag sewing machine.

1945   25 October, Tokyo-Juki Industrial Machine Company begins sewing
        machine production.

1947   Italian made Nechhi sewing machines introduced to the Americans.
        Pfaff introduces an automatic cycling machine.
        Tokyo Juki produces their first sewing machine wherein all parts
        manufactured internally.

1948   Milton Lightner recruits attorney Donald Kircher to supervise
        Singer's legal affairs.
        Pfaff offers its zigzag machine to U.S. consumers.

1949   2 May, 7,000 Elizabethport workers go on strike.
        6 May, 1,500 Bridgeport workers go on strike.
        22 May, Sir Douglas Alexander dies.
        Milton Lightner takes over.
        Reece Company introduces the Speedy Reece S2.
        Wilcox & Gibbs introduces the Model 10A.
        Singer develops Model 95K capable of 4,000 stitches per minute.
        Nechhi's Elna with zigzag attachment joins its product line.
        Singer 451K machines achieve 5,000 stitches per minute.

1950   Tokyo Juki Company awarded first prize in the important Sewing
        Machine Competition.
        Singer opens plant in Anderson, South Carolina.

1951   600 Singer Sewing Centers train an estimated 400,000 housewives.
        6 July, workers strike St. John's Quebec facility.
        American Merchandising Corporation forms a computer
        development committee.
        Juki Company offers the "impossible to make" disc type rotary
        thread take up machine.

1952   Singer introduces the Slant-O-Matic its first zigzag machine.
        All domestic sewing machine sales increase by 21.5 percent.
        6 July 1951, the St. John Quebec factory strikes.
        Elizabeth facility threatens a new strike.
        22 May, Charlotte, SC, distribution and service center opens.
        RCA begins Bizmac design.

1953   Bizmac, a real-time, online computer network system, in operation.

1954   Pfaff rolls its five millionth sewing machine off of its assembly line.
        South Bend, Ind., Singer cabinet plant closes. 1,000 laid off.
        15 Sept. Association of Clothing Machine Engineers.

1955   Lightner opens a new factory in Campinas, Brazil.
        Lightner brings Kircher into corporate offices.

1956   Bizmac in operation in Higbees Department Store, Cleveland, OH.

1957   62 percent of American housewives reportedly sew.

1958   Milton Lightner steps down as Singer Company President.

1958   Donald Peter Kircher (d. 1978), takes control of Singer.

1959   Begin construction of $1.3 million sewing machine factory in
        Istanbul, Turkey.
        Singer succeeds in purchasing the Pine Company, a Japanese
        sewing machine maker.

	Frederick Ambrose Clark, Edward Clark's grandson, sells off 600,000 company shares.
1960	The Singer Company begins diversifying in earnest.
	Pfaff introduces high speed seaming machine.
1961	Corporate offices move from 148 Broadway to 30 Rockefeller Plaza.
1962	17 July, agreement to purchase Panoramic Electronics, Inc.
	Headquarters moved to Rockefeller Plaza
1963	Singer Co. acquires Empire Devices, a maker of electrical and electronic test instruments.
	Singer Company purchases Sensitive Research Instrument Corp.
	Singer Company's $175,000,000 acquisition of Friden, Inc. office machinery maker.
	Singer introduces the "Photo-Line Tracing Unit" that uses electronics to duplicate designs.
	Singer regains 40 percent of the domestic sewing machine market.
	Singer removes "Manufacturing" from its name to reflect its new diverse character.
1964	Singer acquires Empire Electric, Lakeville, IN.
	Singer acquires Wirekraft, Rolling Prairie, IN.
	Singer acquires KLH, hi-fi electronics maker, Cambridge, MA.
1966	14 July, Packard Bell Electronics Corp. acquired for $44 million.
1968	Singer acquires General Precision Equipment Corporation.
1971	40 Japanese companies make domestic machines. Another 10 produce commercially.
1972	Singer introduces the Singer Direct Drive, an original Philip Diehl idea of 1887.
1974	Company sales hit $2.6 billion with a $10 million loss.
	Company debt hits $1.1 billion.
	Singer sewing machine sales now own 54% of the domestic market.
1975	Kircher removed as Singer Company CEO.
	Singer introduces Athena 2000 an electronic home sewing machine.
	Joseph B. Flavin takes control of the Singer Company.
1976	Union Special Machine Company invents a solid state memory chip controlled machine.
	Singer offers Centurion electronic industrial sewing machines.
1977	Singer's sewing machine sales post 10 percent decline for the year.
	Singer introduces the Diana 560, a low-priced electronic model.
1978	Donald Kircher murdered by his mentally troubled brother-in-law.
	Joseph Flavin moves Singer's corporate headquarters from Manhattan to Connecticut.
	A Singer Company report reveals that young American women no longer enjoy sewing.
	Singer introduces the Touch-Tronic 2001, micro-controller in a sewing machine.
1979	Clydebank closes bringing a $130 million write-off.

1980   Singer's aerospace and marine division report 34% profit increase.

1985   Singer's French sewing machine operations sold off.

1986   Singer Sewing Machine Company now a separate entity.
        Singer launches the Fashionmaker advancing decorative stitching.

1987   July, Singer reports $20 million loss because of aerospace division
        R&D investments.
        8 October, Joseph Flavin dies.
        19 October, Black Monday, Paul Bilzerian acquires Singer through
        hostile takeover.

1988   July, Bilzerian begins liquidating; 8 of 12 Singer divisions sold.
        October, Bilzerian left with only four divisions.
        December, Bilzerian indicted on 9 tax and securities violations.

1989   Singer company assets reduced to approximately $445,000,000.
        27 Jan., James H. Ting's International Semi-Tech Microelectronics,
        Ltd. acquires SSMC.
        November, Biocoastal Corp., files Ch. 11 bankruptcy.

1991   STG, Semi-Tech Global, which is SSMC's parent holding company,
        makes a first public stock offering that increases SSMC shares by
        130 percent over the next three years.

1992   SSMC enters agreement to manufacture in China.
        May, Semi-Tech Global, STG, acquires Japanese electronics
        manufacturer, Sansui.

1993   SSMC purchases Pfaff sewing machine company.
        SSMC acquires 80% interest in the Singer Bangladesh.
        SSMC acquires 100% interest in Singer Industries Philippines, Inc.

1994   SSMC begins manufacture in Viet Nam and plans 100 retail centers.
        STG becomes $2.8 billion company.
        SSMC's world market share at 38 percent.
        1 January, SSMC acquires 51% interest in the Singer Hua Nan
        Sewing Machine Co. Ltd.
        SSMC acquires 51% interest in P. T. Singer Industries Indonesia.
        SSMC acquires 100% of Singer Spain S. A. and Singer Turkey.
        SSMC acquires 70% interest in the Singer Viet Nam Company, Ltd.

1995   SSMC buys back its Singer Furniture Company and its Italian
        manufacturing operation.
        STG acquires 55% of Akai Electronics.
        SSMC acquires 51 percent interest in Singer India Limited.
        1 Oct., SSMC acquires Singer India and The Singer Furniture Co.
        SSMC's worldwide market share increases to 41 percent.
        SSMC introduces three new zigzag models.

1997   6 November, The Singer Company agrees to purchase Pfaff Sewing
        Machine Company.

1998   STG increases Akai stake to 71%.

Selected Bibliography

Books

Birmingham, Stephen. *Life at the Dakota: New York's Most Unusual Address,* New York, Random House, 1979.

Bourne, Frederick G., "American Sewing-Machines," reprinted in *1795-1895: One Hundred Years of American Commerce,* ed. Depew, Chauncey M., LL. D., Greenwood Press Publishers, New York, 1968, Vol. II, pp. 525-539.

Brandon, Ruth. *A Capitalist Romance,* New York: J. B. Lippincott Company, 1977. This classic work is the most complete biography of I. M. Singer. The definitive study of the Singer Company origins.

Bunch, Brian and Hellemans, Alexander. *The Timetables of Technology,* Simon & Schuster, New York, 1993.

Carstensen, Fred V. *American Enterprise in Foreign Markets : Studies of Singer and International Harvester,* University of North Carolina Press, Chapel Hill and London, 1984.

Clark, Victor S. *History of Manufactures in the United States,* Carnegie Institute of Washington, 1929. New York, reprinted by Peter Smith, 1949, by permission, vols. I, II, II.

Cooper, Grace Rogers. *History of the Sewing Machine,* Bulletin 254, Washington, D. C: Smithsonian Institution, 1968.
   A good history of the sewing industry's origins along with biographical profiles of the major players. A detailed record of sewing machine sales figures and patent awards. Descriptions of various patented sewing machine models, their workings and improvements.

Davies, Robert Bruce. *Peacefully Working to Conquer the World: Singer Sewing Machines in Foreign Markets,* New York City, Arno Press, 1976.
   This work delivers the minutiae of the Singer company's manufacturing and marketing policies especially as these developed in reaction to European economic nationalism.

Durant, Will and Ariel Durant, *The Lessons of History,* Simon and Schuster, New York, 1968.

Eastley, Charles M. *The Singer Saga,* Brauton & Devon England: Merlin Books Ltd., 1983.

English, W. *The Textile Industry,* Longmans, Green and Co. Ltd., London and Harlow, 1969.

Ewers, William, Baylor, H.W., Kenaga, H.H. *Sincere's History of the Sewing Machine,* Sincere Press, Phoenix, Arizona,

Fayerweather, John. *Facts and Fallacies of International Business,* New York: Holt, Rinehart and Winston, 1962.

Godfrey, Frank P. *An International History of the Sewing Machine,* Robert Hale Limited, 1982.
   Mr. Godfrey, a professional engineer by profession, has provided a comprehensive overview of the mechanical operating details of early sewing machine development. Good photographs and detailed descriptions of a variety of early sewing machines.

Groner, Alex. *American Business & Industry*, New York, American Heritage Publishing Co., Inc., 1972.

Kaempffert, Waldemar, ed. *A Popular History of American Invention*, New York, Charles Scribner's Sons, 1924, vol. II, pp. 313-404.

Parton, James. *Famous Men: Triumphs of Enterprise, Ingenuity, and Public Spirit*, New York, James Miller, Publisher, 1880, c. 1874, p. 139-175.

_____. *Age of Invention*, 1921.

Sampson, Anthony. *The Sovereign State of ITT*, New York, Stein and Day, 1973.

Scott, John. *Genius Rewarded: or The Story of the Sewing Machine*, New York, John J. Gaulon, Printer, No. 20 Vesey Street, 1880.

Singer Company. *The Singer Sewing Machine: America's Chief Contribution to Civilization*, New York, Singer Co., 1911.

Ward, J. T. *The Factory System*, Barnes & Noble, New York, 1970, Vol. 1.

Wilkins, Mira. *The Emergence of Multinational Enterprise: American Business Abroad from the Colonial Era to 1914*, Cambridge, MA: Harvard University Press, 1970.

Articles

"7,000 go on Strike at Singer Factory," *New York Times*, 3 May 1949, 21:3.

"Agreement is Set on Singer Merger," *New York Times*, 20 June 1963, 41:7.

"Another Singer Link," *New York Times*, 8 January 1963, 10:3.

"Archives Picture Sewing Progress," *New York Times*, 2 July 1951, 15:2.

Barron, James. "Joseph B. Flavin is Dead at 58; Led Overhaul as Singer Chairman," *New York Times*, 8 October 1987, 5:2.

"Bridgeport Union Ends Singer Strike," *New York Times*, 3 October 1949, 10:1.

"Brother v. Singer," *New York Times*, 30 March 1955, 41:4.

Burck, Gilbert. "Singer: Hardening of the Assets," *Fortune*, January 1959, pp. 85-89+.

Byrnes, Nanette. "The Ting Dynasty?" *Financial World*, vol. 163, 10 May 1994, p: 28-33.

Curtis, Carol. *CFO: The Magazine for Chief Financial Officers*, "Aftermath of an LBO (Leveraged Buyout)," vol. 6, iss: 4, April 1990, pp. 20-26.

"City Feels Impact of Singer Strike," *New York Times*, 17 August 1949, 3:6.

"Estate To Sell Stock In Singer," *New York Times*, 25 April 1964, 24:4.

"Clerics Urge Strike End," *New York Times*, 13 October 1949, 23:2.

"Current Technology in Light Machinery," *New York Times*, 21 March 1860, 6:1.

"Electronics Count the Stock," *Business Week*, 5 February 1955, p. 57-8.

Engardio, Pete. *Business Week,* 23 November 1987, p: 62, 66.

"Faces Behind the Figures: Flavin of Singer," *Forbes,* 25 January 1977, 119:72:6.

Faltermayer, E. K. "It's a Spryer Singer," *Fortune,* 68:144-8+, December 1963.

Fierman, Jaclyn. "Boone's New Partner," *Fortune,* :89+, March 28, 1988.

"Flavin's Master Plan for Ailing Singer, *Business Week,* May 10, 1976, p. 66.

"For Reasons of Health," *Forbes,* 15 May 1976, 117:102-103.

Gray, Christopher. "Style Standard for Early Steel-Framed Skyscraper," *New York Times,*

Hawkins, Chuck; Lee, Dinah; King Resa W., "Who is James Ting and What Will He Buy Next?" *Business Week,* 13 February 1989, p. 33.

"Home-Sewing Booms Singer," *Business Week,* 14 August 1948, pp. 75-78.

"How the Directors Kept Singer Stitched Together, *Fortune,* December 1975, pp. 100-103+.

"Japan Approves Deal: Singer Sewing Machine to Join with Company There," *New York Times,* 8 October 1959, 57:2.

"Japan Spurs Sales of Sewing Machine," *New York Times,* 9 September 1951, 11:1.

"Japanese Mark Set In Sewing Machines," *New York Times,* 15 January 1953, 36:8.

"Japanese To Push Appliances Here," *New York Times,* 24 March 1955, 45:2.

Kobler, John. "Mr. Singer's Money Machine," *Saturday Evening Post,* 7 July 1951, v224, no. 1, pp. 17-19+.

ibid. 14 July 1951, v224, no. 2, pp. 22-23+.

ibid. 21 July 1951, v224, no. 3, pp. 30, 112-114.

ibid. 28 July 1951, v224, no. 4, pp. 25, 103-106.

Lyon, Peter. "Isaac Singer and His Wonderful Sewing Machine," in *Great Stories of American Businessmen,* New York, American Heritage Publishing Co., Inc., 1954, pp. 147-157.

McNeil Jr., Donald G. "Ex Head of Singer Company Slain In Jersey; Brother-in-Law Is Held," *New York Times,* 2 May 1978, 28:1.

"Miscellany, Nechhi-Elna Sales" *New York Times,* 10 July 1956, 42:3.

Mitchell, Russell. "Can Paul Bilzerian Fatten Singer for the kill "More Industries Score Tariff Cuts," *New York Times,* 4 February 1955, 8:3.

"New Industry Cited," *New York Times,* 29 January 1952, 28:3.

"New Stitching Device Out," *New York Times,* 7 January 1953, 23:5.

"Nixon Tells N. A. M. of Urgency To Counter a Soviet 'Offensive,'" *New York Times,* 7 December 1957, 16:5.

North, Sterling. *New England Business*, "Singer Spins Off Its Homespun Roots for High Tech, Defense Concentration," vol. 8, Iss: 7, 21 April 1986, pp. 39-40.

Obituary, Edward Clark, *New York Times*, 17 October 1882, 4:7.

Packard, Winthrop. "The New England Society in the City of New York," *New England Magazine,*" January 1908, V. XXXVII, no. 5, pp. 523-547.

Plummer, John. "The Sewing Machine; Its Industrial and Social Results," in *The British almanac of the Society for the Diffusion of Useful Knowledge for the Year. . ..*, London: Charles Knight, 1877, pp. 95-115.

"Pfaff To Push Sale of Sewing Machine," *New York Times,* 7 August 1952, 25:2.

"Pfaff Unit Output Surpasses Pre-War," *New York Times*, 8 August 1951, 39:5.

Reckert, Clare M. "Singer Will Make Office Machinery," *New York Times*, 1963, Jl 17, 37:4.

"Sears Turns to Japan For Sewing Machines," *New York Times*, 19 June 1957, 49:3.

"Sewing Machines Here From Abroad," *New York Times*, 9 December 1950, 18:2.

"Sewing Machines Face Record Sales," *New York Times*, 10 December 1952, 56:5.

"Sewing Machines Sales From Abroad," *New York Times*, 8 August 1951, 39:5.

"Sewing Machines Stage A Comeback," *New York Times*, 24 February 1952, III, 11:4.

"Singer Company Special Report," *Forbes*, 15 October 1964, pp. 20-24.

"Singer Adds Two to Board," *New York Times*, 24 June 1954, 45:6.

"Singer Company," *New York Times*, 20 July 1972, 49:2.

"Singer Plant to Close," *New York Times*, 6 October 1954, 17:8.

"Singer Strikers Paid Off," *New York Times*, 13 May 1949, 20:3.

"Singer Plans Bonuses," *New York Times*, 13 December 1949, 36:4.

"Singer Plans Fight of Antitrust Suit," *New York Times,* 24 December 1959, 5:2.

"Singer to Build Charlotte Plant," *New York Times*, 22 May 1952, 46:2.

"Singer Slates Turkish Plant," *New York Times,* 27 August 1959, 36:4.

"Singer's Dividend is Cut 40C to 10C," *New York Times*, 14 February 1975, 51:2.

"Singer's Surprises," *New York Times*, 21 May 1959, 44:2.

Smith, Hedrick. "Soviet Eases Visa Rule; Singer Co. Presses Plan," *New York Times*, 14 April 1973, 43:4.

"Strike Under Way at Singer Factory," *New York Times*, 2 May 1949, 18:1.

"Sewing Machine Prices Cut," *New York Times*, 12 November 1958, 62:3.

"Singer Company Plans Expansion Move," *New York Times*, 17 July 1962, 32:4.

Sloan, Leonard. "Singer Criticized by Shareholders,"*New York Times*, 9 May 1975, 9, 50:3.

Smith, Gene. "Xerox Officer to Head Singer,"*New York Times*, 11 November 1975, 43:6.

Sterba, James P. "Singer Co. Is Moving to Stamford To Surprise of New York Officials," *New York Times*, 14 June 1978, II, 3:1.

"Swedish Concern Plans Drive Here," *New York Times*, 29 May 1952, 21:3.

"The Story of the Sewing Machine. Its Invention - Improvements - Social, Industrial and Commercial Importance," *New York Times*, 7 January 1860, 2:2.

"Up-to-the-Second Inventory: the Distribution," *Business Week*, 3 October 1953, p. 118+.

"Why the Profits Vanished at Singer," *Business Week*, 30 June 1975, pp. 106-108.

"Xerox Officer to Head Singer," *New York Times*, 11 November 1975, 43:6.

Studies and Monographs

Carstensen, Frederick Vernon. *American Multinational Corporations in Imperial Russia*. Yale University Ph.D. thesis, 1976.

Davies, Robert Bruce. *The International Operations of the Singer Manufacturing Company, 1854-1895*, Doctoral thesis at the University of Wisconsin, 1967.
Dr. Davies' well-written doctoral thesis is an important historical document. The analysis of The Singer Sewing Machine Company's first efforts at opening foreign markets is of particular interest.

Godley, Andrew. "Singer in Britain: The Diffusion of Sewing Machine Technology and its Impact on the Clothing Industry in the U.K., 1860-1905."*Textile History*, Sprg 1996, v. 27, n.1.

"Singer Manufacturing Company (B), 9-355-007 Ft-841 in *The Singer Machine Shop, Inc.* Harvard Business School, 9-604-004, EAP 241, 1958, pp. 1-7.

171, 188, 204
Clark, Nathan 68
Clark, Victor S. 90
Class 71 buttonhole machine 118
Cleveland, OH 120, 144
clothes iron 187
clothing factory 44
Clydebank, Scotland 82, 103, 115,
130, 133, 134, 195
Colt, Samuel 78
commission houses 80
Commodore Perry 43
Communist Party 150
cooling fans 144
Cooper, Grace 6
Cooperstown, NY 98
Cowperthaite and Sons 76
Craftsman power tools 174
Crosley 154
Crown Zellerbach Corporation 201
Cuba 81, 130
Dakota 13, 98, 113
Dalmo Victor 199
Davies, Robert Bruce 11, 58
Davis, Ari 55
Debs, Eugene 130
desktop calculators 173
di Scipio, Alfred 170
Diaz, Porfirio 148
Diehl Manufacturing 117, 144
diversification 9, 142, 144, 159, 160,
165-167, 170, 172, 174, 193, 204-207
domestic expansion 76, 93
Eastley, Charles 17-19, 28, 32
Edward Clark Benevolent Society 98
Electric telegraph 36
Electronic Systems Division 198
Elizabethport, NJ 76, 82, 108, 115,
132, 133, 142, 144
Elna 153, 156, 157, 168
embroidering attachment, third thread
25
Empire Devices, Inc. 172
Empire Electric Corporation 174

engineers 7, 139, 149, 175
Eureka 144
Evans, Oliver 59, 60
Everglades Club in Palm Beach, FL 31
Ewers, William 49
eye-pointed needle 49, 52, 53, 56, 61
Factory system 3, 7, 37-42, 89-91,
105, 108, 118, 124, 143
Featherweight Model 221 137
Federal Reserve Act 130
Ferrand 50
Fifth Avenue 12, 27, 29, 31
Fisher, George 55, 60, 112
Fisher & Steiner 112
Flappers 137
Flavin, Joseph 189-196, 199
Franco-Prussian War of 1870 31
Fredericksburg, PA 19
Friden 173, 182, 183
Frister & Rossman 112
GE Credit Corporation 191
Gegauf 153
Geneen, Harold 193
General Electric 83
General Instrument Corporation 199
General Precision Equipment Corp.
174
Genius Rewarded 22, 23
George W. Bliss 60
German Singer manufacturing 5
Germany 5, 81, 105, 133, 139, 143,
155, 176, 177
Gibbs, James A. E. 63, 64, 74
Glasgow 82, 103, 107, 108
Glen Spey 109
Godey's Lady's Book 24
Godfrey, Frank P. 7
Graphics System Division 191
Grasshopper 74
Great Civilizer 4, 36, 65, 73, 79, 98,
136
Great Depression 96
Grimme 112
Grover & Gibbs 63, 64

Point of Sale,(PoS) 167, 175, 178, 180-183, 194
Potter, Orlando B. 85-87
Power tools division 198
Proctor, William 101
R&D 8, 9, 72, 89, 103, 109, 110, 116, 117, 141, 172, 182, 197, 208
ready-to-assemble furniture 205, 207
ready-to-wear clothing 44, 50, 90, 125
Reece, Company 112, 140
repair manuals 5
replacement parts 6, 133, 140
Richardson, patent illustrator 53
Rochester, NY 17
rock drilling machine 19
Rockefeller Plaza 176, 195
Rommel, Field Marshall 139
Roosevelt, Theodore 126
ruffler and tucker 25
Ruhrgas A.G. 198
Russo-Japanese War 126, 129
Ryobi Ltd. 198
Saint, Thomas 49
Sansui 204, 207
Schwab A. G. 177
Scientific American 53, 63
scientific management 7, 89-91, 143
Scott, John 22
Truman, President 129, 131, 161
Sears 135, 136, 157, 158, 174, 180
Securities and Exchange Commission 161, 169, 200
Bank of Nova Scotia 199
Semi-Tech Global 203, 204
Sewing Machine Combination 83
Sewing Machine War 64-67, 84, 85, 87
sewing service centers 158
shuttle-thread controller 25
Sinclair, Upton 130
Singer, Adam 16
Singer Building 11, 145, 160, 162
Singer Business Machine Division 194
Singer (employee) families 5
Singer Gauge 118
Singer, Isaac 1, 2, 12-18, 20, 23, 25-34, 36, 48, 53, 57, 59, 60, 64-72, 80, 86, 91, 102, 161, 189
Singer, Isabella 30-32, 91
Singer Manufacturing Company 4, 10, 23, 58, 88, 144, 147
Singer Nikko 206
Singer, Paris 31
Singer, Ruth 13, 16, 74
Singer Sewing Machine Company 1, 26, 38, 55, 74, 96, 99, 100, 103, 111, 112, 114, 133, 137, 142, 147, 191, 193, 199, 201, 204, 205, 209
Singer, Voulettie 101
single-thread chain-stitch 25, 74
Sino-Japanese War, 1937-1945 154
Slant-O-Matic 175
slop shops 44
Spanish American War 126
spectrum analyzers 172
Sponsler, Mary Ann 18, 27-29, 32, 102
St. John, Quebec 151
Stalin 5
Standard Oil companies 83
Standard Sewing Machine Company 137
Stanford University 201
Statue of Liberty 13, 32, 123
Sterling, Dr. Alexander F. 101
Stone, Thomas 49
Strike of '49 149
Stucchi 112
Summerville, Isabella Eugenie 30, 91
Supermatic 157
surgical stitching machines 144
synchro-system 143
Taylor, A. B. 15, 20, 21
Tele-Signal 191
tension device 25
territorial sales rights guarantee 75
textile industry 2, 35, 39, 40, 42, 44, 54, 57, 58, 78, 136

Thimmonier, Bartheleme 50-52
Thomas, William F. 58
thread-controller 25
ticketographs 173
Ting, James H. 203-205, 207-209
Tokyo-Juki Industrial Machine Co.
    141
Torquay 31
Touch and Sew 177
Tower, the 160, 161
White Rotary sewing machine 145
Turtle Back Sewing Machine 71
U.S. Congress 32
Underwood Tariff Act 131
Underwood-Olivetti 180
Union Special Machine Company 146
United Electrical, Radio and Machine
    Workers Union 149
United Electrical, Radio and Machine
    Workers, CIO 150
vacuum cleaner 207
vapocleaners 207
VerPlanck, Prince, Burlingame and
    Lightner 149
Victor Comptometer 180
Viet Nam 200, 207
Villa, Pancho 31, 148
Wagner Act 142
Walters, Mary Eastwood 30, 32
Wal-Mart 208
water filter 207
West Side Association 67
Wheeler and Wilson 63, 85, 86, 88,
    110, 112, 117, 130, 144
Wirekraft 174
White Sewing Machine Company 144
Whitney, Eli 33, 41
Wigwam, the 31, 32
Wilkins, Mira 104
Williams College 66, 98
Williams College in 1830 66
Wilson 62-64, 73, 74, 85, 86, 88, 110,
    112, 117, 130, 144
Wilson & Gibbs 73, 74, 112

Wright brothers 6, 23
Wittenberg 133, 139
Woodruff, George 81, 82, 93, 103
Woolworth company 180
Worcester, Massachusetts 200
World War I 32, 131, 133-135, 148
World War II 5, 138, 139, 141, 143,
    153, 155, 159, 185, 186
Wycliffe, John 123
Xerox Corporation 190
yielding presser-foot 25
yielding spring 24
Zeiber, George 21-23, 68-72, 95
zigzag sewing machine 9, 118, 140,
    152, 153, 155, 157, 164, 205, 208

ORDER FORM

Please send:

_____ copies of *The First Conglomerate*
@$19.95 each   _____

Shipping: $2.00 first book (bookrate) or
$4.00 (priority); .50 each add. bk.   _____

Sales tax (state of Maine only) 5.5%   _____

TOTAL   _____

Send check or money order to:
Audenreed Press
PO Box 1305 #103   207-833-5016
Brunswick, ME 04011
Orders only: 888-315-0582 (M-F, 9-5)

Name_____

Address_____

_____

_____

Phone_____